HAUSA FOLK-LORE

WANAN LITĀFI TĀTSŪNĪA NE

THIS IS A BOOK OF STORIES

HAUSA FOLK-LORE
CUSTOMS, PROVERBS, ETC.

COLLECTED AND TRANSLITERATED WITH ENGLISH TRANSLATION AND NOTES

BY

R. SUTHERLAND RATTRAY, F.R.G.S., F.R.A.I.

OF EXETER COLLEGE, OXFORD
ASSISTANT DISTRICT COMMISSIONER, ASHANTI, WEST AFRICA
AUTHOR OF 'CHINYANJA FOLK-LORE'
QUALIFIED INTERPRETER IN HAUSA, TŴI, CHINYANJA, MŌLE

WITH A PREFACE BY

R. R. MARETT, M.A.

READER IN SOCIAL ANTHROPOLOGY IN THE UNIVERSITY OF OXFORD
PRESIDENT OF THE FOLK-LORE SOCIETY

IN TWO VOLUMES: VOL. I

NEGRO UNIVERSITIES PRESS
NEW YORK

Originally published in 1913
at the Clarendon Press

Reprinted 1969 by
Negro Universities Press
A Division of Greenwood Publishing Corp.
New York

SBN 8371-1464-0

PRINTED IN UNITED STATES OF AMERICA

PREFACE

It is our privilege at Oxford to be visited from time to time by officers of the Public Service, who modestly apply to us for instruction in Anthropology, more particularly as it bears on the history of the native races of the Empire. Not infrequently, however, they bring with them a previously acquired stock of anthropological information, such as almost takes away the breath of their duly constituted teachers. Thereupon the latter feel inclined to offer to change places; and, instead of teaching, to play the part of learners in regard to them.

Mr. Rattray furnishes a case in point. When he joined our School of Anthropology, he was already a past-master in all that relates to Chinyanja folk-lore, a subject on which he had actually published a useful book. Besides, though but recently transferred from British Central Africa to the West Coast, he was already at close grips with more than one of the languages current in that most polyglot of regions.

To claim, therefore, any share whatever in the origination of the present work would ill beseem one who merely offered sympathetic encouragement when Mr. Rattray proceeded to unfold his latest design. This design was to compass two ends at once—to obtain trustworthy linguistic material, and to explore the inner secrets of the Hausa mind—by giving a somewhat novel turn to an old and approved method.

As regards the collection of folk-lore, the approved method —in fact, the only method likely to satisfy the demands of science—is this: the observer must draft word-for-word reports of what he hears; and must further give the original words, when a foreign tongue is used, so that it may be possible independently to control the version.

Such a method, however, is more easily prescribed on paper than followed in the field. When the witness is illiterate—as commonly happens when there is genuine folk-lore to be gathered—its application proves exceedingly troublesome, for reasons that may readily be divined. A more or less formal dictation lesson has somehow to be given and received; and the several parties to it are only too apt to conspire each in his own way to render it a failure. Thus the story-teller, on the one hand, is probably shy and suspicious at the outset; is put out of his stride by the slightest interruption; and, becoming weary all too soon, tends to take short cuts, instead of following to the end the meandering path of the genuine tradition. The reporter, in his turn, is incessantly puzzled by the idiom, more especially since in such a context archaisms will be frequent; boggles over a pronunciation adapted to a monotonous sing-song delivery, or else, perhaps, to a dramatic mimicry carried on in several voices; and is likely to be steadily outpaced into the bargain.

Mr. Rattray's happy thought, then, was to remedy the practical shortcomings of the standard method by finding some one who, as it were, could dictate to himself; who, in other words, could successfully combine the characters of story-teller and reporter in his single person.

Moreover, as Mr. Rattray was not slow to perceive, the existing conditions of Hausa culture bring it about that the very type of helper needed is with due search to be procured. A *mālam* of the best class possesses all the literary skill which a knowledge of Arabic and of the Arabic script involves. None the less, he remains thoroughly in touch with his own people, a Hausa of the Hausas. In his hands, therefore, the traditional lore loses nothing of its authentic form and flavour. In short, the chance of literary manipulation may be ruled out.

Hence it would seem, if I may venture to say so, that the Government of the Gold Coast was no less wise than liberal in its policy when, by the grant of a subvention, it enabled *Mālam* Shaihu's work to be perpetuated in the fullest way, namely, not only by transliteration and translation, but likewise by actual reproduction in facsimile.

For, apart from its value as a masterpiece of artistic penmanship, this clear and, I understand, correct calligraphy must prove of great assistance to European students of Hausa to whose official lot it falls to wrestle with the productions of the native scribe. Then, conversely, if an educated Hausa aspire, as well he may, to learn the English language, together with the use of the English alphabet, he has here an invaluable means of comparing his own system of written symbols with ours. So much, then, for the more obvious advantages to be derived from a study of the *mālam*'s actual manuscript. Over and above this, it proves of assistance to the philologist, as Mr. Rattray shows, by making clear certain finer points of grammar in regard to which evidence was hitherto lacking. Also, I suppose, simply as exemplifying the characteristic differences between the African and the classical modes of writing Arabic, it would not be without a certain scientific interest of its own.

Concerning the worth of the collected matter to the student of language and to the folk-lorist, I am hardly called upon to speak here, even were I competent to do so. Suffice it to say that, in respect of its contents, the book does not, of course, claim to stand alone. Yet, though a considerable library of Hausa literature is already in existence, it can well bear to be enriched by another volume such as this, which manages to dispense with the middle man of another mental type, and brings us directly into contact with the native intelligence as it witnesses to itself.

For the rest, I take it that the study of Hausa folk-lore offers fascinating problems to the student, if only because it calls for a critical sifting and weighing of the most drastic kind. The culture of the Hausas is not, in any sense of that much abused term, primitive. They have undergone interpenetration on the part of the Fulani and other alien stocks. They have more or less universally embraced Mohammedanism. They engage in trading expeditions which bring them into touch with most of the peoples of West Africa. Altogether, then, they are far away from that state of aboriginal innocence in which a strictly homegrown tradition perpetuates itself by means of stories that almost amount to oral rites, so undeviating is their form, so solemn their import and associations.

On the contrary, the most characteristic feature of Hausa lore, when purged of its more obvious accretions from without, consists in the folk-tale; which some authorities go so far as to regard as typically reminiscent of some degenerated and desolemnized myth. Nor can it be denied that, for example, various survivals in this region of what may be termed in a broad sense totemism lend colour to the view that the animal story may have fallen from a far higher estate, if the criterion of value be the seriousness of the beliefs which it embodies. To the student of folk-lore origins, however, the material available here is at least as good as to be got nearer home; and, in so far as there still exist in Hausaland odd corners where customs lurk of a quite primaeval appearance, the chance of discovering the laws of change involved is relatively the better.

Besides, quite apart from the purely scientific interest in origins, the reader will come to understand the thoughts and ways of the Hausas as they are now. Their notions about right and wrong, for instance, are indicated pretty clearly by many of the animal stories; seeing that each animal tends to represent a type of character calling either for admiration or detestation, and, being more or less humanized into the bargain, affords a nucleus round which a nascent moral philosophy can be observed to gather.

Even more directly, too, may we obtain insight into the present conditions of Hausa culture by studying what the *mālam* has to say about their history, manners, and arts. If brief, his notices are always business-like and to the point; while he plainly has access to information—for instance, in regard to bronze-casting by the *cire perdue* process—for which the European investigator might for the most part snap his fingers in vain.

But, as the Hausas say, 'If you are not going to drink the pap, stop stirring it.' The pap, I am convinced, is excellent. So let us drink without more ado.

R. R. MARETT.

AUTHOR'S NOTE

On first proceeding to West Africa (the Gold Coast), and on commencing a study of the Hausa language, the compiler of this work was struck by the comparatively high standard of education found among the Hausa Mālamai or scribes. Arabic characters are used by them, as by the Swahili of East and Central Africa; but, whereas any natives met with there possessed but a very superficial knowledge of the Arabic language or writing, the Hausas could boast of a legal, historical, and religious literature, which was to be found preserved by manuscripts. The Mālamai were everywhere the most respected and honoured members of the community. It was disappointing, however, at any rate for one who wished to study Hausa, to find that all their manuscripts were written not only in Arabic characters, but also in that language. This appears to be universally the case, even in Nigeria. The use of Arabic to-day among the educated Hausas corresponds to that of French and Latin in England in the middle ages.

The writer's intention was, as soon as he had acquired a sound colloquial knowledge of the Hausa language, to collect some of their folk-lore and traditions, taking down such information as was required verbatim, and translating afterwards into English. This plan he had adopted when collecting his *Chinyanja* folk-lore.

The advantage of such a system is that the original text will help the student of the language to appreciate its structure and idioms, in a way that the best grammars could hardly do. The translator will also be bound down thereby. There will thus be no room for embellishments or errors creeping in, as is liable to be the case when the investigator has had to rely on the vagaries of his cook, 'boy,' or other interpreter for his information. It follows that such a collection will be of more value from the anthropological standpoint. Indeed, of late years many collections of native folk-lore compiled according to this method have been called into being by the demand created by this new science of anthropology.

As is to be expected, there are not many persons who have the fortune—or misfortune—to spend four or five preliminary years in acquiring a knowledge of the language of the people whose traditions they hope to study; yet such a probation is very necessary, if the collection is to be of any real value to the anthropologist.

Stories and traditions collected through the medium of an interpreter are amusing, and might prove of interest in the nursery (though much would have to be omitted or toned down, as savage folk-lore is often coarse and vulgar according to our notions, and hardly fit *pour les jeunes filles*); but for the student of anthropology such collections cannot be considered to possess much value.

The anthropological theorist, who is probably some learned professor at one or other of our great Universities, where he made a life-study of primitive customs and beliefs, has, in most cases, to rely for his data on the field-worker. He needs to feel perfectly convinced that the information on which he is seeking to base some far-reaching generalization is absolutely correct; and this can hardly be the case, however skilled, conscientious, or well trained the field-worker may be, if the latter be wholly ignorant of the language of the people from whom he is collecting his information.

Now the literary skill of the Hausas, already referred to, led the writer to depart somewhat from the *modus operandi* employed in his *Chinyanja* folk-lore, the subject-matter of which was taken down from the lips of the raconteur.

For the present work the services of a learned MĀLAM, by name MĀLAM *Shaihu*, were secured. He himself wrote down, or translated from manuscripts in Arabic, such information as was required. Much of the work contained in the present volumes involved, first, a translation from Arabic into Hausa, secondly, a transliteration of the Hausa writing, and thirdly, a translation into English from the Hausa.

During the writer's 'tours' of service in West Africa, as also during his furloughs in England, this MĀLAM, who was entirely ignorant of English, made a collection of many hundreds of sheets of manuscripts (1907–11).

In the meantime the present writer was making a study of the Hausa language and script, by way of securing the key to their transliteration and translation. He was fortunate, in the course of his official duties, in being stationed for some time at YEGI on the VOLTA river. YEGI lies on the main caravan route between Nigeria and Ashanti. Each month thousands of Hausas from all parts of Nigeria cross the river here, going to and from Nigeria with kola or cattle. Such a position enables a student, even better perhaps than if he were resident in Hausaland, to get into touch with Hausas from all parts of Nigeria. It was thus possible to select such stories or traditions as seemed most generally and widely known, and therefore likely to be of historical value on account of their antiquity.

The Hausa given in the text is that of Kano or Sokoto, where by general consent the purest dialect is spoken.

The Hausa Manuscript. The writing is throughout clear, correct, and legible. It has been written with the *aya* (.˙.) between most of the words to facilitate easy reading. Some of the specimens of Hausa writing that have been reproduced from time to time are obviously the work of illiterate Hausas, or at best are very carelessly written manuscripts, and as such afford little criterion of the best work of these people. The hasty scrawls, which, it is true, form the larger part of the existing manuscripts, in which vowel-signs are missed out and words run together, often cannot be deciphered by the Hausas, and sometimes not even by the writers themselves, unless they know the context or subject by heart. Such manuscripts are therefore worthless for scientific purposes. They cannot, for instance, serve to disclose those nice points of grammatical construction which the perusal of a carefully written manuscript will reveal, though they can hardly be noted in the spoken language.

The Transliteration. This has been given, letter by letter, word for word, line by line. Thus it is easy for the student to follow the original on the page opposite.

The Translation. As literal a translation as is consistent with making the subject-matter at all readable has been given throughout. It is primarily as a text-book for students of the language that this work is intended, and for such a literal translation will be of most use. The author would crave the pardon of the general reader for the baldness and utter sacrifice of the English idiom which such a style of translation must necessarily involve. The latter may, however, find here and there a certain touch of 'local colour' in the phraseology, which may compensate for its other obvious defects.

The value of Hausa writings. Hitherto, perhaps, it has not usually been deemed essential to know much about Hausa writing. (A slight knowledge of it is necessary, it is true, for the higher standard Government examination.) This work attempts to go somewhat fully into the subject of the writing and the signs used, in order to assist the student who desires a knowledge of the writing that will enable him to decipher manuscripts as apart from the printed type. *The writer is convinced that a thorough knowledge of Hausa writing is essential for any advanced study of the language.* Thus he has so far been rewarded for the time spent in the minute perusal of the manuscripts comprising the Hausa portion of this book by the further elucidation or confirmation therein of grammatical structures not perhaps wholly accepted as proved, and by the discovery of some new idioms which, to the best of his knowledge, had apparently escaped the vigilance of previous writers on this subject, or else had taxed their powers of explanation.

The length of vowels, which is so distinctly shown in the written word, does not hitherto appear to have had that attention paid to it that it undoubtedly deserves. Yet the length of a vowel may alter the meaning of a word entirely, e.g. *gūda*, *gŭda ;* *sūna*, *sŭna;* *gādō*, *gădō*, and so on. Indeed, an educated MĀLAM would consider a word as wrongly spelt whenever a long vowel was written where it should have been short, or vice versa. In Hausa writing such an error would amount not merely to the dropping of an accent, as in English, but to the omission of a letter. Moreover such a slip may lead to serious confusion, since the tense of a verb, or even, as has been seen, the entire sense of a word, may depend on the length assigned to the vowel.

The author of *Hausa Notes*, perhaps the best treatise on the language yet written, remarks at some length on the apparent 'absurdity' of the want of any inflexion for the 1st, 2nd, and 3rd persons singular of the past tense, for the plural of which the well-known forms in *ka* exist, and thinks the forms for these persons are the same as those used for the aorist tense. Yet a perusal of almost any half-dozen pages of the present manuscript will reveal the hidden missing forms. Were the student to search for these by ear only, he might easily never discover them, as they are almost indistinguishable in the spoken word.

Again, the definite article,[1] for many years conspicuous by its

[1] First noted by Professor A. Mischlich.

absence, will be met with repeatedly in these pages in the final *nun*, or *ra*, or the *wasali* or *rufua bissa bīū*.

Enough has been said to show the value and importance of a close perusal of Hausa manuscripts; but emphasis must be laid on the fact that such writing must be the work of a learned MĀLAM, or probably these very details, which are of such importance to the scientific investigator, will be omitted, either through carelessness or ignorance.

Proverbs. So far as possible, the endeavour has been made to omit such proverbs as have already been collected and published.

The Notes. The student is expected to be familiar with the well-known works on the Hausa language by Canon Robinson, Dr. Miller, and others; hence only such phrases, words, or grammatical points as are not considered in these works are noticed here.

Acknowledgments. The debt is vast which the student of any language owes to those who have by their labours reduced that language to a definite form. This makes it possible in a comparatively short time for him to master what it has cost the pioneers many years of ceaseless labour to create out of nothing. Availing himself of the fruits of their labour, he can thus move forward to fresh fields of research. Such is the debt that the writer owes to Canon Robinson, Dr. Miller, and others. His thanks are also due to his friend Mr. Diamond Jenness, of Balliol College, Oxford, for revising the English translation; to Mr. Henry Balfour, Curator of the Pitt-Rivers Museum, Oxford, for having had the photographs taken that appear in this work, and for his valuable notes on the same which are again published through the courtesy of the Royal Anthropological Institute; to Professor Margoliouth for having translated the Arabic lines which occur in the Hausa script; to Mr. R. R. Marett, of Exeter College, Oxford, Reader in Social Anthropology, his tutor, who by his wonderful enthusiasm and ability may be said to have organized a school of working anthropologists, building upon the noble foundations laid by Sir E. B. Tylor and Dr. Frazer; to the authorities of the Clarendon Press, who, besides dealing most generously with a work not likely to prove remunerative, have likewise laid the author under deep obligation by their friendly interest and advice.

Finally, the publication of this work has only been made possible by the generous grant from the Government of the Gold Coast, to whom, as also to the Secretary of State for the Colonies, on whose recommendation the grant was made, the writer has the honour to tender his sincerest thanks.

R. SUTHERLAND RATTRAY.

EJURA, ASHANTI,
WEST AFRICA.
Sept. 8, 1911.

CONTENTS OF VOL. I

	PAGE
PREFACE	v
AUTHOR'S NOTE	x
ALPHABET	xix

PART I

A SHORT HISTORY, PURPORTING TO GIVE THE ORIGIN OF THE HAUSA NATION AND THE STORY OF THEIR CONVERSION TO THE MOHAMMEDAN RELIGION, *pp.* 1–35.

PART II

STORIES IN WHICH PEOPLE ARE THE HEROES AND HEROINES

1. The story of the slave by name 'The World' 38
2. How brothers and sisters first came to quarrel and hate each other 50
3. The story of the boy and the old woman, and how the wasp got his small waist 68
4. The story about a beautiful maiden, and how the hartebeest got the marks under its eyes like teardrops . . 74
5. How the whip and the 'māra' spoon (a broken bit of calabash) came to the haunts of men 80
6. A story about a chief, and how his sons observed his funeral, and the origin of the spider 108
7. A story about an orphan, showing that 'he who sows evil, it comes forth in his own garden'. 130
8. A story about a witch, and how the baby of the family outwitted her, and invented the first walled town . . 162

PAGE

9. The doctor who went a pilgrimage to Mecca on a hyena . 186
10. A story about a chief and his cook 200
11. A story about three youths all skilled in certain things, and how they used that skill to circumvent a difficulty . . 204
12. A story about a giant, and the cause of thunder 210
13. A story about an orphan which was the origin of the saying 'The orphan with a coat of skin is hated, but when it is a metal one he is honoured' 232
14. A story of a jealous man and what befell him 248
15. A story of a great friendship and how it was put to the test 254
16. A story about a test of skill 256
17. A story about Miss Salt, Miss Pepper, &c. 260
18. The story of Mūsa (Moses) and how it came about that brothers and sisters do not marry each other. . . . 274
19. A story about a hunter and his son 284
20. A story about a maiden and the pumpkin 300
21. The Gāwō-tree and the maiden, and the first person who ever went mad 312

ILLUSTRATION

Modern Brass Castings . . . . . . *Frontispiece*

ALPHABET AND WRITING SIGNS

The following are the letters employed in the Hausa Text :

Hausa Name of Letter.*	Letter.				Pronunciation in Hausa.	Remarks.
	Standing alone.	Connected with following.	Connected on both sides.	Connected with preceding.		
Alif	ا	ا	ا		—	The bearer of vowel-sounds only, as is also *ain*, really consonants.
Alif baki (black alif)				ـا		
Ba guje	ں				*b*	*Guje*, lit. *ba* with the twirl.
Ba		بـ	ـبـ	ـب		
Ta guje	ت				*t*	Lit. *ta* with the twirl.
Ta		تـ	ـتـ	ـت		
Tsha guje	ث				*tsch*	Lit. *tsch* with the twirl.
Tsha		ثـ	ـثـ	ـث		
Jim karami kōma bāya	ج				*j*	Lit. small *j* with a twirl behind.
Jim karami		جـ				Lit. small *j*.
Jim sābe			ـجـ			Lit. *j* with the part projecting.
Jim sābe kōma bāya				ـج		Lit. *j* with the part projecting and a twirl behind.
Ha karami kōma bāya	ح				*h*	Lit. little *h* pointing backwards.
Ha karami		حـ				Lit. little *h*.
Ha sābe			ـحـ	ـح		Lit. *h* with the part projecting.
Ha sābe kōma bāya						Lit. *h* with the part pointing backwards.

* These names are given by the *mālam* when teaching small children in the *masalachi* (schools) and are in no way classical, just as in English one might say big *A*, little *a*, &c.

Hausa Name of Letter.	Letter.				Pronunciation in Hausa.	Remarks.
	Standing alone.	Connected with following.	Connected on both sides.	Connected with preceding.		
Ha mai-rua kōma bāya	خ				*h* (as in Scotch *loch*)	Lit. *h* with the water (i.e. drop, dot) and pointing backwards.
Ha mai-rua		خـ				*h* with the (drop of) water.
Ha sābe mai-rua			ـخـ			*h* with the projecting part and dot.
Ha sābe mai-rua kōma bāya				ـخ		*h* with the projecting part pointing backwards.
Dal	د	د	ـد	ـد	*d*	
Zal	ذ	ذ	ـذ	ـذ	*z*	
Ra	ر	ر	ـر	ـر	*r*	
Zaira	ز	ز	ـز	ـز	*z*	
Tsa mal hannu	ط	طـ	ـطـ	ـط	*ts*	
Zadi	ظ	ظـ	ـظـ	ـظ	*z*	
Kaf lāsan	ك	كـ	ـكـ	ـك	*k*	
Lam arat	ل				*l*	
Lam		لـ				
Lam jaye			ـلـ			
Lam arat				ـل		
Mim arat	م				*m*	
Mim		مـ				
Mim jaye			ـمـ			
Mim arat				ـم		

Hausa Name of Letter.	Letter.				Pronunciation in Hausa.	Remarks.
	Standing alone.	Connected with following.	Connected on both sides.	Connected with preceding.		
Nun arat	ن				*n*	
Nun guda		نـ	ـنـ			
Nun arat				ـن		
Sodi arat	ص				*s*	
Sodi		صـ	ـصـ			
Sodi arat				ـص		
Lodi arat	ض				*l*	
Lodi		ضـ	ـضـ			
Lodi arat				ـض		
						Like *alif* bearer of vowel-sounds.
Ain baki wōfi kōma bāya	ع				—	Lit. *ain* with the open mouth and the twirl backwards.
Ain baki wōfi		عـ				*Ain* with the open mouth.
Ain likāfa			ـعـ			Stirrup *ain*.
Ain likāfa kōma bāya				ـع		Stirrup *ain* with the twirl back.
Angai baki wōfi kōma bāya	غ				*g*	*Angai* with the open mouth and the backward twirl.
Angai baki wōfi		غـ				*Angai* with the open mouth.
Angai likāfa			ـغـ			Stirrup *angai*.
Angai likāfa kōma bāya				ـغ		Stirrup *angai* with the backward twirl.
Fa guje	ڢ				*f*	*f* with the twirl.
Fa		ڢـ	ـڢـ			
Fa guje				ـڢ		

Hausa Name of Letter.	Letter. Standing alone.	Connected with following.	Connected on both sides.	Connected with preceding.	Pronunciation in Hausa.	Remarks.
Kaf wau	ق				*k* (guttural)	*Mai-rua*, lit. with the water, i.e. drop, dot.
Kaf mai-rua		قـ	ـقـ			
Kaf wau				ـق		
Sin arat	س				*s*	
Sin		سـ	ـسـ			
Sin arat				ـس		
Schin mai-rua arat	ش				*sch*	*Mai-rua, vide* above, *Kaf.*
Schin mai-rua		شـ	ـشـ			
Schin mai-rua arat				ـش		
Ha kuri	ه				*h*	
Ha baba		هـ	ـهـ			
Ha kuri				ـه		
Wau	و	و	ـو	ـو	*w*	
Ya arat	ي				*y*	
Ya		يـ	ـيـ			
Ya arat				ـي		

VOWELS

The vowel-signs in Hausa are :

1. ـَـ (above the line) called *wasali bisa* = *a*.
2. ـِـ (below the line) ,, *wasali kasa* = *i*.
3. ـٜـ (below the line) ,, *guda casa* = *e*.
4. ـُـ (above the line) ,, *rufua* = *o* or *u*.

Long vowels are distinguished from short vowels in writing as in pronunciation, and the length of a vowel is of such importance that the meaning of a word is often entirely changed, or the tense of a verb altered according as a vowel is long or short.

Long vowels are distinguished from short in writing in the following manner:

1. A long *ā* sound by an *alif* following the *wasali bisa* (ـَـ).
2. A long *ī* sound by a *ya* following the *wasali kasa* (ـِـ).
3. A long *ē* sound by a *ya* following the *guda kasa* (ـٜـ).
4. A long *ō* or *ū* sound by a *wau* following the *rufua* (ـُـ).

EXAMPLES :

LONG VOWELS	SHORT VOWELS
1. بَا = *bā*	1. بَ = *bă*
2. بِيـ = *bī*	2. بِ = *bĭ*
3. بٜى = *bē*	3. بٜ = *bĕ*
4. بُو = *bō* or *bū*	4. بُ = *bŏ* or *bŭ*

DIPHTHONGS

There are three diphthongs in Hausa ; they are written and pronounced as follows :

1. ـَيْ = *ai* (like *i* in nice).
2. ـَوْ = *au* (like *ow* in how).
3. ـُيْ = *oi* (like *oy* in boy).

READING SIGNS

1. (ّ) This is known as *karfī* (i.e. strength). It is placed over a consonant, which is then pronounced as if doubled.

2. (ٔ) Called *hamza.* It is put above an *alif* when the *wasali* is above, and below when the *wasali* is below. It has no effect on pronunciation. It is not used after a *wasali bisa* or *kasa bīū.*

3. (ٔ°) *Hamza da dauri* (*hamza* with a *dauri*) is placed over a consonant to indicate that a syllable is of medium length.

4. (°) *Dauri* indicates the end of a syllable or the omission of a vowel, and the vowel over which it is placed is doubled in pronunciation. This is most important as it alters the mood in certain pronominal forms of the verb.

5. (ً) *Wasali bisa biu*
(ٍ) *Wasali kasa biu*
(ٌ) *Rufua biu*

By the doubling of the vowel-signs the final vowel is pronounced nasally, that is, as if followed by an *n* (*nun*). Note the *alif* following a *wasali biu* has no *hamza.* The *wasali* or *rufua bīū* is sometimes used instead of the final *n* to denote the definite article.

6. (ا̄, ا̱) *Alif da tabi*, *bisa*, or *kasa* signifies that the *alif* and the following letter are not to be pronounced at all.

R. S. R.

PART I
HISTORICAL

[1] Bismi alahi alrahmani alrahimi wa sala alahu ala man la nabiu baadahu.
Wanan shi ne lābārin Hausa. Kōwa yā san shi garēsu tun zā-
-manin kākaninsu da uwāyensu, abin [2] karbōwa ne wurin mā-
-lamai(n)su da tsōfafinsu. Wanda ya zama wani, ba wanan ba,
bai zama [3] mai-chāu garēsu ba. Idan matanbaiyi ya tanbaye ka,
'Ana mafārin Hausāwa?' Ka che, 'Gaskīa mafārinsu [4] Barebari
da [5]Arewāwa.' Wada alāmari ya yi ya zama hakanan. Sarkin [6] Barno shi na
da dōki da kafō na zīnāria. [7] Dōkin nan ba shi hanīnia banza banza,
sai rānan jumaa. Idan ya yi hanīnia, sai ka che hadari ne.
[8] Aka-bōye shi chikin gida. [9] Sarkin kūa, shi na da dansa, ya [10] di-
-nga baiwa mai-kiwō nasa kurdi da rīguna, dōmin shi fitō
da dōkinsa, su je, shi gama da gōdīa [11] tasa. Kulum hakanan.
[12] Ranan sai mai-kīwō dōki ya fitō da dōki, ya kāwō. Dan sarki
kuma ya fitō da gōdīa tasa. Su-ka-tafi dāji. Su-ka-yi [13] bāye.
[14] Sarki kūa yā [15] rigāyi, yā fadi. Kōwa [16] aka-gani dan dōkinga

---

In the name of Allah the Compassionate, the Merciful, and may the peace of Allah be upon him, after whom there is no prophet. This is the history of the Hausa (nation). It has been familiar to every one from the time of their grandfathers and grandmothers, (and) is a thing which has been handed down from the malamai (learned men) and the elders. Any account other than this one is not authentic. If a questioner ask of you (saying) 'Where did the Hausa people have their origin?' Say (to him) 'Truly their origin was (from) the Barebari and Northerners'. And this is the account of how this came to pass. The king of Bornu had a horse with a golden horn. This horse did not neigh just at any time, but only on Fridays. If it neighed you would say it was a tornado. It was hidden away in a house. Now the king had a son. He (the son) continually gave him who looked after the horse money and robes in order that (he might persuade him) to bring his horse out, and they should come, and he should mate the horse with his mare. And it was always thus. (And) one day the man who was looking after the (king's) horse took (it) the horse out and brought it. The king's son too took his mare out. They went into the forest and the mare was covered. Now the king has (had) previously said that whoever was seen (with) a foal from this horse

بسم الله الرحمن الرحيم وصلى الله على من لا نبي بعده
ونن شين لابارن هوس كو وايا سنش غم مس تشنذا
مين كد كينفنس دعوا يفنس امن كم بو وابن ووشدا
لتين ع طو فو فنس رفعم يدم ونى بداونب =
بيكم ميشا وغم مسب ادن قشبم ميتشبيك
امنا مقار نهو لسداوا كبث تقسكيا مقاو فسن بم كبم
دا ارم واوا ودا الامر بيدم حكنن سن كن بم فو شد
نع منداوهد
م دوك دكبو دوكنن باشعنيق مينذ بنذ
سن رانم بوم عم ادريو هنيق سن كب حدويق
اكبو ويش تكم غذا سركن كو شنادد فس مد
نغم بيو ميكو فلس كم دي دريغم دو ومن شعنو
م دوكنلس سبكي شغم دغو دبا قسر كلم حكنن
ومن سم ميكيو وكدوك يبقو دوك يكداوو دنسم كم
كم يبقو دغو دبا قسر سكتف داج سكو بايس
سركم كو بيد وغد ميداقب كو واكعنم دفدوكنم

gidansa, shi-na-yanka shi. Yau ana-nan, [17] ranan gōdīa ta haifu. Har dā ya girma. Ranan dōkin sarki ya yi hanīnia. Sai dan dōki ya amsa. Sai sarki ya che, ' Kō gidan wa aka-gani, ayanka shi, kar [18] akāwō shi gabāna.' Sai fādāwa su-[19] ka-wātsu chikin gari. Su-na--neman dan dōki. Sai su-ka-je gidan dan sarki, kamar dōkin sarki da kafō nasa na zīnāria. Sai fādawa su-ka-che, ' Sarki yā che mu [20] tafō da kai.' Sai dan sarki ya dauki takōbi, ya sārē [21] mutun bīū, saura su-ka-[22] wātsē. Sai ya daura ma dan dōki sirdi, ya hau. Sarki ya che, [23] akāmō shi. Gari duka su-ka-hau dawāki, su-ka-bi shi. Ba su chika da shi ba. Yā [24] tafīa tasa. Sar--ki kūa yā che kar [25] ahawa dōki nasa. Idan bā dōkinsa ba bābu dōkin da ke chikāwa da shi. Dan sarki ya tafi, ya sabka kasar [26] Daura. Ya gani yar sarkin Daura, ita ke da [27] garin, shi na wurinta. Sai ranan ta che [28] ta-na-sonsa aure. Shi kūa ya che shi-na-so nata. Sai su-ka-yi aure. Yar sarki ta yi chiki, ta haifu dā, namiji, ta [29] yāyē. Ta yi chiki kuma, ta haifu mache, Mafārin [30] fitar Hausawa

---

at his house, he would have his throat cut. Things remained at this, (and) one day the mare gave birth, (and nothing happened) till the colt grew up, (when) one day the king's horse neighed, then the young horse answered. And the king said, ' At whose ever house they see it let (that person) be killed (lit. be cut), and do not let him be brought before me.' Then the councillors scattered (to make search) in the town. They were searching for the young horse. And they came to the house of the king's son, and behold as it were the king's horse with its golden horn. Then the councillors said, ' The king has said we must come with you.' Then the king's son lifted his sword. He cut down two men, the remainder were scattered. Then he saddled up the young horse. He mounted. The king ordered he should be seized and brought (before him). The whole town mounted their horses (and) followed him. They did not come up with him. He has gone his way. The king, moreover, has given orders that his own horse is not to be mounted, and if not his horse, then there was not the horse to overtake him. The king's son (rode) went on and (eventually) dismounted in the country of Daura. He saw the daughter of the king of Daura, she possessed the town. He stayed with her. And one day she said she wanted him in marriage and he too said he loved her. So they married. The king's daughter became with child. She bore a child, a son. She weaned it. She was again with child (and) bore a girl. And that was the origin of the Hausa nation.

تحيق ميا غودم فمر وفمر آمنا يموا شنكداينا شنا فمس غدم

كر ود مف سرم هيمنق يم كسر كرود رمف رمغيا د مح

كم شاكنيا فنقكا وفو غدم ميجث كسرس سمس فمس ميا كحو

سنا يمرغ كنث طاوكس اوادقا سوكس فغيا شورودا كا

كسرس كرودمحك كسرسف غدمف يجسكس سنس كودمف بقمر

بف يا كمرس كبسكا اوادقا سن يارودنيا مف سرمف وجبك د

سرداس يمبوجكت كودري كسرمف د سس كمكدوجبقم

كودمف امرو يح وينس لجبا اوكسار وسمس يميو قمر

وحكس كود ذمغ شوم ادا ثيم كسرس وحمي مرس

سمس سقمبيا مبيت شكدا بيشم كسيم كاوا د

بسنكو كوده ياز ا سنيكي ودومها كرم بثيا موكم

كيسميس كيت كمركسف مشدا اوكتكعبكدو بابا

شنا غرمغ كبتما او ودركسرم يم فيي اورود كسر

ميث شكو بروع سفقوسنا تمت قمرو سن قفو

شنا [redacted] سوفمث سو سكم عوبرم يم سركم تمرتك تميف

اسوموه رتقبمف رادبم ثمف فيحت محك كنوم يبايت مجنا د

ke nan. Barebari da Daurāwa su ne kākaninsu. Ama wajan Musulumchi
daga [31] Barnō ya fitō. Hausawa, da Barebari, da kōwane iri, duka nan
yanma da wuri kāfurai ne. Saanan mālamai su-ka-che, wada alāmari ya
zama. Akwai
wani mutun, chāna Barnō, daga yāyan sarākunansu, sūnansa Dalāma.
Da ya chi sarauta, ana-che masa Mainadināma. [32] Fasara tasa, wai sarki
[33] maabōchin [34] rinjāya. Saada sarauta tasa ta wuche, watani sai ya a-
-ika manzo, zūa-ga halīfa. Saanan kūa [35] Abūbakari-Sidīku, yarda(n) Ala
shi tabata garēshi, shi ne halīfa. Kā ga mafārin aikāwa tasa, chewa
[36] wanchānanka mutun yā kashe, shi-na-jin lābārin Musulumchi tun
bai chi sarauta ba. Kā ga sūnan manzo nasa, da ya aika, sū-
-nansa Gujālo. Sāilin da manzo ya zo, ya iskē halīfa, batun
yāki yā dauki hankalinsa, bai che ma manzo kōmi ba, sai ya che
da shi zamna nan, saanan bai kōma tuna magana tasa, dōmin
daukan hankalinsa da maganar yāki na [37] mazōwan tāwāye. Manzō ya za-
-mna chāna, har manzō ya mutu. Bāyan wata uku da kwānaki kadan
saanan Halīfa Abūbakari Sidīku shi kuma ya mutu. Bāyan watani
sāilinda aka-aje [38] Umaru Ibunuhutābi. Shi ne Halīfa bāyan Abūbakari

---

The Barebari and Daura people were their ancestors. But the Mohammedan religion, as far as that is concerned, from Bornu it came. Hausas and Barebari and whatever race (you can name) in the West were at first in early times pagans. Then the malamai (scribes) said that this is what happened. There was a certain man away there at Bornu from among the children of their royal house, his name (was) Dalama. When he came to the throne he was called Mainadinama, the meaning of that is, 'a chief more powerful than any other.' After he had reigned for some months then he sent a messenger to the Caliph. Now at this time Abubakari-Sidiku, the blessing of Allah be upon him, he was Caliph. You have seen the beginning of his being sent, referring back to that man (Mainadinama), was that he was hearing about Mohammedanism before he succeeded to the kingdom. Behold the name of his envoy whom he sent, his name was Gujalo. At the time when the envoy came he found the Caliph's attention occupied with a war. He said nothing to the envoy. All he said was, 'Remain here.' Then he did not again remember his words because his mind was so occupied with words of the war of the father of the twins. The messenger remained there till the messenger died. After three months and a few days then the Caliph Abubakari Sidiku he too died. After some months Umaru Ibunuhutabi was set up. He was the Caliph after Abubakari

بكنش ببر كببر دم ورا وا سو فبى محمد كننس هو أمدا وجم مسلمث
دمببر قو يجتوا هو سوا دببر مببر دكو ونى عم دكنس
ينض د وعدا فرينى سعنن مد امنم سكث ود الأمير يخما كو
ونفش ندر ببر فو دغ ميا ميم سر اكننس سو فنس د لماهم
د ميت لسر وت أما بعلس هسمر د ندا م قسرا قس ومسر كي
ما ابو شر فجار سعد سر وتا قس قوب وقنغ اسر بما
يك منذ و د وغلب سعنن كو ابو بكر صديق ميرد آل
شتنت غمر مش شيبر خليق كدغ مجا ونداكد وا قس قوا
ونتا فنك متر يعبش يشناجر الاما ور مسلمث متس
ميث لسر وقاب كدغ سو فمر منذ و فسر دميا يك سو
منسر فجال سا ولند منذ و ميذ و ميا سكي قليق بتس
ميلك ميا د وك حنكلنس بيشمذ وكو مي هسر يث
د شم كمنتا مس سعنر بكو م قمر معنذ قلب دوس
دو كر منكلنس د معنر ياك نمذ و ونتا وا يس منذ و يم
مرنا ر قم منذ وينا بد امير وق أك دكوانكم كدن
سعنر خليف ابو بكر صديق شيكم يمث بدامير وتينه
سد ولند اكا جي عمر ابن خطاب شيبر خليق بدامير ابو بكر

Asidīku. Sai ya tuna alāmarin manzō da mutūa tasa. Saanan su-ka-yi shāwara su sauran [39] sahabai. Su-ka-gama kai bisa aaika, zūa Barnō manzō. Aka-aiki Umaruasi, da takardū na Alkorani. Aka-che rubūtun Abdulāhi dan Umoru halīfa, da rawanī, da takōbī, da [40] kasausawa, da [41] garkūa, da [42] fūlar sarauta, da tarkache ma--suyawa, da akushī. Dukanta keauta ne, daga halīfa, zūa Maina--dināma. Sāilin da manzō ya kusa, sai ya aika garēsu, wanda [43] kāsanashe su lābārin zūansa. Sarkin Barnō, da mutāne(n)sa, su-ka-hau dawāki, su-ka-gamū da shī nīsa. Sāilin da ya shiga gari--nsa sai ya nada masa rawanī, ya [44] sābunta sarauta tasa, ya sa masa sūna, Sarkin Barno, ya ba shi dukan abinda aka-che shi ba shi, dōmin kyeauta wanan da aka-aiko da ita garēshi. Ya zamna garēsu. Shi-na-sanashe su adīnin Ala, da sunnō--ni manzō nasa, tsīra da aminchin Ala, shi tabala garēsu. Sun kashe, su-na-girmama shi, [45] matukan ban girma, su-na-neman albarka da sauran kalāchi nasa, da abinchinsa, da wurin aje.

Asidiku. Then he called to mind the report of the envoy and his death. Then they held a consultation, they his friends who remained. They joined their heads about the question of sending an envoy to Bornu. Umaruasi was sent with manuscripts of the Koran. It was said the writing of Abdulahi the son of Umoru the Caliph, and turbans and a sword and spears and shields and the kingly fez and such things and plates; all these presents from the Caliph to Mainadinama. When the envoy drew near he sent to them one to acquaint them of the news of his coming. The king of Bornu and his men mounted their horses and met him afar off. When he (the envoy) entered his town, then he bound the turban on him, he was established in his right to the kingdom, he was given the name of the king of Bornu, he (the king) gave him everything he was told to give him, because of the presents which he (the envoy) had been sent with for him. He lived among them. He was instructing them (the people of Bornu) in the creed of Allah and the names of His messengers, may the salvation and trust of Allah be assured to them. They continued to honour him, to the extreme that honour could be carried. They sought a blessing (by eating) the remains of his meals and his food and from the spot (he) se

الصِّدِّيقُ سَرْكِنْ يَقِّ الأَمِيرُ مُنْذُرْ دَ مُتَوَامَسَ سَعَنْ سَكِي
ڢَدَوَرْ سُو سُو رُحَمَّبُو وَالِسِعِفُوا سُكَّعُمْ كَيْ مَشَيْ أَيْكِ
دُوَبَرْ ڢُو مَنْدُ وُ أَكَ أَيْكِ عُمَرُ الْقَاضِي تَقْكَمْ دَوَمَا الْفُرْءَانِ
أَكَنْ وُبُوتَنْ عَبْدُ اللّٰهِ دَنْ عُمَرُ خَلِيفَ دَرُوَفِ دَتَكُوبِ
دَكَسُو سُوَا دَعَمْ كُو دَفُولَنْ سَرَوْتَ دَقَرْكَنْ هَدَ
سَيْوُ دَأَكَشِ دُكَنْتَ بَجُوقَدَفِي دَعَ خَلِيفَ دُوَمَيْسَ
دِقَدَمَ سَدَ لِقَدَ مَنْدُ وَيَكَسَ سُنْ يَدَأَيْكَ عُمَرُ مُكَسُ وُڢَدَ
كَدَ اسَنْبِشَ لَابَارْ ڢَدُو ڢَسَ سَرْكِنْ بَرْ ڢُو دَمَتَابِسَ
سَكَّتُو دَوَاكِ سُكَّعُمْ دَبِشِ ڢِيَسَ سَدَ لِقُمْ يَشْغَ ڢَمْ
ڢَسَ سَنْ وَتَخَدَ امَسَ رُوَفِ يَسَدَ بَنْتَ هَسَرْ وُقَدَ اقَمَسَ يَسَدَ
مَسَ سُومَنِ سَرْكِنْ بَرْ ڢُو يَبَدَ لِشِ دُكَمْ أَبِنْدَ أَكَنْ
شِبَدَ لِشِ دَوَمَرْ بُكُوتَ وَمْ دَ أَكَدَ أَيْكُو دَ إِتَ عُمَرُ مَشِ
يَخَ مَرْعُمَرُ مَسَ شِنَدَ سَنْبِشَ أَدِ يِمَنْرَ أَلْ دَسَنْفُو
فِمْ مَنْدُ وُفَسَ حِيرَادَ أَمِنْشِرَ أَلْ شِنْتَ عُمَرُ مَسَ بِ
سُنْكَيْشِ سَنَاغِمْ مَحَاشِ مُتَكَمْ بَنْغَمْ مِسُ سَنَابِمْ
أَلْبَرْكَ دَسُو وُنْكِنَدَ اشِيعَسَ دَ أَبِنْشَنْسَ دَوُرِنَاجِ سِ

kafāfu nasa. Sāshensu su-na-neman albarka da fīātachen mājina tasa da mīawunsa. Su-na-hawan [46] shigifū, dōmin ganinsa. Su-na-neman alberka kuma da shāfan tufāfi nasa, da tākalminsa, da būlala tasa, har aka-che, su-na-neman albarka da daba tasa, da sauran harāwa tasa, da tōrōso nata. Ya rubūta masu takardū kuma, da rubū--tun hannu nasa, mai-alberka. Ya zamna bisa hakanan matukan zāmani, har aka-che garēshi, wadansu mazōwan kasa su-na bāyanka, su-na-sō Musulumchi indaa sun gane ka, daa sun bi ka. Bai gaskata ba, sai ya aiki mai-tōnō bōyē, ba asan sūnansa ba. Ya tafi, ya yi yāwō chikin kasan Hausa. Ya tōnē ya ji su-na-yabo Musulumchi, su-na-sō nasa. Ya kōmō, ya baiwa Umaru Ibunua--si lābāri. Umaru Ibunuasi ya gaia ma mutānensa, ya che su tafi. Su-ka-yarda. Saanan ya yi shiri. Ya aiki Abdulkarīmu--Mukaila zūa Kanō. Kwatamchin mutun dari uku, Lārabāwa, su-ka-bi shi. Sāilin da Abdulkarīmu ya kusa da su, sai ya aiki wanda ke-gaia masu. Ya zō, ya che, 'Gaia masu manzō na manzō yā zō.'

---

his feet. Half of them were seeking blessing from the mucus from his nose and his spittle (by rubbing it on their persons). They were climbing the roofs in order to see him. They also sought blessing by touching his robes and his slippers and his whip, until it was even said they looked for a blessing from his beasts, and the remains of their fodder and their dung. Now he wrote manuscripts for them in the writing of his own hand, the blessed one. He lived amid such works up to the very end of (his) sojourn (and this went on) till he was informed that, 'Other owners of (another) land are behind you (and) are wishing for the Mohammedan religion, should they see you they would follow you.' He did not give (this report) credence until he had sent one to spy out (the land), his name is unknown. He (the spy) went and travelled over Hausa-land. He made secret inquiries, he heard they were praising the Mohammedan faith and that they wished for it. He returned and gave Umaru Ibunuasi the news. Umaru Ibunuasi told his people. He said they must go (and preach the Mohammedan religion). They agreed. Then he made preparations. He sent Abdulkarimu-Mukaila to Kano. About 300 men, Arabs, followed him. When Abdulkarimu was near to them (the people of Kano) then he sent one to inform them. He (the messenger) came and said, 'Tell them the envoy of the envoy has come.'

كبد فو قنس سد بنفنس سند بمر البرك دبيا قنبش مدبنا
قنس د ميا وفنس سند حور شغبو دوم غنس سند بمر
البرك كم دشد قنتجا فينس د قدكلينس د بولال
قنس حر أكب سند بمر البرك ددبتس د سحو وحرارا
تنس د ثور وطو فت يربو قدامس تكرد وكم د زبو
ثر هنو فنس ميا لحبرك يد مر وبلس حكنمر متكس
دامن حر أكب غمرمش ود فسر مد ونكسو سند
بايتك سند سو مسلمث إزم أسنفنك د أسنيك
بيفسكتاب سن يايك ميثو فو بدوبى بأسنسو قنلسب
يتف يو يدوو تكرك سو هو لس يثو بن يج سند ييو
مسلمث سند سو فنس يكو مو ييبو عمر ابن القا
ضي لابدوش عمر ابن القاضي يقيد مهتد قنس مينا
تستفي سكيرد تسعنم مو شر يأيك عبد الكريم
المغيلي ذوكغو كتفش مترد ري أك لاربدا وا لسكيش
تسهلن عبد الكريم يكسر سو تسو يأيك وم
بكفيا مس يد ذو يبشغيا مس منذ ونمند ويادو

Sāilin da ya zō masu ya gaia masu abinda aka-aiko shi da shi. Su-ka-gaskata shi, su-ka-karbi abinda ya zō da shi. Sāilin Kanō tā kashe alkaria che, ama bābu birni, sūnan [47] mutānen Kanō, Muhamadu-da-Jākara, sāilin da Abdulkarīmu ya sabka garēsu. Ya rubūta masu litāfi da rubūtun hannu nasa, mai-albarka, dōmin bai zō musu da litāfi ba, daga wajen Umaru Ibunu(l)asi. Dōmin hakanan alāmari yā kashe, dukan wanda ke sō shi iya rubūtu mai-chau, sai shi tafi zūa Barnō, shi zamna chāna, saanan shi kōmō. Ama Abdulkarīmu yā kashe shi-na-sanashe su sharaa Ala, da hukumchin sharaa, har su-ka-tanbaye shi abūbua da ba su kasan Lārabāwa. Bai san jawābin da zaa shi gaia masu ba. Sai ya che da su, su bari har shi kōmo. Akwai daga abinda su-ka-tanbaye shi, tunkū da yanyāwa, da gafia, da būdāri, da tsāra, da waninsa. Ya zamna garesu watani, kōwache rāna shi-na -sanache su Alkorani da Hadisai, masu-chau, har aka-che da shi, 'Akwai wata alkaria kusa da alkaria nan, ana-che mata Kāshina,

---

When he came to them he told them what (message) he had been sen with. They believed him, they received the thing which he had brough Now at this time Kano was an unenclosed town but not a walled towr the name of the men (man) at Kano (was) Muhamadu Dajakara at the tim when Abdulkarimu alighted amongst them. He (Abdulkarimu) wrot them books in the writing of his own hand, the blessed one, because h had not come to them bringing books from Umaru Ibunu(l)asi. And thu it has come to be reported that every one who wished to be able to writ well let him set out towards Bornu and remain there (till he had learned t write) and then return (home). But Abdulkarimu continued to instru them the laws of Allah and the commands of the law until they mad inquiries about things which were not (to be found) in Arabia. He di not know what answer to give them. Then he said to them to leave th matter open till he returned (to Arabia). Among the things they we asking about were panthers, and civet-cats, and rats, and servals, and tig cats, and such like (whether clean or unclean). He lived with them (man months (and) every day instructed them well in the Koran and th Traditions, till at length he was informed, 'There is another town near th town, it is called Katsina,

تس دهلند يفرو قس يفيا قس ابند اكا ايكو شد شم

سكفسكتدا شر سككزب ابند يفرو دشم تس دهلنكو

تداكشو الفد يدب اما باف بيرفي شوقمر فتدا قمر كنوا

محمد دباكد تس دهلند عبد الكريم بلسبك غمر قسر دع

بير بجوتدا قس يتا فجو دو بجوقمر هنو قسر قيبا ابرك

دوقمر بيقد و قس دلتا فكب دغ وجر عحمر ابرعا صح

دوقمر قكنز الامد ييا كشو دكم وقد بكسو شخو

زبوقت قيتو سرشتف ذو مبرقو شغمر قدر سعنر

شكوقو اما عبد الكريم يا كبتو شنداس تبشس

• شدع ال د قكفشر شرع حمر سكتنبشر ابو بجو

د بداسر كسرلاوبداوا بيلسر قجوابر دذا اشغيا قسب

تسر قيشد تسو سبير حمر شكوقو اكور دغ ابند =

سكتنبش تنكوا دينيدا دغجو د بجو كروى دطاوا

دونفسر يغ مرغم مكسر وقسنه كجوب رامى شقا

تسنبشس الفد ار د حد يغر مداستدا و حمر اكب

دشم اكور وت الفرتو كسرد الفريتر اقد يقن كداشر

indaa sun gane ka, mutānen [48] garin, daa sun bāda gaskīa garēka da wa ya aikō ka. Sāilin da ya ji hakanan, sai ya yi shiri, ya tafi da kansa, zū garēta. Sāilin da su-ka-ji lābāri zūansa, sai su-ka-gamu da shi nīsa. Sāilin da ya sabka garēsu, ya sanashe su abinda ya sanashe su, ya fōri wanda ke rubūta musu litāfi. Aka-che, chewa shia, bai rubūta musu Alkorāni ba da hannu nasa, dōmin hakanan ne, mutānen Kanō sun Alkorāni, sun fi mutānen Kāshina har yau. Saanan bāyan kārēwa tasa daga alamarin Kāshina, sai ya kōma zūa Kanō, ya zamna kadan. Saanan, sāilin da ya yi nufi kōmāwa zūa Barnō, ya che da su, 'Da sannu naa kōmō garēku da jawābai abinda ku ka tanbaye ni garēta.' Saanan ya tāshi, ya tafi. Ama dayawa chikin mutānensa ba su bi shi sai kadan su-ka-bi shi chikinsu. Saura su ka zamna, su-na abin girmam chikin Kanō. Danginsu sun kashe mabayana sananu chikin Kanō har yau, har mutāne su-ka-che masu sharifai, aa ba sharifai ba ne su dai Lārabāwa ne. Hakikan Abdulkarīmu yā sainya alkāli chikin Kanō, da shugaban sala, da mai-yanka, da wanda ke sanada yār

---

should the people of the town see you they would believe you and who sent you.' When he heard (them speak) thus, then he made re He set out himself to go to it (the town). When they got news o coming, then they met with him afar off. When he alighted among t he taught them about what (he had come) to instruct them in. instructed one who was to write books for them. It was said, speak of him, he did not write the Koran with his own hand, and because of the Kano people surpass the Katsina in their knowledge of the Kora to-day. Then, after the completion of his work at Katsina, he went b going to Kano, (and) remained there a short time. Then when he tho of returning to go to Bornu he said to them, 'Shortly I shall retur you with the answer to what you were asking about.' Then he ros and went away. But many among his people did not follow him, a few among them followed him. The rest remained and continue perform great deeds in Kano. Their descendants are found (and) kn in Kano until to-day, till people called them seraphs, but surely they not seraphs, they were just Arabs. Of a truth Abdulkarimu has se a judge in Kano, and one to lead in prayers, and one to slaughter stock), and one who was to instruct the youths

إن د أسنغنك متانبن غمز د أسنباد غنسكيا غمبك د ونم
يا أبكوك سدلفن بج حككن سنو يمو بشر يتي د ككنس د ور
غمبمت سدلفن سكج لامباور دولفس سنو سككم د بشم فيس
سدلفن ميسنبك غمبس يسنشبس أبند يلسنشبس يجور
وند بكرمبوقا مسر لتدفكي أكث قوالشم بنرمبوقا هد
مسر الفرء افيب دهننوفس دوفم حككنز بن لسنفس
الفرء ار سنف متانبر كداشر مرميو سنفنز بابين كدابر موا
قسر د م الامر فكداشر لسن بكوم دوككو يند مر كدن
سنفنز سدلفن د يمي نجركه ماوا دومبر فوا ميشد سو
د سنفوفنا كومو غمبكه د جواب أبند ككنعمبي
غمبمت سنفنز ميتاشر بتف آما د ميو ثكر متابنس بهيلشي
سوكدن سكميش ثكنس سو السكد مر سنا أبرغم قمدا و
ثكرككنو د نفنس سنكشو مبنا سنفو ثكرككنوا
حرميو حرمتا بنو سكنمس سرفو عدء وداشر فحبو
سود نا لاورداوا بي حكيكر عبد الكريم ميا سنر الفاضم
ثكرككنو د شو غمبنحمل د مبينكى د وفنم بكسنم يادا

Alkorāni, da mai-kiran salla. Ya halalta masu abinda Ala ya halalta, ya han masu abinda Ala ya hana. Sāilin da ya kōma zūa ga Umaru Ibunula--si, ya ba shi lābāri da abinda su-ka-tanbaye shi. Sai Umaru Ibunula--si ya yi kurum, har ya kōma zūa ga halīfa, saanan ya aikō da jawā--binta, bāyan wata shida. Ya halalta masu sāshenta, ya hane su sāshe. Ama Abdulkarimu bai kōma zūa Barnō ba, bāyan kōmāwa tasa zūa garinsu, kō zūa Kanō. Hakanan Umaru Ibunulasi, ama yā yi sarautar Masar, bāyan kōmāwa tasa gida. Ama sauran garūrūa, su-na-zūa, sāshe zūa Kanō dōmin sanin adīni, sāshe kūa zūa Kāshina, har adīni ya chika kasan Hausa dukanta. Sai kasan [49] Kabi, chewa su, sun ki Musulumchi, su-ka-tabata bisa Kāfirchinsu. Su-ka-tabata chikinsa. Sarākunansu sun kashe, sūnansu, Barbarma, Argōji, Tabāriu, Zartai, Gōbari, Dadafāni, Katāmi, Bardo, Kudamdam Sharīa, Bādōji, Karfu, Darka, Gunba, Katatar, Tāmu. Wadanan dukansu sun ki Musulumchi bāyan shiga tasa kasan

---

in the Koran, and one to call (them) to prayer. He made lawful for the: that which Allah had made lawful, and forbade that which Allah ha forbidden. When he returned to go to Umaru Ibunulasi he gave him a account of what they had asked him about. And Umaru Ibunulasi w silent (on the subject) till he returned to go to the Caliph and then he se an answer to it (the question) after six months had elapsed. He ma lawful for them half of it, half he made unlawful. But Abdulkarimu d not return to Bornu after his return to their (his, Abdulkarimu's) tov or to Kano. Thus (also) Umaru Ibunulasi, but he ruled over Egypt aft his return home. Now the remainder of the towns were coming in, h of them to Kano in order to know about the (new) religion, and half al to Katsina, until the creed filled all Hausa-land. Now the Kibi countr speaking of them, they refused (to adopt) the Mohammedan religion, th continued in their paganism. They persisted in it. Their kings, (the: were their names, Barbarma, Argoji, Tabariu, Zartai, Gobari, Dadafa Katami, Bardo, Kudamdam, Sharia, Badoji, Karfu, Darka, Gunba, Katat Tamu. All these refused the Mohammedan creed after his advent in the land

الفزاري د مينكير فحل يعلنتا مس أبنعم اليعلنتا يهنتا
مس أبنعم أليهمر لسدملنم يكوم دو غعمر ابن العا
ص ميباشن لابدو د أبنعم لسكتنبيش بين عمر ابن العا
ص ميبي مكرم حز يكوم دو غليق لسكتنرما يكوم دجو
ابمنت ماييرو فشم يعلنتا مس لسد بشنت يهنبس
سدبشو أما عبد الكريم بيكوم دو بر فوب باين
كومدوا امس دو غيم فنس كودو وعنوا امكن عمر
ابن العاص وأما يدن لسرو متز محمد بداين كومدوا امس
غدا أما هسو زغم ورو لسنا فطو لسدبشو ركنو دوفس
لسنن ادمير لسدبشو كو دو كداشر حز ادمير يشك كلس
هولس د كننت لسو كسم هحو كسب شوالسو سنو
فسلفنت سككتبت بمسكاو فتنس سككنبت تكفس
لسد اكنفس سنكبشو سو فتنس بربزم ؞ ازعوج
فبدورن ؞ زوفتو غو بم ؞ دكجلو كنام برندوا كلدمدم
شرما بادوم كرفجو دزك غنبي كتنز متدموا
وهمن دكنس سنو معلنث بايرشفا منسر كلس

Hausa. Saanan sāilin da Zaidu ya chi sarauta, sai ya musulumta da wada ke tāre da shi, kasan Kabi ta musulumta, zūa wakatin Bata-Musa; wada su ne sarākai Kabi chikin Musulumchi. Fārinsu, Zaidu, Muhamadu, Namakāta, Sulaimāna, Hisrikōma, Abdulāhi, Dunbāki, Alia, Usmānu, Chisgari, Barbarmanaba, Muwāshi, Muhamadu-Karfi, Bata--Musa. Bāyansu Fūmu ya yi sarauta. Ya juya Musulumchi da Kāfurc Wadanan su ne wadanda su-ka-kāfurta. Fārinsu, Fūmu, Kautai, Gunba, Sakana-Murtāmu, Kanta, Rātaini, Gaiwa, Gado, Māsu, Chidagora, Gabangari, Maikebe, Marshākoki, Lazimu, Māshirāna, Makata. Wadanan su ne dukansu sun tabata chikin Kāfurchi. Sāilin da Kanta ya chi sarauta, ya sābunta Musulumchi, ya tanb mālamai abinda ke chikin litāfi. Ya tsaida adīni chikin zāmaninsa da wa-nda ke bie da shi, har kasan Kabi duka ta musulumta. Wanan shi ne -nansu. Kantāhu, Gōfe, Dauda, Hamidu, Sulaimāna, Mālu, Ishāka, Muhamadu-Nashāwi, Amuru, Muhamadu-Kābe, Kantanabaiwa, Muhomadu-Shīfāya, Hāmidu. Wadanan dukansu sun tabata chikin Musulum

---

of the Hausas. Then at the time when Zaidu came to the throne [th he became a Mohammedan and those who were with him. The K country became Mohammedan up to the time of Bata-Musa. These w the kings of Kabi under the Mohammedan régime. The first of t was Zaidu, (then) Muhamadu, Namakata, Sulaimana, Hisrikoma, Abdu Dunbaki, Alia, Usmanu, Chisgari, Barbarmanaba, Muwashi, Muhama Karfi, Bata-Musa. After them Fumu ruled. He turned Mohammedan into paganism. These were they who became pagans. The first of t (was) Fumu, (then) Kautai, Gunba, Sakana-Murtamu, Kanta, Rat Gaiwa, Gado, Masu, Chi-da-gora, Gaban-gari, Maikebe, Marshak Lazimu, Mashirana, Makata. These were they who all continue paganism. At the time when Kanta ruled he revived the Mohamme religion (and) inquired of the learned men the contents of (their) bo He established the faith in his time and in that of them who follo him, till the whole of the Kabi country became Mohammedan. T were their names, Kantahu, Gofe, Dauda, Hamidu, Sulaimana, M Ishaka, Muhamadu-Nashawi, Amuru, Muhamadu-Kabe, Kantanaba Muhamadu-Shifaya, Hamidu. All these continued in the Mohamme faith.

هولس سغنن لسدهلنغ زنيم ميث سروت لسي يمسلمت دارد مقد
بتد رمعشي كسنكب قمسلمت دروفتر بتامولس ودمن
سوبني لسراكوكب تكرمسلمف قدروفسر ارنيم .:. محمد .:. =
نمكات سليمان حيسكوم عبد الله دنبايكم علي
عثمان فشفم يبمرم نبي مواشي محمد . كربج بنم
مولسو مدانفس قوم يبي سروت يبجوبر مسلمت دكدبرق
نبي ودنر سوبني ودنم سككا بنرت قدروفس قوم =
كومتي غمنبي سكرفر قدامو كنتا واتيم عنبوا غدوا
قدلسوا نيع غور غمبرغمر مموكب هم شدكوك لازم
مدشرانا مكات ودنر سوبني دكنس سنتبت نكركا
بنرف لسدهلنغ كنتا بيث سروت يلسابمت قسلمت يتبنو
مدالقع أبنغ بكيكر يشداقي مطيعادمير فكر وامتنس درع
قدكبيور نشم قركلسركيجدك تمسلمت ومرشبنو لسو
فنسر كنتاه غوبكر دراد حيكم سليمان قبالو
السعار محمد فشداو آدم محمد كدامي عنتا نبيو .:.
محمد فيكاور قامد ودنر دكنس سنتبت فكر مسلمف

Sāilin da Barbarma ya yi sarauta, ya musāya Musulumchi, ya zama Kā--furchi. Kāfurchi ya tabata zūa wakatin Hūdu. Shi ne wananda Usmānu dan Fōdio ya yi yāki da shi. Ya kōre shi, har ya kashe shi kusa da Kebi. Buhāri dan Abdu-Salāmi, shi ya kashe shi. Shi ne sarkin Jega. Danginsu su ne sarākaita zūa yau. Yā kāre.
Ama chikin Kanō adīni ya tabata bāyan kōmāwa tasa, shi Abdulkarimu, adīni ya dinga dadūa kulum, da girma da daukaka.
Ya tabata bisa hakanan shekaru dayawa, zūa wakatin [50] Mainamugabadi. Shi ne wanda ya juya abinda Abdulkarimu ya aje. Ya walakanta suna, ya daukaka sarauta, ya walakanta Musulumchi, ya girmama gumākai, ya yi girman kai, ya yi shishigi. Māsu-waazu su-ka-yi masa waazu, bai anpāne shi ba waazunsu sai ya dada gir--man kai. Shi-na-[51]alfahari. Ya tabata bisa hakanan har ya mutu. Dan uwa--nsa Kunbāri ya zamna mazamninsa, ya bi tafarkinsa.
Ya tabata ga wanan har wakatin Runfa. Shi kuma ya dada Kāfurchi da shishigi. Shi ne wanda ya aure būdrūa alif. Ya yi fōrō da yin afi da turbīa gaba garēshi, saan gaisua. Ya che,

---

When Barbarma became king he changed the Mohammedan religion (and became a pagan. Paganism lasted up to the time of Hudu. He was th one Usmanu the son of Fodio made war against. He drove him out (an pursued him) till he slew him near to Kebi. Buhari the son of Abdu -Salimi, he it was who slew him. He was the king of Jega. His famil are its kings till to-day. It is finished. But as for Kano in (it) the fait continued after his, Abdulkarimu's, return (home). The faith continued t increase always with force and power. And it lasted on such footing fo many years until the time of Mainamugabadi. It was he who change the order of things Abdulkarimu had set up. He set at naught the la (of Mahomed), he made the kingship all powerful, he disregarded th Mohammedan faith, he exalted fetish worship, and was arrogant. H surpassed (all his predecessors in evil). Instructors endeavoured to instruc him, but their admonitions were of no avail against him, but he increase in pride. He was vainglorious. He continued thus till he died. Hi brother Kunbari reigned in his stead and followed in his ways. He to continued in this (evil) till the time of Kunfa. He also spread paganis and evildoing. It was he who married 1,000 maidens. He instructe (people) to prostrate themselves and put earth on their heads befo saluting him. He said,

لَسَالِنْغَ بَرْمَمْرَمَ مِيَ سَرْأَتَ يَفْسَدَا نَسْلَمْثِ مِيغَمْ كَا
فُرْثِ كَدَافُرْفِ يَبْثَتَ دُرُوَفْتِنْ هُودَ شِيِنُو وَفْرْ دَغْثَمَارُ
دَنْفُودِنْ مِيِي يَاكِ دَشِ يَكُورْمَشْ حَمْرَكَبْشِسْ
كُسَرْ دَكَبَّ بُعَادَرْ دَنْعَبْدِ السَّلَامِ شِ يَكَبْشِسْ فِينُ
سَنْكَنْ جِخْ دَنْغَنْسَ سُوفُ سَرَاكِيْنَ دُوَّيُو يَاكَابُرُ
أَمَّا تَكِرْكَنُو أَلّذِي مِيرِّ يَقْبَتْ بَالْيِمَّرْ كُوهَدَا وَاتَّسَ شِم
عَبْدُ الكَرِيمُ أَلّذِي مِيرِّ يَدِ دَنْغِ دُوَا كُلُّمْ دَغِمْ هَادَا دُوَرُوكَ
يَفْثَبْ مَسَرْ قَكَنْفُ شُكَرُ وَدَمِّيُو دُرُوَفْتِنْ مَيْرْ فَجْمِ
شِنْ وَفَدَ يَجُوْتِرْ أَبَنْدَ عَبْدِ الكَرِيمِ مِيَاأَبِي يُوَلَاكُنْتَ
سُنْرْ يَمْ وَكَكْ سَرْأَوْقْ مِيُوَلَاكُنْتَ فَنْسَلُهْثِ يَفْغُرْ مَمْ
غُمْدَاكُو مِيِي غِمْرْ مَرْكِي بِيِي شِشْغِم مَاسُوعَظ سُك
يَمَسَرْوَعَظْ يَبِيَا أَمْجَدْ فَشِبْ وَعَظُنْسِ سَرْ مِيَدْ دَغِمْر
مَنْكِي شِنْدَ الْفَخْرِ يَقَبْتَ مِسَرْ هَكَنُّ حَرْيَفْثَ دَنْفُو
مْسَرْ كُنْبَارِ يَذْ مَرْ مَدْ مَنِنْسَ يَبِ تَقَبْ كِنْسُ
يَقَبْثَ غُوفُنْ هَمْ وَفْتِنْ رُنْقْ شِيكُمْ مِيَدْ دَكَافُرْثِ
دَشِشْفِ شِيِينِ وَمْدَ يَعُوْوبُدْ زُوَا أَلِفْ مِيِي فُورُ رَا دَمْ
يَفْسْرْ أَفِ دَنْتُرْ بِيَا غَبَا غَمْ مَشْ لَسَعَرْ غَيْسُوَا يَبِ

kar akirāyi wanda sūnansa yā katarta da sūnan
uwāyensa sai da [52] alkunia. Ya bāta adīni dukansa, ya sai da
yāya, ya ginan gidan sarauta, wanan da sarākai Kanō ke shiga
har yau. Ya aikata abinda ya sō. Hakanan mutānen kasan Kanō
dukansu, sai dai daia chewa su, su-na-rikō [53] suna,
bābu girma garēsu, [54] fa che mutānen kasan Kanō ba su
san dafūan gīa ba, sai kadan chikinsu, mutānen kauye.
Hakanan ba su chin mushe. Su-na-[55]kāchia mātansu, su-na-
-rufe kānunsu da lulubi. Ba su wani aiki sai wanan. Su-ka-
-tabata bisa hakanan har aka-sāmu mālamai chikin Kanō, mai-gudu-
-ndūnia, mai-tsōrō Ala. Sūnansa Muhamadu-Zāri. Ya tsaya
da waazu, Runfa bai ji ba kōwanin abinda ya ke yi masu waazu
da shi. Sai su-ka-yi dabāra chikin kashinsa, har su-ka-kashe shi
da dare, kashin [56] gīla, chikin tafarkin masalāchi, ya kwana [57] yankake,
yā [58] sashe, har gari ya wāye. Aka-bisna shi wakatin luha.
Kushewa tasa [59] sananīa che chikin Kanō. Ana-zīāra tata

---

let not him whose name happened to be the same as that of his parents be called so, but (let him be called) by some sobriquet. He completely destroyed the creed, he sold free men, he built a palace, the one which the kings of Kano enter to-day. He did what he wished. And it was so with all the people of Kano except a very few, speaking of them, they kept to the Mohammedan faith, they were not powerful, only the Kano people did not know how to make beer, except a few among them, men in outlying villages. Thus they did not eat any animal that had died a natural death. They removed the clitoris of their women, they covered their heads with a veil. They did nothing else but this. They continued in such (conduct) until learned men were found in Kano, who had renounced the world, who feared Allah. (Of these learned men one) his name was Muhamadu-Zari. He stood up and preached. Rumfa paid no heed to whatever admonitions he admonished them. But they planned to kill him, till at last they did kill him in the night by slaying him from behind, in the road to the mosque, and he lay (there) murdered, cast aside, till dawn. He was buried about eight in the morning. His grave is known in Kano, it is visited

كز أكرابي وفد فسوفنس يا كترق د سوفس
عوا اينس لسغ د الكلق يباق الى يير د كنس يليد
يديا يكرفي عفسرق وامر د سرالحي كنوا بكلبغي
قرميو يانكت أبنع يسو ككنز متابمز كسركنو
د كنس لسيغ يد تن ثبوا سو سنا ركو سنس
جب غمدا غم مس قدثي متابي عسر كنو يلر
سعر د قو نعيلب سيكح زكنس متابز كوس
ككنز بلسنز مثبل سنا كداثي مدا قنس سند
وفي كد فنس ع للبيه بدا سوفد اك سيوفنز سك
تبث بسى ككنز مر أكعسدام مداقغ ثكن كنو منكد
فد وقى ميثلو وال سوفنس معهد زاري يبلس
د وعد زنف بمجب كوفنز أبند يكبهس ومكد
د شم سز سكع بدا زنكن كقنس مر سككبشش
دمرز كشر غيلح ثكن تقم فكنز مصاليم بكو زتكلو
يلسشن مع غم ميوابس أكيسنوا ش وفتر نحى
كبشوا قنس سنيبا ثني ثكن كنو أقد زياد اقد =

ana-tsarō nata, ana-che da shi [60] mai-kalgō, ana-neman albarka da ādua garēshi. Saanan Abdulāhi-Sako ya tsaya bāyansa. Shi-na-waazu, ba su ji ba garēshi, sai walākantatu, ama mainya mainya ba su ji ba. Sai su-ka-ba shi tsōrō, har ya fita, ya gudu, zūa kauye, dōmin shi yi ma mutānen kauye waazu. Saanda sarki ya aiki wanda ke kā--mō shi. Su-ka-kāmō shi, su-ka-dinga bugunsa, har su-ka-kāwō shi. Shi-na maras lāfia. Ya mutu bāyan kwānaki kadan. Kushewa tasa sananīa che bāyan [61] gwoboron dūtsi, ama ba azīāra tasa, ba atsarō nasa. Kāfurchi ya tabata hakanan har wakatin Muhamadu-Alwali. Shi ne wanan [62] Usmānu dan Fōdio ya yi yāki da shi, bāyan zamansa chikin sarauta shekara gōma sha bakwoi. Ya fita shi da mutānensa, ya gudu, zūa [63] sāsan dāma. Wani bai san wurin da ya zamna ba har yau, aka-che Barnabarna, aka-che ba nan ba. Mālami su-ka-che tun zuan Abdulkarīmu, har zūa zāmani Usmānu dan Fōdio, saraki sabain da shida. Kushewansu dukansu tā tabata chikin birnin Kanō, bīu, Bāwa da Muhamadu-Alwali, ama chikin Kāshina. Adīni ya tabata bāyan

---

and watched over, he was called 'the Kalgo man', blessings are sought by prayers being made for him. Then Abdulahi-Sako stood up (to proclaim the creed) after him. He was admonishing them but they paid no heed to him, except some people of no importance, but those in authority did not hear. And they frightened him so that he fled to the outlying towns in order to instruct the people of the lesser towns. Then the king sent one to seize him. They seized him, and continually flogged him till he was brought before (the king). He was (by this time) ill and died after a few days. His grave is known, (it lies) behind the rock (known as) 'the single rock', but it is not visited or watched over. And so it came to pass that paganism existed till the time of Muhamadu-Alwali. It was he Usmanu, the son of Fodio, made war on, after he had ruled in the kingdom for seventeen years. He (Usmanu-dan-Fodio) drove him out and his men, he fled in the direction of the country on the right and none know where he settled till this day, (some) say Barnabarna (some) say it was not there. The learned men said that from the coming of Abdulkarimu till the coming of Usmanu, the son of Fodio, there were seventy-six kings. All their graves have remained in the town of Kano, but two of them, that of Bawa and Muhamadu-Alwali, are in Katsina. The creed continued after

أَمَا طَرُوفَتَ أَمَا بَقِمْ شِمْ مَيْكَلْفُو أَمَا بَقِمْ الْبَرْكَ دَعَمْدَعَ

غَمْ مُشِ سَعَفَنْ عَبْدُ اللّٰهِ سَكُو يَطُو مَا يَنْسَ شِنَا وَعَظْ

بِسَجَبْ غَمْ مُشِ سَنْ وَهْ لَاكَنْتَتُو أَمَّا مَفُنْ مَفُنْ مِسَجَبْ

سَنْ سَكَبَا شِ طُورُرْ حَمْ يَجِبْتَ يَقُدُ دُرْكَوَيِي دُورِقَنْ

شِيمَمُتَا بَمْ كَوَيِي وَعَظْ سَعَفَنْ سَرْكِي يَا أَيْكِ وَنْعْ بَكَكَا

مُوشِرْ سَكَكَا مُوشِ سُكَعَ مَغْ يَفُنْسَ هَمْ سَكَكَا وُرُو

شِ شِنَا مَرْسَلَا فِي يَمُتَ بَا إِيَّمْ كُوانْكِمْ كَدَنْ كُشُوَا

قَمْسَ سَنْيَاقْ بَا إِيَّمْ غَمْبَرْزَدُ وَطِ أَمَّا بَا أَزْيَا وَاقَنْسَ بَا

أَطَرُوفَنْسَ كَا أَبُرْ فِي يَتَّبَتَ تَكَنْ تَزُوَفْتِنْ مُحَمَّدُ الْأَوَّلْ

شِينِنْ وَفَمْ دَعْشَمَارْ دَفَجُودِ نِ بِيِي مَا كِيدِ شِ بَا إِيَّنْ

دَمُنْسَ نَكُمْ سَرُوتَ شِمْكَمْ غُومَ شِبَكُو شِ يَعْتَ شِمْ

دَمَتَا فُنْسَ يَقُدُ دُرَ سَسَنْ دَامَ وَفِيبْيَسْرُو وَتَعَدِيمْ فَنْ تَابْ

تَرِيَوْ أَكَشْ بَمْرَ يَجُمْ وَ أَكَشْ بَا فَنْتَابْ مَا أَلَمْ سَكَبْ تَمَدُرُونْ

عَبْدُ الْكَرِيمِ حَمْدُ وَدَا امِيرْ عَشْمَارْ دَفَجُودِ نُ أَسَرْكِ

سَبَعَنْ دَشِعَ كُشُو فُنْسَ دَكُنْسَ تَدَ تَبْنَا نَكُمْ مَمَ فَنْ كُو

بِيُو بَاوَرْ مُحَمَّدُ الْأَوَّلْ أَمَا نَكُمْ كَا أَشَرْ أَلَدِ مِيرِ يَتَّبَتَ يَا إِيَّنْ

kōmāwan Abdulkarīmu. Adīni ya dinga dadawa kulum, ya tabata
da girma. Mutānin [64] Gōbir su-ka-dinga zūa Kāshina, su-na-
-karban adīni garēsu, da gaskīa, da kōkari. Su-ka-shiga
chikinsa bāki dai. Adīni ya tabata garēsu kuma,
tamkar da ya tabata chikin Kāshina. Ama Musulumchi ya tabata
chikin Kāshina; hakanan zūa wakatin Agarga. Shi ne farko
wanda ya juya abinda Abdulkarīmu ya aje chikin Kāshina.
Māsu-waazu su-ka-yi masa waazu. Bai ji ba. Ya tabata ga Kā-
-furchinsa har ya mutu. Kaura ya yi sarauta, da dansa,
ya bi hainyar ubansa. Kāfurchi ya tabata har zāmanin
Wāri-mai-kworia. Shi ne wanda ya yi shishigi, ya yi gir-
-man kai, girman kai baba. Ya auri budrūa alif. Ya [65] kinkumu
chikin barna, bai bari ba. Shi-na-neman māgani dōmin
shi [66] dawama chikin dūnia, kar shi mutu, har wani [67] bōka ya rū-
-de shi, wai ba shi mutua harabadi. Wanchananka mai-
-māgani ya aikata masa abinda ya aikata daga māgani.

---

the return of Abdulkarimu. The faith continued to grow always and took firm hold. Men from Gobir continued to come to Katsina and were adopting the Mohammedan faith with (in all) truth and earnestness, they embraced it, all together. The faith took hold among them also as it had taken hold in Katsina. And so it was until the time of Agarga. He was the first who changed the state of things that Abdulkarimu had established in Katsina. Instructors (strove) to admonish him. He heard not. He remained in his heathenism till he died. Kaura ruled the kingdom, and (then) his son; he followed the path his father had taken. Paganism continued till the time of Wari-mai-kworia. It was he who did evil and was most arrogant. He married 1,000 maidens. He embraced evil (and) did not cease. He sought for (a) medicine in order that he might go on living in the world and not die, till (at last) a certain wizard deceived him, saying he would never die. That doctor did for him what he did from (his knowledge of) medicines.

بِتَّنَ اَعْلَمْ وَادُدُ فُغْ قِدِ مِيرِ اَدِ مِخْ الْكِرِ غِبْفُ وَمَدُ كُو

سُنَا شِرِ كَدَا وَذُ مُغْ سُكِدِ بِمْ عُو غَمْ فِيْ مَتَا مُتَا مَطَا غِرِ دِ

سُكِشِعْ كُوكُمِ دِ غَلِسْكِيَا دِ مَسِ غِبْ مِيرِ اَلِدِ بِمْ كَمْ

نَهْ كُمَّ مَسِ غِبْ مِتَّبَ مِيرِ اَلْدِ نُ كِيعِ بِدَا ثِكِنْسَ

مُنْتَبَّ يَا ثِلْمُسَ اَمَّا شِرِ كَدَا ثِكِرْ مِيتَّ دُ تَكْرْ تَقَ

كُو كَرْ فَرْ شِيبِنُ غُعْ عِرْ اَعْ فِنْشِ وَرُ فُرْ كَكْنَرْ شِرِ كَدَا ثِكْرِ

ثِشْ كِدَا ثِكِرْ بِي مَا مِيحِ الْكِرِ عَنْبَمْ اَبِنْدُ نُو بِجُ فِنْدَ وُ

كَدَ غَمْكَ بِتَّنْ بِبْجَبَ خَا عَ وُرُ مَسَ يَكِ سَكْ دُعَ وُرُسْ مَا

مَسْ فُ دُ دُ وُفْ سَرْ بِيُّ وُ كُو بَنْدُ حَرِ تَسْ فِنْسَ فُرْ

مِشْمَ اَرَ حَرْ تِسْتَّ مِيتِّ فِرْتْ اَدَكَ سَنْسَ اَبِنْسَ حَنْفِيرْ بِبْ

غِرْ بِيرِ شِخِي شِي مِيوْ فَدْ وُرُ شِيبِلْ بِيَا وُرْ كُو مِيكُو اَرْ وَ

بِكَنْكَمْ [redacted] وَارُ زُ بُمْ جُو وُ مَعْ بَبَّ كَوْنْ كَمْ غُمَّ غِمْرِ يَكُوْنْ هَمْرْ آلِفْ

مَقِّنْ دِرْ غِنِمْ غَمَعَا قَصَّ شَنَّدَ بِنْبَمْ مِيبْ مِبْتَبَ فُرْ بِرْ نِكِرْ

وُمِرُ كُوِيبُو حَرْوُ شُمْدُ شُمْكَمْ مُرْ كِرْ دُو ثِكِرْ دُورِ شَدْ

مَنْ غَكْنَ مَنْ قَشَّانْ وَرَ بِحْ اَرَحَرْ وَ شُمْشُو شِبَا بَيْبَ وُرَ مِكْشِ دُ

غِمْ غَعَا غْ دِ نَكَنْتَ يَنْيَ دَرِ يُتْبِي اَرِ مَسَ مَتَّكَنْ اَيْ مَ فُنْعِنْ غَمْدَ

Sarkin nan ya ba shi dūkīa dayawa, aka-che bāwa dari, kuyenga dari, da dōki dari, da kōre dari, da sānia dari, mache da bajinin sānīa dari, da rāgō alif, da akwia alif. Ya ba shi tufāfi wadanda ba su [68]kidāyuwa dōmin yawa, da wanin wanan, Ala shi ne masani. Chikin zāmaninsa ne aka-sāmu mālami bīu chikin Kāshina, māsu-gudu dūnia, māsu-tsōrō Ala. Sū--nan guda Muhamadu-Ibnumusina, sūnan guda kūa, Muhamadu-Dunmurna. Kōwane daia chikinsu ya yi waazu, waazu mai-shiga chikin zuchīa, bai [bai] ji ba. Sai su-ka ba shi tsōrō dōmin su bar waazu. Ba su bari ba. Sarākai kūa, ba su ji ba, har mālamai nan su-ka-mutu. Chikin Kāshina kushewa tasa sananīa che har yau, wurin yārō da baba ana-zīyāri tasa, ana--kīwo, ana-neman albarka da adua garēsu. Ama Wari-mai-kworia, chewa shia, ya zamna shekara tokwas bāyan an-yi masa māganin, kar shi mutu. Ya mutu chikin shekara ta tara. Sāilin da ya mutu gardaman sarauta ta a--bko tsakānin yan sarākai. Sāshe su-ka-kashe sāshe, har aka-kashe kamar mutun alif chikin birnin Kāshina, tsakānin dā da bāwa. Saanan kanin Wāri ya chi sarauta, bāyan ya kashe dan Wāri.

This king gave him much wealth, it was said one hundred slaves, one hundred female slaves, a hundred horses, a hundred black tobes, and a hundred cattle, cows and bulls a hundred, and a thousand rams, and a thousand goats. He gave him robes which could not be counted by reason of their number, and things of this description, Allah he know (what all). In his reign two learned men made their appearance in Katsina, men who renounced the world (and) who feared Allah. The name of one was Muhamadu Ibnumusina, the name of the other also was Muhamadu Dunmurna. Each one among them gave instruction, (such) instruction as enters into the heart. He did not hear them. Then they made them afraid in order to dissuade them from preaching. They did not desist. The kings also did not pay any attention till these learned men died. In Katsina their graves are known till to-day, where young and old visit and guard, and at which blessings are sought by prayers for them. Now Wari-mai-kworia, speaking of him, he lived eight years after he had had the medicine made for him to prevent his dying. He died the ninth year after (taking) it. When he died a quarrel about the kingdom arose among the king's sons. Half were slaying the other half until about 1,000 men were killed in the town of Katsina among both free men and slaves. Then the younger brother of Wari ruled after slaying the son of Wari.

اوفلبكر دؤاب بكبأ جيمد ايكود شيابم مقشنكر نس

ايفلدقنجيبر د ثبمق يوركدايلثقد يروكمبوكد يرد كيرودد يرد

اويمإكسملبمعف ودو فاقثشابميم فلاىكاد فلاوغارد يرد

مسلاكأ لونبسنتثمازركث نيسم نيبيشلاأ مثقرمثقود اوجيمفود

وسوأ لاوروطسام يرثيود مثعسام رشيكاثركيثويبم ملادم

ادرفمنمد دمحم وكاعمغرفوس ينسمرمبإدمفحما عغرفم

بم ايثدركيثفشيمم ذعو ذعاويم سنفنثيتمو دميفوكو

بيبزنجبسيب ذعروبمرسيمود روطشابكسل مكلاوس بجنيم

اوثيكرشالكرثكيثشمكسرمنعلاملم مرح بجيلبمكوكمعلاوس

امأرسقماويبزامنأ بقدرزاميفود ويمرح يقابينفس سمق

اويثكيمروايمأ سحم مبغ عدعد كرزبلاأرمفيثادمأ ويك

شهنثمك منعاقرسمقنأمرميماب سوكنثمكشرمم غني يشي

امثقوررسلرمرمغ ثفيب معلبهاس رثمق مكشبرثكيث ثمي

مر يلشاسد وبشكس يلشاس يكارسر ريبرفمكاه كب

ادنم ركهث رشاكرفمرب رثيكث فلارثم رمعمع لبشكماأ

=راومد وشبكهبميرمياب فرسر ثيباوارنفرفعس رابد

Shi kuma ya tabata bisa Kāfurchinsa. Kāfurchi ya tabata chikin Kāshina har wakatin Bāwa-Dungaimāwa. Shi ne wanda Usmānu dan Fōdio ya fita daga Kāshina, shīa da mutāninsa su ka nufi [69] Marādi, su-ka-zamna chāna har yau. Danginsa sun kashe, su-na-yāki da dangin Usmānu dan Fōdio har yau. Ama Gōbir su-ka-tāru, su-ka-tabata bisa adīni, su-ka-tabata chikinsa har wakatin Bābari. Shi ne fārin wanda ya musāya suna, ta zama [70] bida, ya daukaka ginin Kāfurchi, ya yi girman kai. Māsu-waazu su-ka-yi masa waazu, bai karba ba, sai ya tabata bisa Kāfurchinsa har ya mutu. Bāchira ya chi sarauta, ya aikata kaman aikinsa, sai ya dada barna da batarwa, kunfan Kāfurchi ya daukaka chikin kasar Gōbir, sarā-kanta su-ka-yi girman kai, su-ka-sai da dīa, su-ka-aikata abinda su-ka-sō, har alāmari ya zama, kōwane sarki ya chi sarauta, sai shi auri budrūa dari. Sai su dai ba su san dafuan gīa ba, sai kadan chikinsu. Ba su chin musai, ama sāilin da zaa gaisua su-na-zuba kasa ga kainsu, su-na-bauta ma tūru, māsu-rikō

He again continued in heathenism. (And) heathenism continued in Katsina till the reign of Bawa-Dungaimawa. It was he Usmanu, the son of Fodio, drove out of Katsina, he and his men, they went to Maradi, they settled there until to-day. His descendants continue to make war on the descendants of Usmanu, the son of Fodio, till to-day. But the (men of) Gobir assembled together and continued in the faith and dwelt in it till the reign of Babari. He was the first who changed the true faith, it became lax, he exalted (and) set up paganism (and) was arrogant. The preachers (of the faith) preached to him but he would not receive (their instructions), but persisted in his heathenism till he died. Bachira ruled over the kingdom, he did what his predecessor had done, he added to the evil he had done, and the harm, the foam from the wave of heathenism rose in the land of Gobir, its kings were proud. They sold free men, they acted as they wished until report had it that every king that ruled married one hundred maidens. But (the only redeeming point was) they did not know how to make beer, except a few among them, (and) they did not eat animals that had died a natural death, but when they greeted (their kings) they poured earth over their heads, they served idols. (Some) who cleaved to the faith

ثكر يثبت فرق ابركد قنس كد ابر كد مسر يتبت يكم شي

عثمان ونع شيني والا غنيد ادر ورج فتر ور قر كداشر

مراد سكنف قنس قتا م شي كداشر م د يجت بن مجوم م

مفكر م د كياد سند شي كنس سنفنس م يو قرر قار م سكم

سكتبت وسكتا سكر مير غو اما بيو قر بن مجوم دو عشما

شبني مرج ماجم قتر ور قر شكنس شكتبن سكر مير الد بسر

غفر كك كرد يد م م د تنغم سنر سدسيقر ونع در قار

وعما سكيمس ماسوعة م مركك غم يبي رف ابر كد

يمت قر قنس ف كد مسر يبتبت سن باب كم بي

ملي م د بم قر سن ينس اكتع يكت يد رف سر وف يث م بت

اسر ا جوم قرع مكتب نكر كك يد رف اتبر كد كنفر اولا تبد

ابقم يكت اكت س سكت يد سكتبع كر قر غم سكي عنت

سرف يث يم كم سر قبل كو م م يغم اما ي الا قر سكسو

فنياب قوف د سم بسن بر سو سن دوي الا زبدم وقو شعو سن

اغيثوا م ا نم ملي ساد اما مسو سثر م باسير شكنس كم كر سو

كو مسر م د قورو قتا م بو سنا كنس كعو كسو كب م سنا

su-na chikinsu, sāilin kadan ne, walākantatu, bābu girma
garēsu. Su-ka-tabata bisa hakanan har wakatin [71] Bāwa-jan-gwarzō.
Ya dada Kāfurchi, ya yi girman kai, har aka-sāmu mālami chikin
zāmaninsa, mai-gudun dūnia, mai-bautar Ala, ana-che masa Alhaji Jibrīlu.
Aka-che, chewa shīa, ya tafi tun Gōbir, ya je Maka, ya yi haji, ya zamna chana kama shekara ishirin. Aka-che ya zamna Masar shekara
gōma sha takwas. Ya zamna chikin Maka shekara bīu, saanan
ya kōmō zūa Gōbir. Ya waazche su sābunta dare da rāna,
bōye da bayene. Su-ka-ki abinda ya fadi, sai su-ka-nufi kashinsa.
Sarākunan Hausa duka su-ka-gama kai bisa su-kashe shi.
Ba su iya ba. Mālamai sun kashe Kālāwa, sāilin ama
ba su iya fadin wani abu chikin sani, sai bōye, dōmin
tsōrō sarākai. Sai Alhaji-Jibrīlu, chewa shia, yā
tsaya da waazu, ya yi kōkari bayane, ba su iya sun kashe shi ba.
Shi kūa bai iya yā hane su ba ga abinda su ke chiki.
Sai su-ka-dada shishigi da Kāfurchi-chikin wakatin nan.

---

were (still) among them, at that time only a few (and) without power or influence among them. And they continued thus till the time of Bawa-jan-gwarzo. He went on (living) in heathenism. He was arrogant till a learned man was found in his reign, one who had fled from the world, one who served Allah. He was called Alhaji-Jibrilu. It was said, speaking of him, he went from Gobir, he came to Mecca and performed the pilgrimage and resided (away) there twenty years. It was said he lived in Egypt eighteen years. He stayed in Mecca two years, and then returned to Gobir. He instructed them each new day and night, in secret and openly. They refused the thing (message) he brought and thought to kill him. All the kings of Hausa(land) plotted to slay him. They could not. The malamai were in Kalawa at that time, but they could not speak from their (store) of knowledge for fear of the chiefs. Only Alhaji-Jibrilu, speaking of him, he stood (fast) in (his) preaching and strove openly (and) they were not able to kill him. He could not, however, prevent them (doing) the evil they dwelt in. And they continued in evildoing and heathenism in this reign.

سُنْرَتِكُنْس سَامِلِنْ كَدْفَنِنُوا وَلَاكُنْتُو بَدَابِ غِرْمَى
غَمْ مَسَنْ سَكَنْبَتْ بِسَرْ مَكَنْتَنْ صَرُوفَتِنْ بَاوَجِنْ غَمْرَزُوْ
يَدَمْ كَدَابْجَمْ ثِ مَيُوغَمْرَمَرْ كَهْوَ فَرْ أَكَسَدَمْ مَدَالِهِمْ تِكَمْ
زَامِنَنْسَ مَنِكُدْ زُدُوفَيْ مَيَبُوْمَتْرَالْ أَمَا بِتَمَسَ أَلِجَمْ جَبْرِيمْ
أَكَبُ بُنُوَاشِيَ يَـ تَنِ تَنْرَعُوبِمْ بَجُومَكَ بَيْ جَمْ يَمْ
مَرْتَنْ كَمَرْ بِشَكَمْ عَشِرْ أَكَبُ مَـ دَمَرْ مَجَمْ بِشَكَمْ
غُومْ شَا تَكُوسْ يَغْ مَرْتِكَرْمَكَ بِشَكَرْ بِنُو سَعَنْرْ
بَكُو مُوْدُ وَغُوبِمْ مَيُوعَغَبَسْ سَا بُنْتَ دُوْرَعْرَافَسَ
بُوبِيْ دَمَتِبَنْ شَكَكَ أَبِنْدَ بِجَ سَرْ سُكَنِي كَشَمْنَسْ
تَسَرَاكُنَرْ مَوْسَرْ دَكْ سَكَغَمْ كَتَيْ مَسَرْ سَكَشْمَنْ
بَسُعِيَابْ مَدَالِهِمْ سُنكَشْبُوفَدَ تَغْدَوْا اسَامِلِنْ أَمَد
بَدَاسِعَوْ قِحِ فُوحْنَا بْ تِكَرْ تَسَرْ تَسَنْ بُوبِيْ دُوقْمْ
طُووْ تَسَرَاكَنْ تَسَ أَلِجَمْ جَبْرِيمْ شُوَاشَسْ بَيْ
طَعْ وَعَطَ مِيْ كُوكُرْ بَتِنِ بَسَعَيْ سَنْكَبْشِبْ
تَنِيكُو بَنْكِ بَامَنْسَبْ غَمْ أَبِنْدَ سَبْكَتِيكَ
تَسَرْ سُكَدْ دُشِشُغِ دَعَدَ ابْرِثِ تِكَرْوَفَتَنْقَمْ

Aka-haifi Usmānu dan Fōdio, sāilin da Alhaji Jibrilu ya mutu. Usmānu dan Fōdio ya fāra waazu kadan kadan, har Bāwa-jan-gwarzō ya mutu. Dan uwansa, Yaakubu, ya zamna mazamninsa. Sāilin Usmānu ya bayana waazu sarari, har ya aikata abinda ya aikata, yā kāre.

Mun[72] takaita zanche nan. Ala
shi ne mai-katari. Yā kāre.
Tsīra da aminchin Ala
shi tabata ga anabi.
Amin.

(Then) Usmanu, the son of Fodio, was born at the time when Alhaji-Jibrilu died. Usmanu, the son of Fodio, began to preach little by little till (the time when) Bawa-jan-gwarzo died. His brother Yaakubu reigned in his stead. Then Usmanu proclaimed (his) preaching openly till he did what (all the world knows) he did (and) finished. We have drawn the history to a close.

Allah, he is the one who knows all. It is finished.

The salvation and blessing of Allah be upon the prophet. Amen.

أَكَمِيِ عُشْمَارِمْفُودِن لَسَامِلِنْدَ أَلِمِج جِمْمِيش

يَمُتْ عُشْمَارِمْفُودِن يَقَارَوَعَظْ كَدَرِكَدَ ن

تَرْمَبَاوَجَمْغَمْزُوِيَمُتْ رِمْفُوفَسَرِيمْفُوبْ =

يَغَمْ مَرْمَغْ مِنَنْسَ سَامِلِرْ عُشْمَارِ يَمَبِيَّرَوَعَظْ

سَرُوِي حَرْمِيَأَنْيِكَتَ أَبْنَعْ مِيَأَنْيِكَتَ يَاكَمُوِش

مُتَنَكِنْتَ رَمْنَبْ فَمْ ال

شِينِس هِمِكِتِش مِدَكَدِرِي

طِيمِرَادَامِشَرَال

شَتِيمَتَغَرَانِب

دَامِسِير

PART II

'STORIES ABOUT PEOPLE'

No. 1.

[1] Bismi alāhi alrahmami alrahimi, wa sala alāhu ala mam la nabiu baadahu

Wanan [2] bābi ne na gātanar mutāne.

[3] Gātanan, gātanan, ta je, ta kōmō. Bāwan sarki shi ke da [4] maatansa, aka-che ta-na-neman maza. Ya che karīa, maata ta ba ta neman maza. Sai ranan wata tsōfūa ta che masa, 'Kulum idan ka tafi fādanchi, sai ta je wurin maza'; sai tsōfūa ta che, 'Yau ka hau dōkinka, ka che zaa ka kauyē, ka kwāna.' Sai bāwa sarki ya damra sirdi, ya hau, ya kāma hainya, ya tafi. Da marenche ya yi, [5] bai zaka ba, shi kūa ya che,

---

In the name of Allah, the Compassionate, the Merciful, and may the peace of Allah be upon him, after whom there is no prophet. This is the beginning of a story about people. A story, a story. Let it go, let it come. A slave of a chief had a wife, and it was said of her she was of a loose character. He (the husband) said it was a lie, (and) that his wife did not go after men. At last, one day, a certain old woman said to him, 'Always when you go to the council then she (your wife) is after the men'; and the old woman said, 'To-day mount your horse (and) say you are going to an outlying village (and) you are going to sleep there.' Then the chief's slave saddled up, mounted, took the road and went off. When evening came he had not come, for he had said,

بِسْمِ اللَّهِ الرَّحْمَنِ الرَّحِيمِ وَصَلَّى اللَّهُ عَلَى مَنْ لَا نَبِيَّ بَعْدَهُ

وَمَّنْ بَعْدِ مِنْكُ :: مَغَدَاقَتَنْ ::

مُتَانْبِكِ

غَدَاقَنْ :: غَدَاقَتَنْ تِجِي :: تَكُو مُوشْ بَدَاوْ

سَرْكِ :: يَشْكُدَ مَا اُقَنْشَنْ اَكْبْ :: مَغَدَا فَجَرْ ::

مَغَدَا :: يِتْ فَرِيَا :: مَدَا اُقَاتَا :: بِدَاتْ :: بَعْمْ مَغَدَا ::

سَنْ وَمَّنْ زَقْطَلُو فُوَا :: تَشْبْ مَسْ :: كُلَّمْ :: اِذَنْ ::

كَتِيفْ بَادَ مُشَمْ :: سَنْ تِجِي :: وُرُ مَغَدَا :: سَنْ طُو فُوَا

تَشْبْ :: يِجُو :: كَعَوْ :: دُو كِنْكَ :: كَكَبْ :: دَ اُكَ

فَوُيَسْ :: عَكَوَا اَنْ سَنْ بَدَاوْ :: سَرْكِمْ ::

بِدَ مَرْ :: سَرْدِ :: يِعَوْ :: يَكَامَ :: تَعْمَ :: يَتَّفِ

رَقَمْ مُسْبْ :: يِسْنَ :: بِنْ كَبْ :: شِيكُو :: يَابْ

'Ina je, baa ni kōmōwa,' [6] Maatar kūa, ashe [7] galādīman gari, da wāzīri, da wani bāwa(n) sarki, sūnansa Dūnīa, [8] baubāwa ne, da fitar mai-gida, sai maata ta aika gun farkonanta, ta che 'Mai-gidana yaa tafi kauyē, ama baa shi kōmōwa yau, sai gōbe.' Sai [9] galādīman ya sai nāman arba da shinkāfar alfin, wāzīrin gari ya sai nāman arba da shinkāfar alfin. Bāwan sarki Dūnīa ya sai nāman arba da shinkā--far alfin, aka-kai mata. Dare ya yi, sai galādīma ya zo, aka-sainya masa shinkāfa da nāma, shi-na-chi. Sai ya ji mōtsin tākalmin wāzīri. Sai ya fāda karkashin [10] gadō, aka-dauki shinkāfa, aka-rūfe.

'I am going and shall not return.' Now the wife (possessed some lovers), the galadima and the vizier, and a certain of the chief's slaves, a foreigner, by name 'The World', and on the master of the house going out, then the wife sent to (these) her lovers, she said, 'My master will go to an outlying village, and he will not return to-day but to-morrow.' Then the galadima brought four thousand cowries worth of meat and two thousand cowries worth of rice to bring to the woman. When night came the galadima arrived, the meat and rice was set out, and he ate. Then he heard the sound of the slippers of the vizier, and down he fell under the bed, and the rice was lifted and covered up.

اِنْ قَادِ بِيَ ∴ بَدَا نِكُو مُو وَا ∴ هَا قَمْ نِكُوَّ ∴ أَشِنْ ∴ غَمْنَا دِيَمَ

غَمْرِ ∴ دَوَا زِيمِ ∴ دَوَ فِنْبَا دَوَّا ∴ لَسَمْ نِكِمِ ∴ لَسُو قَمْنَسَ ∴

دُو فِتَّ ∴ بَجُو بَدَا وَ فِنِ ∴ دَ بِتَمْ مَيْخِدَا ∴ تَسِنْ قَدَا أَمْ ∴ مَ

تَمَا نِكِ ∴ غَنْجَمْ كُنَّنْتَ ∴ مَتَشْ هَلَا مَيْخِدَ أَقَا ∴ بَدَا أَنْفِ

تَكْوِبِ ∴ أَمَّا ∴ بَدَا أُشْكُو مُو وَا ∴ بَيَّخْ ∴ لَسَنْ غُمُو بِسَ ∴

تَسِنْ غَمْنَا دِ يَمَا ∴ يَلَسِنْ ∴ قَدَا مَمْ ∴ أَوْبَ ∴ دَ شِنْكَا بَقَمْ ∴ أَلْبِقَرْ

وَازِيمِ فُغَمْرِ ∴ يَلَسُنْ قَدَا مَمْ ∴ أَوْبَ ∴ دَ شِنْكَا بَقَمْ ∴ أَلْبِقَرْ ∴

بَدَا قَّ ∴ لَسَمْ نِكِمِ ∴ دُو فِتَّ ∴ يَلَسِنْ ∴ قَدَا مَمْ ∴ أَوْبَ ∴ دَ شِنْكَا

بَقَمْ ∴ أَلْبِقَرْ ∴ أَكَكِيَّمَتَ ∴ دَ وَمِبِيَّتَ ∴ لَسَنْ غَمْنَا دِيَمَ

يَخْرُو ∴ أَكَسَنْبَا مَسَرْ ∴ شِنْكَا بَقَا ∴ دَ فَدَا مَ ∴ شِنْدَا فِ ∴

لَسَنْ بَيَجِ ∴ مُو جِمْ ∴ قَدَا كِلِمْ ∴ وَزِيمِ ∴ لَسَمْ بَقَادَمْ ∴

فَمْ كِشِنْ ∴ غُدُوا ∴ أَكَدَ وَكِ ∴ شِنْكَا بَقَا ∴ أَكَرُو بَمْ

Ashe wāzīri ne. Sai ya zamna; shi kuma
aka-ba shi shinkāfa da nāma, shi-na-chi. Sai ya ji
mōtsin tākalmin Dūnīa, shi-na-che
mai-gida ne. Sai ya fāda karkashin-gadō.
Sai ya iskē [11] galādīman [12] zamnē. Sai ya-che,
'aa galādīma ne?' Ya che, 'I,' ya che, 'mu rufa ma kaimu
asīri,' ya che, 'Bābu laifi.' Su-na-nan, zamnē.
Sai aka ba Dūnīa nasa rabō; shi kuma
shi-na-chi. Sai su-ka-ji mōstin kōfatō
dōkin mai-gida, [13] yā zō. Sai Dūnīa ya yaada
akoshin tūō; ya fāda karkashin gadō.

Sure enough it was the vizier. Then he sat down, (and) he also was given rice and meat. He ate. Then he heard the noise made by the slippers of him called 'The World'. He thinks it is the master of the house. So he fell under the bed, when he discovered the galadima sitting (there). Then he said, 'Oh, it's the galadima, is it?' And he said, 'Yes,' (and) said, 'Let us keep this secret.' And he said, 'There is no harm in that.' They were sitting there then, (and the one called) 'The World' was given his share, and he also was eating. Then they heard the hoofs of the horse of the master of the house; he has come. Then 'The World' threw away the plate of food (and) fell under the bed.

أبشر :: وأزمير فبو :: سس يغ مر :: شيكم :: =

أكبداش :: شكدا قم :: دقدام :: شناف :: سر بجم

:: موطن :: قد اكلم :: دوفيد :: شناب ::

مينجدا ابن :: سس :: يقدام :: فركشر :: غمدو ::

سس :: يالسكم :: غدادي يمد :: دمبن :: اسريب

أأ :: غدادي يمبن :: يب :: إي :: ميب :: مرقمكيم

أسيمي :: ميثا :: مداب :: أليقي :: سنافر :: دمبن

سس :: أكبد دوفيا :: قداسر موا :: شيكم ::

شناف :: سس :: لسكج :: موطن :: كوقبو

دوكر :: ميفدا :: يدا دو :: اسس دونيد :: ييدام

أكشر قدوو :: يقبادر :: فركشر :: غمدو ::

Sai Dūnīa ya gani mutum. Sai ya che, [14]'Ke wācheche anan?' Sai galādīma da wazīri su-ka-che, 'Mu ne.' Sai Dūnīa ya che, 'Galādīma me ta kāwō [15]ki nania?' Sai su-ka-che, 'Dōmin Alla, Dūnīa ka bari mu rufa makanmu asīri.' Sai Dūnīa ya che, 'Tō, ku yi kulum.' Sai su-ka-yi shirū; mai-gida kūa shi-na wurin dōkinsa, [16]shi-na-kunche sirdi; bai sani ba. Sai ya che maata ta ba shi rūa, shi yi wanka. Ta ba shi rūa, ya yi wanka. Sai ya shiga dāki, ya zamna bisa gadō. Sai maata ta che, 'Sannu da zūa.' Sai ya [17]gaza amsāwa, shi-na-mamāki, shi-na-che, 'Dūnīa, Dūnīa.' (Dōmin da aka-yi masa karīa, aka-che [18]mātasa ta-na-neman maza, ga shi ya zō bai ga kōwa ba), shi-na-fadi, 'Dūnīa, Dūnīa.' Maata tasa ta-na-che,

---

Then 'The World' saw a man (there). He said, 'Who are you?' Then the galadima and the vizier said, 'It is we.' Then 'The World' said, 'You, galadima, what brings you here?' And they said, 'For the sake of Allah, World, let us keep this secret among us.' And 'The World' said, 'All right, keep silent.' Then they kept still. The master of the house meanwhile was at his house taking off the saddle, he did not know. Then he told his wife to give him water to wash. She gave him water and he washed. Then he entered the house and sat on the bed, and his wife said, 'Greetings to you on your coming.' He did not reply, he was wondering and saying, 'The World, the World' (because he had been lied to and told his wife went after the men, and behold, he had come and saw no one). And he kept saying, 'The World, the World.' His wife said,

سن دُ وفيبا ∴ يخيم ∴ متُم ∴ سن ميبث ∴ بكو اثبث ∴ أقمن ∴

سمو ∴ غملا ديمحم ∴ دورزيم ∴ سكبث ∴ موفمن ∴ سن

دُ وفيبا ∴ ييف ∴ غملا ديمحم ∴ متّكدا وركِ ∴ فيتو ∴ سن

سكبث ∴ دُ وقمن ∴ آن ∴ دُ وفيبا ∴ كجبر ∴ مر قمكنم ∴ أليبيرِ

سن دُ وفيبا ∴ ميبث ∴ فو ∴ كجن ∴ كلقم ∴ هم ∴ سكمّ ∴

فرو ∴ ميفكدا ∴ كو ∴ شنداو وفدو كمس ∴ شند ∴

كنبث ∴ ليسرح ∴ بمنسينيب ∴ سن ميبث ∴ مدامن ∴ قبالش

زوا ∴ شيجمكمن ∴ قبالش زوا ∴ ييو نكمن ∴ سن ∴

ميشخ ∴ داكِ ∴ ميخ فمر ∴ مسفدو ∴ سن ∴ مدامن

قبث ∴ سنو ∴ دذر ∴ سن يعخ ∴ أمسداوا ∴ شند

مادكِ ∴ شداب ∴ دُ وفيبا ∴ دُ وفيبا ∴ دُ وقمن

دا كيمسن ∴ كمر ∴ أكنبث ∴ مدا قمس ∴ قندا مقمن ∴

مزا ∴ غداش ∴ ميا دُوا ∴ بنيخ ∴ كخوا ∴ ب ∴ شند

قبحِ ∴ دُ وفيبا ∴ دُ ونيبا ∴ مدا فدا تمس ∴ قندا قب ∴

'Me ya fāru mai-gida?' Sai Dūnīa baubāwa shi-na-che
da shi ake yi. Ashe ya yi fushi. Sai ya che, [19] 'Ke ya dulin wa-
-nan Dūnīa ki ka lena, Dūnīa kadai ki ka gani,
ba ki gani galādīma da wāzīri ba, sai Dūnīa, dōmin
kin lena Dūnīa?' Sai kōkūa ta kable chikin
dāki. Sai galādīma da wāzīri su-ka-fita da gudu,
su-ka-bar Dūnīa da mijin maata, su-na-kōkūa.
Tsōfūa ta-na-kuwa, ta-na-che, gudunmawa, har
aka-zō, aka-raba su. Gari ya wāye, aka-kai sharaa
wurin sarki. Sai mai-maata ya [20] maida magana. Sai
fādanshi ya pashe da dārīa. Sai sarki ya che,
'Ina galādīma da wāzīri?' Aka-che ba su zō ba. Sar-
-ki ya che 'Atafi, agani lāfia'. Aka-je

'What is the matter, master?' Now he (by name) 'The World', the foreigner, thought it was to him he was speaking. Truly he waxed angry, and spoke, saying, 'You ——, is it (him called) "The World" only you have to find fault with? Look, do you not see the galadima and the vizier, but only "The World", seeing that it is "The World" you are finding fault with (only)?' On that all was confusion in the room, and the galadima and the vizier ran out, and left him called 'The World' and the woman's husband fighting. The old woman was shouting and calling for help. They (people) came and separated them. Next morning the matter was brought before the chief, when the woman's husband stated the case, but the councillors split themselves with laughing, and the chief said, 'Where are the galadima and the vizier?' and he was told they had not come. And the chief said, 'Let some one go and see if all is well with them.' (And) they went

جيقدا و ∴ منغدا ∴ سئ د وفيا ∴ بحوبدا و ∴ الشدا ب

د شيا بحئ ∴ اشيا بفشم ∴ سئ ميث ∴ بكيد و الشكو

تمن ∴ د وفيا ∴ يكحلبن ∴ ع ونيا كحمن ∴ يككغنم

بيكغنم ∴ غمدا د يم ∴ د وا ز ميرب ∴ سئ د ونيا ∴ د وقمن

يكنلبن ∴ د وفيا ∴ سئ كو كحوت تكبلبن ثكسن

دا ك ∴ سئ ∴ غمدا د يم ∴ د وا ز ميم ∴ سكبت ∴ د غمد

سكبم ∴ د ونيا ∴ ع مجنمدا فئن ∴ سندا كو كحو ∴

هو فوا ∴ قندا كو ق ∴ قندا ث ∴ نمد نمهوا ∴ حسم

ا كغد و ∴ اكم بداس ∴ غمر ميو اپن ∴ اككن ∴ شنم ع

و ر فسم كم ∴ سئ فيمدا فتن ∴ يحبكم ∴ هكم ∴ سئث

قدا د نشم ∴ بيقبشن ∴ د دا ريا ∴ سم سم كم ∴ ميث

إمدا غمدا د يم ∴ د وا ز ميم ∴ اكث ∴ بملغد و ب ∴ سم

كم ∴ ميث ∴ امنف ∴ اغمنم ∴ لا بفعن ∴ اكحكي ∴

aka ishe galādīma da waziri, baa su gida. Ashē sun shiga dāji, har wayau ba agansu ba, dōmin kumia. Dōmin hakanan mutum mai-girma bai kamāta shi yi aikin da bai kamāta ba. Shi ke nan. [21] Kungurus kan kūsu.

---

and found that the galadima and the vizier were not at their house. Of a truth they had gone to the bush; and until now they have not been seen, for very shame. And the moral of this (is that) it does not behove a man of position to act improperly. That is all. Off with the rat's head.

أكحا شبر ∴ غملا ح ميحم ∴ دوازيم ∴ بحاسر ∴ غحدا ∴ أمبشى

سنشغم ∴ دابر ∴ حمر وتجو ∴ بأغمبلسب ∴ دوقسر

كحمن ∴ دوقمر قحكقن ∴ مشرش ∴ منيخمرمن ∴ بمه

بنكحا ما ∴ شين ∴ آيكمر ∴ دبينكحا امب ∴ شيبكقر

خنغمرمن ∴ كحمر ∴ كحوسن

No. 2.

[1] Gātanan, gātanan. Wanan tāsūnīar
yārinya che. Wani mutun ke da yāyansa uku,
bīū maza, daia mache. [2] Machen ita ake sō.
Sai [3] baban wansu ya tafi da su dāji. Ya che
su je itāche. Da su-ka-je dāji, sai ya kāma ta.
Ya hau itāche da ita; ya-damre bissa itāche;
ya zō, ya-che, 'Yārinya [4] tā batche dāji, (ba su)
ba su gane ta ba. Sai su-ka-kōmō gida.' Su-na-
-kūka. Sai ubansu ya tanbaye su me ya fāru.
Su-ka-che, 'Kanwamu che ta batche chikin dāji, (ba mu)
ba mu gane ta ba, munyi nema mun gaji, ba mu gane ta ba.'

A story, a story. This tale is about a maiden. A certain man had three children, two boys and a girl, (and) it was the girl he loved. Then (one day) their big brother went with them to the forest (bush), telling them to come for sticks. And when they had reached the forest, he seized her (the girl), climbed a tree with her, (and) tied her on to the tree, (and) came (and) said, 'The maiden has been lost in the forest,' (and said) they did not see her, so they came home. They were weeping. Then their father asked them what had happened, (and) they said, 'Our young sister she was lost in the forest (and) we did not see her. We searched until we were tired, but we did not see her.'

غما اتنّس .: غما اتنّس .: رمّس تا طونيّم .:

يلو رميث .: رمتشن .: كد ميا مبيّن .: عُك

.: ميثو .: مخدا .: درّن .: مبث .: مبثم .: اِمتّ .: اكسو

لسن مجبّن .: رمسن .: متعِد سوا .: داجِ .: مبث .:

سجي .: اِما بن .: د سكجي .: داجِ .: لسن يكا اما

يمجو .: اِماث .: داِتّ .: مجّ مجرّ .: مسن .: اِماث

يدوا .: مث .: مجد رمّن .: مقا مث .: داجِ .: مسك

مسغبنب .: لسن لسكو مووا .: غدا .: سنا

كوكن .: لسن امنسن .: متجبيلسن .: مقدرُ .:

سكث .: كنوم .: ثمبث .: نكم داجِ .: مخمخ

بخلبنب .: منسن .: مفمر .: مفنعج .: مجكبنب .:

Sai ubansu ya che, 'bābu laifi.' Ana-nan wata rāna sai fatāke su-ka-zō, su-na-wuchewa chikin dāji. Ta ji magananansu. Sai ta-che, 'Kū, kū, kū, ma--su gōrina, idan kun je [5] unguan tudu, ku gaida wana Hallabau, ku gaida wana Tanka-baka, ku-gaida wana Shadusa?' Sai fatāke su-ka-ji hakanan. Sai su-ka-che, tsuntsūa ke yin wanan abu. Sai kuma, ta kāra. Sai mādugun ayari ya-che, [6] shii-je shi-gani, kō menene ke yin hakanan. Sai ya tafi; ya je; ya iske yārinya bisa itāche, [7] daure. Sai ya-che, 'Masūrai kō masū-mutūa?' Yārinya ta che, 'Masū-

---

Then their father said, 'It cannot be helped.' Then one day traders came and were passing in the forest. She (the girl) heard their voices and she (sang) said, 'You, you, you, who are carrying kola nuts, if you have come to the village on the hill, greet my big brother Hallabau, greet my big brother Tanka-baka, (and) greet my big brother Shadusa.' When the traders heard this they said that birds were the cause of this (singing). Then again she repeated (the song). Then the leader of the caravan said he would go (and) see what it was that was doing (singing) thus. So he went off (and) came across the maiden fastened to the tree. And he said, '(Are you) alive or dead?' The maiden said, 'Alive,

تسن أبنفسن ؞ مثبنا ب ؞ أليهم ؞ أمّا فمن ؞ وتمران ؞

تسن قتدابكن ؞ تسكذر ؞ تسندا وشوا ؞ تكير دام

ثبج ؞ مغقفسن لسع تثب كوكوكو ؞ ما

سكوروش ؞ إدرن ؞ كنج ؞ نمنعوقتد ؞ كغيم

وقمن ؞ حلبو ؞ كغيد ؞ وقمن ؞ قنك ؞ بكن

كغيم ؞ وقمن ؞ شدلس ؞ تسن قتدابكن ؞ لسكم

تكنفس ؞ لسنلسكب ؞ طمطوا ؞ بكيم ؞ الوقمن

أب ؞ لسن كتم ؞ تكدار ؞ لسن مادغم ؞ أيم ؞

يمب ؞ لشنجم ؞ لتخنم ؞ كومبتن ؞ بكيم

تكنفن ؞ لسن يمتف ؞ يجم ؞ يدابسكم ؞ يداوفمن

بتسن ؞ إمّا ب ؞ دم ورسن ؞ لسن يمثب ؞ فمسواوسي

كوفمسو ؞ فتو ؞ يداوفم ؞ متب ؞ فسوا

rai (masurai).' Sai shi mādugu, dakainsa ya hau bissa itāche, ya kunche ta. Da wuri kūa, shi, [8] mādugun ya nemi haifua, bai sāmu ba. Sai ya che 'Wanan yārinya daka ina (daga enna)?' Sai yārinya ta che, 'Ubamu ya haife mu, mu uku, bīū maza, uwarsu guda. Ni kūa, ni kadaiche, gun uwata. Ubamu kūa da uwamu su-na-sō na, ba su sō yan uwana, dōmin hakanan baban wamu ya tafō da ni nan, ya rūde ni ya che mu tafi itāche, ya zō da ni nan, ya daure ni bisa itāche, ya tafi, ya bar ni. Ubanmu atājiri ne, dōmin hakanan, ya yi mani hakanan.' Sai mādugū

---

alive.' So the leader of the caravan himself climbed up the tree and untied her. Now long ago the caravan leader had wished for offspring, but he was childless. Then he said, 'Where is the maiden from?' And the maiden said, 'Our father begat us, we were three, two boys by one mother, I also alone, by my mother. Our father and mother loved (me), (but) did not love my brothers. And because of that our big brother brought me here, deceiving me by saying we were going for sticks. He came with me here, tied me to a tree (and) left me. Our father is a wealthy man, and because of that, he (my brother) did this to me.' Then the leader of the caravan

وتر : آسم : شيبعا ذ عمر : ذ كيلس تيحو : مس :

إقماف : يكنبت : ذور : كو : شيبعا ذ عمر :

يا ذبم : تيبقوا : بيقسدا م ب : آسم مب : ذ قمش

85

يا ذ رتر : ذ كعامر : آسم يا ذ رقم : قتبث : أبسم

يتميهم : مواك : مبيو متذا : امو وبلس :

عذا : فيكو : نيكذ يبث : عمذ كو اقمر

أبيم : كو : ذ عوم : سنذا سو فمر : نبذ اسن

سو : يبفعو اقمر : ذ وقمر : تكنمر : مبتر : ذ رم

يتفو ذ فيبتمر : يا ذ و وذ مش : يبث : متقيم :

إقماف : يمو ذ فيم : قمر : مذ و رمر : مبلس

إقماف : يتقي : مبنر و : أبتغم : آقما جـ هر مبتل

ذ وقمر : فكنمر : يتمر : تكنمر : آسم قما ذ عمو

sai ya che, 'Ni kūa, kin zama dīāna.'
Sai mādugū ya kai ta gida; ya yi jinya,
har ta warke. Ta-na nan gunsa har ta issa
aure. Ta zama budrūa, bābu irinta kō-
-ina. Da kōwane [9] bigire ana-jin lābāri-
-nta, ana-zua garin kalō(n)ta, har ranan
shi baban wansu, ya balaga, bai sāmu
maata ba. Sai ya ji lābāri, aka-che wani a-
-tājiri shi-na da dīansa, gari kaza,
sararin nan, bābu kamanta. Sai shi kuma ya je gun
ubansu, ya che ya ji lābārin dīar wani atājiri,
ita shi ke sō. Sai ubansa ya gama masa

---

said, 'As for me, you have become my daughter.' So the leader of the caravan took her home (and) nursed her till she recovered. She remained with him until she reached a marriageable age, and grew into a maid whose like was nowhere. And whenever she was heard of, people came to look on her, until a day (when) her elder brother reached manhood. He had not found a wife. Then he heard the report which said that a certain wealthy man had a daughter in such and such a village; in all the country there was not her like. Then he went to their (his) father (and) said he had heard about the daughter of a certain wealthy man (and) it was her he wished (to marry). So his father gave him

لَسْ يَبَّثْ ∴ قِيكُو ∴ كِنْغَمْ تَمَ ∴ دِيَ قَامِي ∴

لَسْ قَادُ غُوا ∴ يَكَبَّتْ تَمِدَا ∴ يَيِّجِنْ ∴

تَمْ قَتُو بَكَّى ∴ قَتَقَا أَقَمْ ∴ غُقْسَنْ ∴ تَمْ قَبِلَسْ

أَوْرَسْ ∴ قَتَغَمْ ∴ بُمُدْ وُو ∴ يَقَابُ ∴ إِرْقَتَ ∴ كُو

إِقَا ∴ دُ كُو وَقَّاِرْ ∴ بِيخِرْبَنْ ∴ أَقَّا جِرْ ∴ لَأُبَادِرْ

قَتَ ∴ أَقَادُرَ ∴ غَمِ قَكَلُوتَ ∴ تَمْ وَقَّمْ

قِيمْ ∴ تَبَّبْرْ ∴ وَقَسْ ∴ يَجَابَلَغَ ∴ يَيْلَسَامْ ∴

مَا أَقُ بَ ∴ لَهْنِ قَيْجِ لَأُبَادِرْ ∴ أَكْثِ ∴ وَقِدَ

تَقَا جِرِ ∴ يِشَنَادِ ∴ دِيَّنْلَسْ ∴ غَمِ كَدَا

لَسْ وَقْتَمْ ∴ يَقَابْ ∴ كَقْتَتَ ∴ لَهْمْ شِبْكُمْ ∴ يَجِنْ ∴ غُمْ

أُبْنَسَ يَبَّثْ ∴ يَجِ ∴ لَأُبَادِرْ قَدِيِّمْ ∴ وَقِدَ أَقَّا جِرِ

∴ إِقَا ∴ شِبْكُسُوا ∴ لَسْ أُمَّنْلَسْ ∴ يَغَحَا قَلَسْ ∴

kāyā; ya je wurin neman aure. Da ya tafi Ala ya yi masa katar, ya sāmu. Aka-ba shi yārinya. Su-ka-yi aure. Su-ka-zō gida, zaa shi [10] sa yārinya zane, yārinya ta kia. Kulum kakanan, sai idan su-ka-tafi gōna, sai ta daukō turmi, da tabarīa na zīnārīa, da ubanta ya ba ta. Ta daukō hatsin, da uwar miji ta ba ta, wai ta yi fura. Sai ta zuba-chikin turmi(n) zīnārīa, ta-na-daka, ta-na-fadi, 'Daka, daka, turmīna, [11] uba yā kōmō uban miji, waiō kaitōnia, uwa tā kō-
-mo uwar miji, waiō turmīna.' Hakanan har ta kāre daka. Ta-na-kūka, ta-na-wāka

---

gifts, (and) he came to seek a wife in marriage. And Allah blessed his quest and he found what he sought, and the maid was wedded to him. They came home, but when he would consummate their union, she would not give herself to him; (and) it was always thus. Only, when they (all) went off to the farms she would lift her mortar and golden pestle which her father had given her, saying she was going to make 'fura' cakes. And she poured the grain into the mortar of gold and pounded and (sung) said, 'Pound, pound, mortar, father has become the father of my husband, alas for me! Mother has become the mother of my husband, alas, my mortar!' And so on till she had finished pounding. She was weeping (and) singing.

كَدَايَدْ ⁖ يَجُلُ ⁖ أُوفُنْجُمَّ ⁖ أَوْرُسَ ⁖ ءِ مَتَّبِ ⁖ أَلَّ يَبَّهْسِ

كَتَّرْ ⁖ مَيْسَدَمُ ⁖ أَكَبَدَاشِ ⁖ مَدَارِفْمِ ⁖ سُكَمَّ ⁖ أَوْرُسَ

سُكُدْوَا ⁖ غِدَا ⁖ دَأُشِ ⁖ سَبِدُوسَّ ⁖ دَفْمُ ⁖ شِبِدَارِفْمِ ⁖

⁖ تِفِمَّ ⁖ كُلُّمْ ⁖ حَكَنَّمْ ⁖ سَمْ إِدَّرْ ⁖ سُكَتِفِ ⁖ غُوشَمْ

سَمْ تَدَّ وُكْوَا ⁖ شُرْمِمْ ⁖ دَتَبَرْيَا ⁖ فَدِ مِنْدَارِيَدْ

دَأُمْشَتْ ⁖ مِبَادَتْ ⁖ مَدُوكُو ⁖ حَطِمْدَ غُورْ ⁖

مِجِّ ⁖ تَبَادَتْ ⁖ وَبِتَّمَّ فُرَ ⁖ سَمْ تَدُّبَ ⁖ تِكِمْ

تُمْرِمِ ⁖ دِ مِنْدَارِيَدْ ⁖ شَنَادِكْ ⁖ تَمَدَا قِدِ

دَكَمْ ⁖ دَكَمْ ⁖ شُرْمِبِنْدَا ⁖ أَبَدِيَاكُرْ مُو ⁖

أُمْرَجِّمْ ⁖ وَمِيُّوا ⁖ كِيَشُو ⁖ فِمْ ⁖ أُوَا ⁖ قَدَاكُو

مُو ⁖ غُوَّرْ مِجِ ⁖ وَمُبُّوا أَشُرْمِينْسَ ⁖ قَكَنَّمْ

تَمْ تَكَابَرْ ⁖ دَكَ ⁖ تَنَاكُوكُ ⁖ تَمَنَاوَاكِ ⁖

Ashe wata tsōfūa na nan ta-na-ji abinda,
ta ke fadi. Kulum hakanan, sai ranan ta kwarmata
ma uwāyan miji. Sai ta che, 'Idan zaa ku gōna,
ke uwar miji ki fita, ki ba ta hatsi, ki che,
ta daka fura, zaa ki gona, idan kin fita,
ki labe, ki kōmō, ki shige daki, ki yi
kurum, ki ji abinda ita ke fadi.' Yau uwar miji
ta fita, ubansu ya fita, yāra da māta duka
su-ka-fita, su-ka-che, zaa su gōna. Aka-jima,
sai uwar miji ta kōmō, ta shiga dāki,
[12] ta-na-kunche. Sai yārinya ta dauko turminta
na zīnārīa, da tabarīanta na zīnārīa, ta-na-

Now a certain old woman of the place heard what she was (saying). It was always so, until one day she told the mother of (the girl's) husband, and she said, 'When you are all about to go to the farm, do you, mother of the husband, come out, give her grain, (and) bid her pound "fura", as you are going to the farm. When you get outside steal away (and) come back, enter the house, (and) remain silent (and) hear what she says.' So the mother of the man came out, their father came out, the boys and the woman all came out, and said they were off to the farm. A little while after the man's mother came back (and) entered the hut (and) crouched down. Then the maiden lifted her mortar and golden pestle. She was

أَبِشَ ؞ يَقَ طُوبُوَا ؞ قَدَقَّرْ ؞ قَتَاجِ ؞ أَمِنْدَ ؞

تَبَكَ ؞ قَدِ ؞ كُلُمْ ؞ تَكَنْ ؞ لَسَّرْ وَقَّرْ ؞ تَكُرْ مَتَ

مَعُوَايِمْ ؞ يَجِ ؞ لَسَرْ تَبْ ؞ ه إِدَّرْ ؞ دَاكُ ؞ غُوقَ

بَعُوَرْمِج ؞ كِبِتَ ؞ كِبَاتَ ؞ تَطِم ؞ كِبَ ؞

تَدَّكَ ؞ بُقَرَا ؞ دَ أَكِ غُوقَمْ ؞ إِدَّرْ ؞ كِنْبِتَ ؞

بِلَبَ ؞ بِكُومُو ؞ كِشْجِرْ ؞ دَاكِ ؞ كَسِّ

كُرْمْ ؞ يَجِ ؞ أَمِنْدَ ؞ تَكَبْجِ ؞ مِيوْعُوَرْمِج

تَبِتَ ؞ أُبِنْسُ مِبِتَ ؞ يَدَوَا ؞ دَمَا قَمْ ؞ دُكَ

لُسَبِتَ ؞ سُكَبْ ؞ دَ أَسْ ؞ قُوقَلَ ؞ أَكِجِمْ ؞

لَسْعُجُ مِج ؞ تَكُومُوَا ؞ تِشَغْ ؞ دَاكِ ؞

تَقَا كُنْبْ ؞ لَسَرْ يَدِ وَقَرْ ؞ قَدَّ وَرْكُوا ؞ قُمْ مِقْتَ

قَمِ مِنْدَرْ تَرَّ ؞ دَ قِيَمْ يَمْتَ ؞ قَمِ مِنْدَ وَرْتُو ؞ قَمْتَ

wāka, ta-na-fadi, ‘ Daka, daka, turmīna, uba
ya kōmō uban miji, wayō turmīna uwa
ta kōmō uwar miji, wayō kaitōnia.’
Ta-na-yin wāka hakanan, ta-na-kūka da hawāye.
Uwa kūa ta-na dāki, ta-na-ganinta, har ta gama
abinda ta ke yi duka. Mutānen gida, da su-ka-tafi
gōna, su-ka-kōmō. Uwa ba ta che kō-
-mī ba. Da dare ya yi, sai ta gaya ma mai-gida, ta che
‘ Kā ji, kā ji, abinda yārinya nan ke yi.’ Uba,
ya che, ‘ Kō yārinya da ta bache, kō ita che ? ’
Sai su-ka-che, ‘ Ama idan ita che, akwai wani tambō
ga bāyanta, tun ta-na [13] jārīriya, aka-bar ta
dāki wurin wuta, ya kōne ta ? ’ Aka-kirāwō ta.

---

singing and saying, ‘ Pound, pound, my mortar, father has become (my) husband’s father, alas, my mortar ! Mother has become (my) husband’s mother, alas for me ! ’ She was singing thus (and) shedding tears, the mother also was in the room and was watching her until she had done all she had to do. When the people of the house who had gone to the farms came back, the mother did not say anything. When night came, then she told her husband ; she said, ‘ Such and such the maid did.’ The father said, ‘ Could it possibly be the maid who was lost ? ’ Then they said, ‘ But if it is she there is a certain mark on her back ever since she was an infant, she had been left in a house with a fire (and) it had burned her.’ She was summoned.

أَبَرْ ؞ قُرْمِينَا ؞ ثَمَّكَ ؞ ءِكَ ؞ قَنَاقِجِ ؞ وَاكَ

= ؞ عُوَارْ ؞ رَبِيُّو مُتَرْمِينَا ؞ أَبَنَّزْمِجِ ؞ يِدَكُو مُوَا

قُمَّنْ ؞ أُكَيْتُوا ؞ رَبِّجَا ؞ عُوزْمِجِ ؞ قَدَكُو مُوَا

دَقَوَابِرْ ؞ قَنَاكُوكَمْ ؞ تَكَتَّرْ ؞ وَاكَ ؞ قَنَدَبِرّ

تَمْقَرْقُمَ ؞ قَنَدَغِيتَّ ؞ قَنَدَاكِ ؞ عُوَاكُوَّ

دَلُسَكَبِّ ؞ غِمَدَا ؞ مُنَابَكْ ؞ دُكَ ؞ قَتَكَمَّ ؞ أَبِنْدَ

كُو ؞ بَتَشْ ؞ عُوَا ؞ سُكَكُو مُوَا ؞ غُوقَلْ

قَشْ ؞ مَقِيكِدَا ؞ لَسُنْقَغَمَّ ؞ ءَدَرُمَبِيَّ ؞ مِيبَ

أُبُرْ ؞ كَمَّ ؞ أَبِنْغَ بِيدُنِيَّتَمَّرْ ؞ كَدَمِ ؞ كَدَمِ

إِقَّشْ ؞ كُوَا ؞ دَبَتَّشْ ؞ كُوَابِدُوقْمَّ ؞ بِيثْ ؞

قُوقَتْبُو ؞ أَكُوسْ ؞ إِمَّشْ ؞ أَمَدَإِدَّرْ ؞ لَسُرْسُكَبْشْ

أَكَبَرْقَا ؞ بَدَرِجِمِتِرْ ؞ قُنْقُسْنَا ؞ غَبَدَبِيَنْتَ ؞

أَكَكِرَاوُوَتَّهْ ؞ يَكُوقَتَ ؞ نُرْقُوقْ ؞ دَاكِ

Aka-gama ta da Ala da anabi aka-che, 'Mutume nan,
da ya yi maki aure nan, ubanki ne, kō kūa
anba shi rikō ne?' Sai yārinua ta kīa
ta fadi. Aka yi, aka yi, ba ta fadi ba. Sai [14] uban
ya che, 'Kāwō bāyanki en gani.' Ta juya
bāyanta. Su-ka-ga tanbo, wanda wuta
ta kōne ta tun tana jārīria. Sai
su-ka-che, 'Ashe hakana ne, tunda fārin
da ki-ka-zō dōmin me ki (ki) gaia mani?'
Sai su-ka-sani diarsu che. Sai
su-ka-aike gun ubanta, wanda
ya tsinche ta, aka-gaia masa kaman da aka-yi.

They adjured her by Allah and the Prophet (and) said, 'This man who gave you in marriage, is he your father or were you given to him to be brought up only?' But the maiden refused to answer. Try as they could they could not get an answer. Then the father said, 'Present your back that I may see.' She turned her back, (and) they saw the scar where the fire had burned her when she was an infant. Then they said, 'Truly it is so. From the first when you came why did you (refuse) to tell me (us)?' And they knew it was their daughter. And they sent to her (foster) father, the one who had found her, and he was told what had happened.

أكفماق ∴ دأل ∴ دأقب ∴ أكب ∴ مبتر ∴

ديبهك ∴ أورمتر ∴ أمنكبر ∴ كوكو ∴

أبدليش رفوبي ∴ لسني مدر ومر ∴ قنفر

تبجد ∴ أكبر ∴ أكمر ∴ بتقديب ∴ لسع أمر

يب ∴ كدأور ∴ بدأينك ∴ إتفيم ∴ تجوس

بدأينت ∴ لسكغ ∴ مبجو ∴ ومدر وقر ∴

تكوفت ∴ منتدأبار ميرس ∴ لسر

لسكب ∴ أبشر مكتر ولم ∴ ثمد قأور ∴

دعكذوأ ∴ دومر جمر ∴ كخيأ مر ∴

لسر لسكسر ∴ دميز لسب ∴ لسر [redacted]

لسك أيبكر ∴ عمر ∴ أمنت ∴ نومد [redacted]

يطنبت ∴ أكفيأ مسر ∴ كحمر ∴ دأكي

Sai shi kūa ya che, 'Bābu laifi ina rōkō
ku ba ni yārinya, idan nā ga wani, in ba shi.
Sai su kuma su-ka-ki yarda.' Miji kūa, da ya ji
hakanan, sai ya dauki kwari, da [15] bakā tasa,
ya shiga dāji, ya rataye kainsa, ya mutu. Mafārin
kiyaya [16] yan uba ke nan. Shi ke nan, [17] kungurus
kan kūsu.

And he said, 'There is no harm done. I beg you give me the maiden. If I have found another I shall give her to him (the husband).' But they (the girl's real father and mother) refused to consent to this. As for the husband, when he heard this he took his quiver and bow. He went into the forest (and) hanged himself. He died. And this was the beginning of hatred among the children of one father by different mothers. That is all. Off with the rat's head.

سَنْ شِيكُو ∴ يَبْ مَاطُبْ ∴ آيِنْجِمْ ∴ إِقَادَارُوكُو

كَبْدِرْ ∴ يَطُو وُمْعَ ∴ إِدَّنْ ∴ فَاطُمَوِنْ ∴ إِنْبَاشِنْ ∴

سَنْ سُو كُحَمَّ ∴ لَسْكِيرِ دَ ∴ مِجْ كُوَّ ∴ دَ بِيجِ

مَكَمَّنْ ∴ سَنْ يَدُوكِ ∴ كُوُوَ ∴ دَ تَيْكَا تِسَنْ ∴

يَبْلِثْغُ دَاجِ ∴ يَمَاتِيبُ ∴ كَيْلِسَنْ ∴ يَمُثُ ∴ مَقَارِنْ ∴

فِيَنْ ∴ يَمْغَلُّبُ ∴ كَبْسَنْ ∴ شِيكِنَّنْ ∴ فَنْكُرُسْ ∴

كَمْقُوسْ ∴

No. 3.

Wanan tātsūnīar kōnan dāji che.

[1] Gātanan, gātanan, ta je, ta dāwō. Sarki ya bari aka-sa ma dāji wuta. Aka-gewaye, ba asāmu kōmi ba, har dāji ya kōnē duka. Sai wani mugun yārō ya gani wani rāmē. Ya gina, bai ga kōmi ba, sai wata tsōfūa ta fitō achiki. Da fitowa, sai ta pasa kūwa, ta che, 'Sarki [2] yā sa ma dāji wuta, kōwa yā gani rāmenga yā wuche, sai kai ka gina, yau [3] kaa gani. Sai ta fāfari yārō. [4] Sai yārō ya buge ta da gatari. Ta tuma bisa, ta zama shāfō, zaa ta fauche shi, sai ya halbe ta;

This tale is about a bush-burning. A story, a story. Let it go, let it come. A chief gave permission for the grass to be burned. They went all round but did not see anything (game) until all the grass was burned. Then a certain bad boy saw a hole and dug (there); he did not see anything. But an old woman came out, and on her emerging she screamed (with rage) and said, 'The chief has set fire to the bush; (hitherto) whosoever has seen this hole has passed on, and now you must dig it up. To-day you will see.' Then she sprang on the boy, but the boy struck her with his axe. Up she leaped and turned into a hawk, and when she was about to swoop down on him he shot at her;

وَقَّرْ قَدَا طُوفِيَّرْ كُوقَرْ دَابِ ؞

غَمَا قَنَّرْ ؞ غَمَا قَنَّرْ ؞ تَجِّسْ ؞ قَدَ اُورُ ؞ لَسَرْكِ ؞

يَبَيَّ ؞ آكَ لَسَامَ ؞ دَاجِ ؞ وُقَالَ ؞ آكَجْغُوبِيَ ؞

بَأَلَسَامَ ؞ كُوجِبَ ؞ قَمْ دَاجِ ؞ يَكُوبِيَ ؞

دُكَ ؞ لَسَرْ وَفِمُوغُرْ ؞ يَادَاوُرُ ؞ يَغَيِنِ ؞ وَفِمَ امَ ؞

يَفِمْ ؞ مَيَغِ كُوجِيبَ ؞ لَسَرْ وَنَطُو فُوَا ؞ ==

قَبِثُوا ؞ أَلَيْكِمْ ؞ دَرْفِثُوا ؞ لَسَرْ قَقَسَكُوَرْ ؞

قَثَّ ؞ لَسَرْكِ ؞ يَدَلَسَحَدَاجِ ؞ وُقَمْ ؞ كُوَا ؞

يَاغَنِمْ ؞ وَابَّنْغُ ؞ يَادُوثُ ؞ لَسِيكِمْ ؞ مَكَخِرَ ؞

يَبُو ؞ كَأَغَيِمْ ؞ لَسَرْ قَبِلَقِمْ ؞ يَادُورُ ؞ لَسَ

يَادُورُ ؞ مَبُغُمْ ؞ دَغَا قَمْرَ ؞ قَتُّمْ ؞ بِمَسَ ؞

قَدَهِمْ ؞ شَابِفُوَا ؞ ذَامْبَقُوبِشَنْ لَسَرْ يَعْلَبَّ

hakanan har ta rinjāye shi. Ya gudu. Shi-na-gudu, ya je, ya iske zanzarō, shi-na-sāka. Sai zanzarō ya che, 'Ina zaa ka.' Ya che, 'Wata tsōfūa ta korō ni.' Sai zanzarō ya che, 'Zamna nan ta tafō.' Sai yārō ya za-mna. Shi-na nan, sai tsōfūa ta zō, bābu shāwara, sai ta zābura, zaa ta kāma yārō. Sai zanzarō ya hade ta. Sai zanzarō ya dauki sīlīli guda daia, ya ba yārō, ya che, shi damre tsakar bāyansa. Sai yārō ya damre shi, har bāyansa zaa shi tsumke. Mafārin ka gani chikin zanzarō da girma ke nan, tsōfūa ke chiki. Bāyansa kua, da ya zama sīlīli, yārō ya damre shi

---

and so (they fought on) until she got the better of him. He ran away. (As) he ran he came across a wasp, he was weaving cloth. Then the wasp said, 'Where are you going?' He said, 'An old woman chased me.' Then the wasp said, 'Sit here (till) she comes.' So the boy sat down. He was there when the old woman came sure enough, and she sprang to catch the boy; but the wasp swallowed her. He lifted a single thread and gave it to the boy (and) said he must tie it round his middle. So the boy tied him up, until his back was almost cut in two. That is the origin of what you see; the wasp's belly is big, the old woman is inside. His back, which has become a thread, the boy bound it

تكنّ قم تم فنجا ميش ⁖ يغم ⁖ شنا غم ⁖ يجس

يا إنسبكن ⁖ ذ مغ ور ⁖ شنا السا اكن ⁖ لسم ذ مغ ور ⁖

يشا إما ذ أك ⁖ ييش ⁖ وقطح فوا ⁖ تكو ور ⁖ تسي

ذ مغ ور ⁖ ييش ⁖ ذ مم قمّ ⁖ تقو أ ⁖ لسم يما ور ⁖ يبم

مم ⁖ شنا قمّ ⁖ لسم طو فوا ⁖ مغ وا ⁖ يما بشا ور ⁖

لسم تغ أم مم ⁖ ذ أتكام ⁖ يما ور ⁖ لسم ذ مغ ور ⁖ يجم مة

لسم ذ مغ ور ا ⁖ يم و ك ⁖ سيليس ⁖ غما ذ تم ⁖ يبا

يما ور ا ⁖ يش ⁖ تبنّ مم ⁖ طكم بما يتس ⁖ لسي

يما ور ⁖ يمّ مم مشن قم بما ينلسو ⁖ نشطمكي ⁖

مبا ور ⁖ ككفتم ⁖ تكن ⁖ ذ نم ور ⁖ ذ غم مس ⁖

بكنّ ⁖ طو فوا ⁖ بكنكي ⁖ مبا ينلس كو ⁖

كميقّ مم ⁖ لسيليم ⁖ يما ور ⁖ يبم مم مشن

ga [5] tsara bāya. Shi ke nan, [6] kungurus
kan kūsū. Kūsu ba ya chi
kaina ba, sai in chi
kain dan banza.

---

at the middle, behind. That is all. Off with the rat's head. The rat will not eat my head, rather will I eat (its) head, son of a worthless fellow.

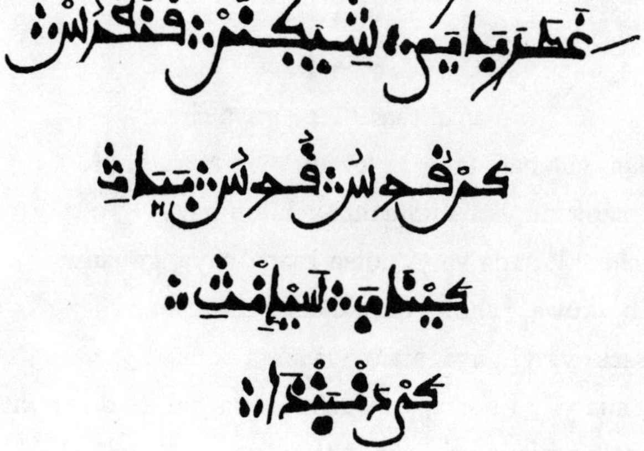

No. 4.

Wanan tātsūnīar [1] gayā che.

[2] Gātanan, gātanan, ta je, ta kōmō. Sarki ya haifi
dīansa mai-keau, bābu kamanta achikin gari.
Sai ya che, ' Wanda ya yi nōma raana-gaya, gōnansa
ya wuche-kōwa, [3] shi ka aure dīa sarki. Yau,
ranan sarki ya yi gaya, atafō ayi masa nōma,
ama wanda ya yi nōma, ya wuche kōwa, shi ke da [4] maatā.'
Yau ashe hawainya ya ji tundadewa,
ya je, shi-na-chin māganin nōma. Yau da raanar gaya
ta zō, hawainya shi-na gida, bai fitō ba, har mā-
-sunōma su-ka-yi nōma, su-ka-yi nīsa. Kāna
hawainya ta zō. Da ya sāra hauya kasa sō daia,

This is a story about an alliance. A story, a story. Let it go, let it come. A chief begat a beautiful daughter; she had no equal in the town. And he said, ' He who hoes on the day the people come together and whose area hoed surpasses every one else's he marries the chief's daughter. So on the day the chief calls his neighbours to hoe (*gayā*), let them come (the suitors) and hoe for him. But he who hoes and surpasses every one else, to him a wife.' Now of a truth the chameleon had heard (about this) for a long time past, (and) he came along. He was eating hoeing medicine. Now when the day of the hoeing came round the chameleon was at home. He did not come out until those hoeing were at work and were far away; then the chameleon came. When he struck one blow on the ground with the hoe,

وَمِنْ قَمَاطُو قِيَّنْ غَيَابُ ⁖

غَدَ اَقَنْ نَيْ دَاقَنْ ⁖ يَجِ يَكُوْ مُوَا ⁖ اَسَرْكِ ⁖ يَحِيْبِي ⁖

دِمِنْسَنْ ⁖ مَيْكُوْ ⁖ بَابُ ⁖ كَحَقْتَ ⁖ اِقْكِرْ غَمِيرِ ⁖

لَسَرْ يَبْ ⁖ وَاْقِعْ مَيْبِنُوْ مَوْ ⁖ زَاقَنْقِيَا ⁖ غُوْ قَنْسَرَ ⁖

يَيُوْبْ ⁖ مُكُوَا ⁖ شِيَكَوْ بِنُوْ ⁖ دِمَّسَرْكِ ⁖ يَيُوْ ⁖

وَقَّنْ ⁖ لَسَرْكِ ⁖ بَبِيَّ غَمِيدَ ⁖ اَقْبُوَا ⁖ اَيِبَسَرْ قُوْ مَيْ ⁖

اَمَّارْ قَعْ ⁖ بَيَّنْ قُوْ مَيْ ⁖ يَيُوْبْ كُوَا ⁖ شِيبَكَدْ مَاقْنَرْ

نَيُوْ ⁖ اَشُيْ ⁖ حُوْ بِيَنَّ ⁖ يَدَاجْ ⁖ قُنْعْ دِمَكُوَا ⁖

يَجِي شِنَا قَنْ ⁖ هَدَ غَمِيَنْ قُوْ مَيْ ⁖ مِيُّوْ ⁖ دَرْ اُقَنْ غَيِّيَنْ ⁖

قُدُرَ ⁖ حَوْبِيَنَّ ⁖ لِشَنَا غِدَا ⁖ بَبِيقُوْبَ ⁖ حَرْمَا

سُقُوْ مَيْ ⁖ لَسْكَرَّ ⁖ قُوْ مَوْ ⁖ لَسُكَرِّ فِبِسَلَمْ ⁖ كَدَانْ

حَوْبِيَنْ ⁖ تَبْغُرَا ⁖ دَمَّيْسَدَوْ ⁖ حَوْمَنْ ⁖ كَسَنْ ⁖ سُوْدَرَّ

sai ya hau bisa hauya ya zamna. Sai hauya
ta kāma nōma, ta-na-tafia tar! har ta chika
da manōma, ta wuche, ta kai bākin [5] kunya.
Hawainya ya sabka, ya zamna, ya fūta, kāna
manoma sun-ka-kāwō. Saanan sarki,
shi bai yarda ba, sai wanda ya yi gudu, ya tsēre
kōwa duka, shi ke aure dīarsa.
Sai [6] gumki ya che shi ya fi kōwa
gudu. Sai su-ka-yi gudu, sai hawainya ta zama
[7] tanpasua, ta tuma, ta mane ga wutsīar
gumki. Sai gumki shi-na-gudu, har ya wuche
kōwa, har ya kāwō kōfar gidan

---

then he climbed on the hoe and sat down, and the hoe started to hoe, and fairly flew until it had done as much as the hoers. It passed them, and reached the boundary of the furrow. The chameleon got off, sat down, and rested, and later on the (other) hoers got to where he was. Then the chief would not consent, but now (said) he who ran and passed every one, he should marry his daughter. Then the hartebeest said he surpassed every one in running. So they had a race. But the chameleon turned into a needle; he leaped (and) stuck fast to the tail of the hartebeest, and the hartebeest ran until he passed every one, until he came to the entrance of the house

لسن يعوش ∴ مسن قوتن ∴ يغمر ∴ اسن قوسن ∴

تكام قومو ∴ قسنا تفين ∴ قمر ∴ قرميك

كنيا ∴ كمر بدا تكي ∴ قوب ∴ منومو د ∴

حوفين ∴ يسبك ∴ يغمر ∴ يقوق ∴ كلق

منومو ∴ سنككاو ∴ سعقم ∴ اسمركم ∴

شبيبير عب ∴ اسن وقدبير غد ∴ يجبري

كوا ∴ دك ∴ شيبكر اور ∴ ح ميرلسن ∴

سن غمكم ∴ يمب ∴ بشي بداف ∴ كوا ∴

غد ∴ اسن سكر غد ∴ اسن حوفين ∴ تغم ∴

تنقبسوا ∴ يتم ∴ يقبن ∴ غحليم ∴

غمكم ∴ اسن غمكم ∴ شنا غد ∴ حم يوب

كوا ∴ قمر يعداور ∴ كوقم ∴ يغم م

(gidan) sarki. Ya wuche. Sai hawainya ya saki
wutsīar gumki. Ashe hawainya ya gani
yārinya. Sai ya rungume ta. Kāmin gumki
shi kōmō, sai ya tarda hawainya shi-na-
-rungume da yārinya. Sai gumki ya rika
kūka da hawāye. Mafārin abinda ka ke gani
ga idānunsa, kaman hawāye ke nan, tun ranan
ya ke kūka, bai share hawāye ba.
[8] Kungurus kan kūsu.

---

of the chief. He passed it. Then the chameleon let go the hartebeest's tail; of a truth the chameleon had seen the maiden. So he embraced her, and when the hartebeest came along he met the chameleon embracing the girl. Thereupon the hartebeest began to shed tears, and that was the origin of what you see like tears in a hartebeest's eyes. From that day he has wept and not dried his tears. Off with the rat's head.

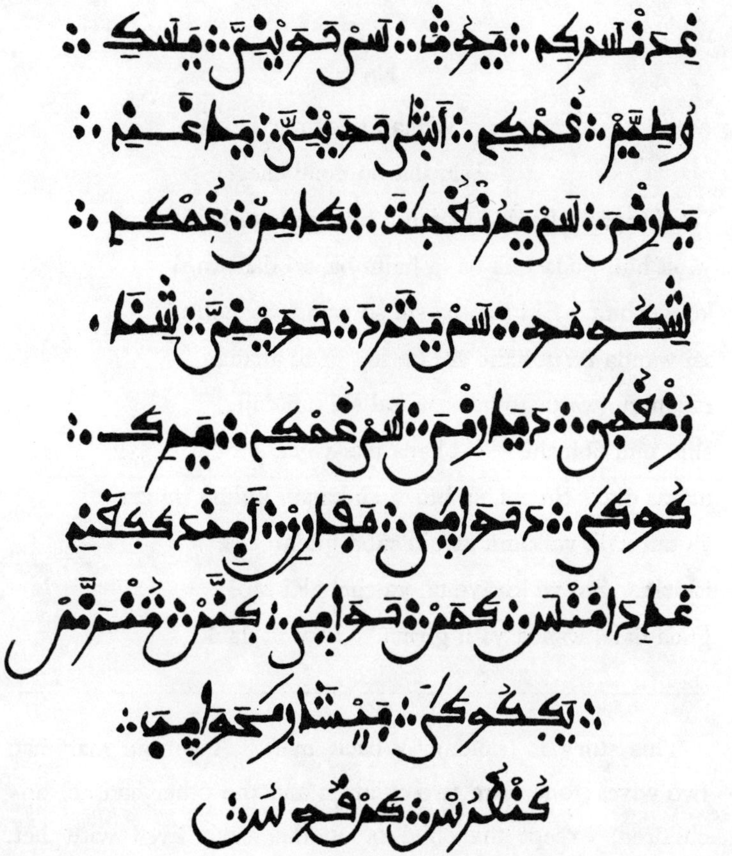

No. 5.

Wanan tātsūnīar
[1] shasharbō mani che.

Wani mutum ke da [2] mātansa bīū, guda tā haifu yāya bīū, guda kūa ba ta haifu ba, sai dan wani ke wurinta. Shi kua ba shi sō wanda ta haifu, sai wanda ba ta haifu shi ke so. Yau ananan ranan yunwa ta zō garinsu, sai shi tafi dāji, shi sāmu abinchi. Shi hana mai-yāya, shi bai maras dīa. Su chi, su bīū. Hakanan kulum, ranan ya tafi dāji, ya sāmu kwain zābō gūda ishirin. Sai ya kirāye ta, ya che, 'Ki zābi guda daia, wanda ya fi girmā.' [3] Sai ta dauki

---

This story is (called) 'Whack me'. A certain man had two wives; one bore two children and the other had not any children, except the child of another who lived with her. Now he (the husband) did not like the one who had borne, but the one who had not borne. Now it came about that a day of famine came on them. Then he (the husband) went to the bush (and) found food, and refused the one with children and gave to the one without children, (and) they two ate; and it was so always. And one day he went to the bush and found guinea-fowl's eggs, twenty in number. Then he called her (the one he did not love) and told her to choose the largest of them. So she took

وَ فَرَقَاطُوفِيَرْ ؞

شَشَرْبُومَيْثْ

وَفِمُتُرْ ؞ بَكَدَ مَا تَنَّسْ ؞ مِيُوا ؞ غُمَدَا ؞ فَاقَيْفْ

يَدَايَمِ مِيُوا ؞ غُدَاكُو ؞ يَتَّعَيْقُبَ ؞ اَسْرِ دِفْمَوْ

بَكَمُوفَنْتَ ؞ لِشَيكُو ؞ بَدَاشَسُو ؞ وَفْمَ تَّمَيْكَ

سَرْ وَفْدَ ؞ بَتَّعَيْفَ ؞ شِكَسُوا ؞ بَيُوْ أَفَا فَّمْ ؞

وَفَّمْ ؞ بَيِفُو ؞ فَغُدُو ؞ غُمْ فَسُنْ سَبِيشْتَفِ ؞ دَاجِ

شِبَسَا مُوا ؞ أَمِنْثِ ؞ لِاشَمْرِ ؞ مَيْرِ ؞ يَدَايَمِ ؞ لِشَبَرْ

مَرْسِحِ يَمِي ؞ لُسَثِ سُوبِيُو ؞ حَكَنَّمْ كُلُمْ ؞ وَفَّمْ

يَتِفِ ؞ دَاجِ ؞ يَسَامُوا ؞ كُوَيْغِ اَبُو ؞ غُمَدَا ؞

عَشِمِرْثْ سَرْ يَكَرَاكِمْتَ ؞ يَيِثْ ؞ كَخَاوِ ؞ =

غُمَدَامْ تَوْثْ ؞ وَفْدَ يَفِ ؞ غُمْ نَمُو ؞ اَسْرِ فَدَوْكِ ؞ =

guda, ta je, ta dafa, ta ba yāra. [4] Su-ka-chi.
Ranan ita kuma [5] ta je dāji, ta sāmu
hatsinta, ta [6] talga kunū, ta kirāye shi,
ta che, 'Dūba chikin yan [7] farutanka,
ka tsōma guda daia wanda ya fi girma ka lā-
-she, ka tāshi, ka bar ma yāra saura.' Sai
ya rika dūba yan yātsa, shi-na-jujuyāwa,
shi-na-fadi, 'Wani [8] zaa ni tsōmāwa chiki?' Shi-na-
-fadi, 'Wanga kō wanga?' Ashe hannunsa
guda shi-na wurin gūtsunsa, shi-na-kunta walki.
Sai ya kunche [9] walki maza maza, ya tūra chikin
kunū. Idānun maata shi-na-dūban wani wuri,

---

one, she went and boiled it, and gave it to the children to eat. And on that day she too went to the bush, she found corn, and stirred (it into) gruel. And she called him (her husband) and said, 'Look among your nails and dip (into the pot) one, the largest one of all, then lick (it), rise up, and leave the rest to the children.' Then he began to examine his nails, he turned them about, saying, 'What one must I dip in?' (and) he kept saying, 'Is it this one or that one?' But all the time his one hand was between his legs loosening his skin waist covering. Then he swiftly unfastened it, and plunged it into the pap, (in the pot) (when) the woman's eyes were looking the other way;

غمدرا ؞ قجى ؞ تعرف ؞ تبايدرا ؞ لسكث ؞

وقمّ ؞ إتكم ؞ قجى داج ؞ قسدموا ؞ =

كطنت ؞ تقالغ ؞ كنوا ؞ تكراپشر

تث ؞ دوبس ؞ قكم ؞ ينقم تنك ؞ =

كطوم ؞ غداتر ؞ ومد ميف ؞ غمرمو ؞ كلا

شبر ؞ كنداشر ؞ كبمر ميدرا ؞ لسورا ؞ لس

يمرك ؞ دوب ؞ ينيا ط ؞ بشنا جو بجويارا ؞

شنا قبـ ؞ وبدا ؞ طومدوا ؞ ثك ؞ شنا

قبـ ؞ ورفغ ؞ كورفغ ؞ اشر قتنفس ؞

غمدا ؞ شنا ورفوطنفس ؞ شنا كنت ولكم

؞ لسريكنث ؞ ولكم ؞ مغمغ ؞ يثوو ؞ ثكم

كنوا ؞ إدا قمرما قمر ؞ شنا دوبنوقوري ؞

ba ta gani ba. Sai ya tāshi ya che, '[10] Nā tsōma dai.' Sai ta che, '[11] Kai ka ji da abin fadi.' Sai ta [12] kyale. Wata raana ta tafi dāji, ta ganō [13] māra. Sai ta wuche. Sai māra ta che, 'Kāka ki ke wuche ni ba ki gaishe ni?' Sai ta che, '[14] Sannū.' Sai māra ta che, '[15] in gwiya.' Sai [16] maatar nan ta kyale, ta wuche. Sai māra ta che, 'Ba ki tanbaya na sūnana?' Sai maatar nan ta che, 'Kāka sūnanki?' Sai māra ta che, 'Sūnana, [17] Shibshibtō mani,' Sai maatar nan ta kyale, zaa ta wuchewa. Sai māra ta che, 'Ba ki tanbaya sūnana?' Sai maatar nan ta che, 'Kāka sūnanki?' Sai

---

she did not see. Then he stood up and said, 'I have put one in.' And she said, 'You will get put to shame over this,' and she refrained from saying any more. Another day she went to the bush, and saw a spoon and she passed on. But the spoon said, 'How is it you would pass on and not salute me?' So she said, 'Greetings to you.' And the spoon said, 'Greetings.' Then the woman would have let it go at that, and passed on, but the spoon said, 'Will not you ask my name?' So the woman said, 'What is your name?' And the spoon answered, 'My name is Help me.' And the woman did not speak again, and was about to pass on, but the spoon said, 'Will not you ask me my name?' So the woman said, 'What is your name?' And

بتقينيب .. لسنى متنالش .. ميجب مط طو مو ىش ..

لسن قث .. كيجى .. دأمن قح .. لسن تبكلبو ..

وقمرأن قتقحماج .. تقفنوا .. مدرا .. لسن

قوف .. لسن مدوأمث .. كداك .. كجكوش

مداكقنبشن .. لسن قث .. لسنفنوا .. لسن مدرا ..

قث إقفن .. لسن مدقن قن .. تكجبى أقوف

لسن مدرا .. قث .. بداكتشبيا .. لسو مدوق

لسن مدقن قن .. قث كداك .. لسو قنك

لسن مدوا .. قث لسو مدرن .. ششبتو من

.. لسن مدقن قن .. تكجبى .. دأقوقوا ..

لسن مدرا .. قثبداكتشبيلسو مدو .. لسن

مدقن قن .. قث كداك .. لسو قنك .. لسن

māra ta che, 'Sūnana Shibshibtō mani.' Sai māra ta che, 'Ke kūa che, Shibshibtō mani in jia.' Sai ita kūa ta che, 'Shibshibtō mani in jia.' Sai māra ta che, 'Kāwō kworianki.' Ta kāwō kworianta, sai māra ta rika zuba mata tūō, ta zuba mata har kworianta ya chika. Ta tafō gida, ta dī-ba, ta bai mijinta. Saura kūa ita da yāra su-ka-chi. Gari ya wāye, sai mijinta ya zō. Sai ya che, 'Dōmin Ala ina ki-ka-sāmū abinchi nan?' Sai ta che, 'Na sāmu kudi ne, na gani hatsi, na saye, na daka, na [18] tūka tūō.' Sai ya che, 'Bābu laifi.' Sai ya tāshi, ya fita, ya bar ta.

---

the spoon said, 'My name is Help me'; and the spoon said, 'You too say, Help me that I may taste.' So she also said, 'Help me that I may taste.' Thereupon the spoon said, 'Bring your calabash.' She brought her calabash. Then the spoon kept filling it with food, he poured it out for her till her calabash was full. She went home, took it out, and gave her husband, and the remainder she and her children ate. Next day her husband came and said, 'For the sake of Allah where did you get that food?' Then she said, 'I got money, I saw grain, I bought it, I pounded it, and made food.' And he said, 'That is all right,' and stood up, and went out, and left her.

مدارا ∴ قب لسوقدار ∴ شبشبتو أمن ∴ لسن قدارا ∴

تب ∴ بككو ∴ قبشبشبتو من ∴ إفجن ∴ لسن

إتكو ∴ قب شبشبتو من ∴ إفجن ∴ لسن قدارا ∴

تب كدارو ∴ كن ينك ∴ تكدارو كن يقت ∴ لسن

مدارا ∴ تم كذ باقت ∴ قذورو ∴ تذ باقت

∴ قم كن يقت ∴ ينك ∴ قتبو أغدا ∴ تحي

يب ∴ قبن يقت ∴ لسوراكو ∴ إقد ميلوا ∴

لسكن ∴ غم ∴ يجوا ابكن ∴ لسن يقت ميذرن ∴ لسن

يبادو من ارن ∴ إفما كك لسامو ∴ أمنشتن ∴

لسن قتب ∴ قد لسامو ∴ كحي يبن ∴ تغنم قطم

قلسبن ∴ قدك ∴ قنوك ∴ قجورو ∴ لسن يقب

∴ بلب ليبجم ∴ لسن يقتالشن ∴ يجت ييبرما ∴

Ita kūa sai ta tāshi, ta dauki kworianta,
ta fita, ta tafi dāji, wurin da māra ta ke,
ta iske māra, ta che mata, 'Kāka sūnanki?'
Sai māra ta che, 'Sūnana Shibshibtō mani.'
Ta che, 'Shibshibtō mani in jia.' Sai māra
ta rika zuba mata tūō, har kworianta
ta chika. 19 Ta daukō, ta tafō gida, ta dība,
ta ba shi, ya chi, da shi da maatansa guda, (sk)
su-ka-kōshi. Kulum hakanan, sai ranan ya che,
'Dōmin Ala ba ki kai ni wurinda ki ke sāmu
tūō nan.' Sai ta che masa, 'In garin Ala ya wāye
ka zō.' Yau, da gari ya wāye sai ya zō, su-ka-je wurin

She also got up, lifted her calabash (and) went out, and went off to the bush where the spoon was. She came to where he was and said to him, 'What is your name?' And the spoon said, 'My name is Help me.' She said, 'Help me that I may taste.' Thereupon the spoon commenced to pour out food for her until her calabash was full. She lifted it and went oft home, took (the food) out and gave him. He ate, with his one wife. They were filled. And this happened again and again, till one day he said, 'For the sake of Allah will you not take me to where you are finding this food?' Then she said to him, 'When the dawn of Allah appears, come.' So when it was dawn, he came, and they went to the place

إتكو :: لسن تتداليَن قدوركي :: كم ميتة :: =

تمقة :: تتبي كراج :: وودفد مادرا انجكن :: بلا

تالسكن مادرا :: تتبقة :: كداك :: لسوفنكي

تسن مادرا اتب :: لسو فادرن :: شبشبتو ممن ::

تتب شبشبتو ممن :: اقجن :: السن مادرا :: مد

تمركد بامة :: تتدورو :: حمركم ميتة ::

تشك :: تتدوركوا :: تتبقوا :: غدا :: تتدميبا

تبداليَن :: ميتا د شيد ما فتنسن :: غدا :: سك

لسكو لين :: كعلم حكمن :: السن وقمر ميت

دو قمرا :: بما اكتين :: ورفد كجكسا موا ::

تغ وومر :: تسم قج مسن :: ا مغفر فدالبيا وايير :: ك

كدرا :: ميوج غم :: ميجو ايمن :: تسم وقدر :: تسكمين :: وزن

māra ta che, 'Gaishe ta.' Sai ya gaida māra. Sai maatarsa ta che, 'Tanbaye ta mana, che, Kāka sūnanki?' Sai ya che, 'Kāka sūnanki?' Sai māra ta che, 'Sunana Shibshibtō mani.' Sai [20] maatar kūa ta che masa, 'Che, Shibshibtō mani in jia.' Sai ya che, 'Shibshibtō mani in jia.' Sai māra kūa ta dinga zuba masu tūō, har korainsu su-ka-chika. Su-ka-dauki, sa-ka-kā-wō gida, su-ka-chi. Da dare ya yi, sai mijin ya kōma, ya dauke māra, ya kāwō gida, ya sainya chikin [21] rufēwa. Idan yā ji yunwa, sai shi che maa-tansa ta shiga chikin rufēwa, ta gani me

---

where the spoon was. She said, 'Salute her,' so he saluted the spoon. Then his wife said, 'Ask her, can't you (her name)? say, What is your name?' So he said, 'What is your name?' And the spoon said, 'My name is Help me.' And the wife said to him, 'Say, Help me that I may taste.' And he said, 'Help me that I may taste.' Thereupon the spoon commenced to pour out food for them until their calabash was full; then they lifted it and took it home. They ate. When night came then the husband returned. He lifted up the spoon and came back to the house, and put the spoon inside the grain store. When he felt hungry then he told his wife to go into the grain store and see what

مَارَا اِشْقَبْ ⁖ غَيْبُتَ ⁖ لَسِنْ وَقِّنْجِمْ مَارَا ⁖ لَسِنْ

مَاقْمُ لَسِنْ قَشْ ⁖ قَنْبِيقَمَ ⁖ نْكَادَ ⁖

لَسُوقَّنْكِ ⁖ لَسِنْ يَبْ كَادَ ⁖ لُسُوقْنْكِ ⁖

لَسِنْ مَارَا ⁖ قَشْ لُسُو فَامُ ⁖ لِشْبِشْبُتُو قَمِ

سَنْ مَاقْمُ كُو ⁖ قَشْ مَسَ ⁖ شِبِشْبُتُو قَمِ

إِقْجِي ⁖ لَسِنْ يَشْ ⁖ لِشْبِشْبُتُو مِيِ ⁖ إِقْجِي ⁖ لَسِيْ

مَارَا كُو ⁖ تَدِي نْغَ ⁖ دُبَا مَسِ ⁖ قْخُوْرُ ⁖ تَمْ

كُخْوَرِيْ لَسِ ⁖ لَسَكَيْكِ ⁖ لُسَكَدَّرْكِ ⁖ لُسَكَكْمْ

وُرْغِدَا ⁖ لُسَكَشِ ⁖ دَدَّرْ مُيِّيى ⁖ لَسِنْ مِيمَ ⁖ يَكُومَ

⁖ يَدَّوْكَيْ ⁖ مَارَا ⁖ يَكَاوُرْ ⁖ غِدَا ⁖ يَلَسْنِيلُ ⁖

شِكِرُ وُسَوَا ⁖ إِكِّمْرِيَامِ ⁖ يُمِنْوَ ⁖ لَسِنْ شِبْ مَا

تَنْسَ قَشْغَ ⁖ نْكِسِ ⁖ رُوسَوَا ⁖ قَقْخِيمْ ⁖ مَبِيْ

ke chiki. Sai ta shiga rufēwa, ta iske māra.
Ta che, 'Kāka sūnanki?' Sai māra ta che,
'Sunana Shibshibtō mani.' Sai ta che, 'Shibshibtō
mani in jia.' Sai māra ta chika mata kworia
da tūō. Ba su bai wachan maata da ta gwoda masa.
Ita kūa ba ta sāmun abinchi, hakanan kulum.
Sai ranan maatansa wa(n)da shi ke sō, mai-gida
ba shi gida, ya je dāji. Sai ta dauki
māra ta kai raafi, ta-na-wanki. Sai [22] mātan
sarki su-ka-zō, su-ka-gaishe ta, su-ka-che
'Me ki ke yi?' Ta che, 'Gā shi dai.' Sai su-ka-kyale.
Sai ta che, 'Ba ku gaishe ta?' Sai su-ka-che, 'Sannu, sannu.'

---

was inside. When she entered the store she met the spoon. She said, 'What is your name?' Then he said, 'My name is Help me.' And she said, 'Help me that I may taste.' And the spoon filled her calabash with food. And they did not give that wife who had told him all about it. She also did not find any food. It was always so, until one day his wife, the one the man loved, when the husband was not at home, he had gone to the bush, took the spoon. She came to the stream and was washing it, when the chief's wife came and greeted her and said, 'What are you doing?' She said, 'Look at that.' Then they said nothing more. Then she said, 'Are you not going to salute her?' And they said, 'Greetings, greetings.'

بَكِلِيكِي :. لَسَمْ تَشِعْرُ وَبِلُوَا :. قَدْ اِسْكِي مَدَارَا :.

تَبْ كَاكَ :. سُوقَنْكِ :. لَسَمْ مَدَارَا :. قَبْ :.

سُونَدَاقَنْ :. لِشَبِشْبُو مَنْ :. لَسَمْ قَبْ شِبِشْبُو

قَمَنْ :. اِفْجَنْ :. لَسَمْ مَدَارَا :. قَيْكَامَتْ :. كُرَيْنْ :.

ءُمْكُو وَ :. بَالَسْبَنْ :. وَقُمْ مَا اَتَدْ قَفُدَا اَمَسَنْ اَبَ

إِنَّكُو :. بَمَاتَقَسَا مُنْ :. أَبِمْنِتْ :. تَكَمْنْ :. كَلَمْ

لَسَمْ وَقَمَّ :. مَا اُتَنَسَ :. وَقَمْعَ شِبَكْسُوَا :. قَيْخَدَ ا

:. بَدَالِشَغَدَا :. بِيَدَا جَبَنْ :. دَرَاجِ :. لَسَمْ قَدَّ وُكِ

مَدَارَا :. تَكَنْ :. رَأْبِمْ :. قَنَدَا وَقَنْكِ :. لَسَمْ مَا اَقَّمْ

سَرِكَمْ :. سَكَكُو :. لُسَكَخَيْبَنْتَ :. لُسَكَبْ

بَمَكَجَنْ :. قَبْ :. نَمَا شِدَمُنْ :. لَسَمْ لَسَكَبْلُو

لَسَمْ تَشَبَا :. بَمَاكُغَيْبَنْتَ :. لَسَمْ مُسَكَبْ لَسَنْسُو السَّنُو ..

Ta amsa gaisua. Sai maatar nan ta che, 'Ku tanbaye ta ku che, Kāka sūnanki?' Ta che, 'Sūnana shibshibtō mani.' Sai su-ka-che, 'Wani abu kuma aka-che masa Shibshibtō mani?' Sai maata nan ta che, 'Ku che, Shibshibtō mani in jia.' Sai su-ka-che, 'Shibshibtō mani in jia. Sai māra ta dinga zuba masu tūo. Wadansu sun dēbi rūa, sai su-ka-zuba, su-ka-kāwō, ta zuba masu tūō, su-ka-dauki, su-ka-kai gida, Sarki ya tanbaye su. 'Ana ku-ka-sāmu abin nan?' Sai su-ka-che, 'Raafi mu-ka-je, mu-ka-ishe maatar wāne, sai ta che, Ba ku gani ina wanki māra ba? Mu-ka-che, Mun gani. Sai ta che, Ba ku gaishe ta?

It answered the salute. Then this wife said, 'Ask, What is your name?' It answered, 'My name is Help me.' Then they said, 'What sort of a thing now do they call Help me?' Then this woman said, 'You say, Help me that I may taste.' And they said, 'Help me that I may taste.' Thereupon the spoon kept pouring out food for them. Some have (had) drawn water, but they poured it out, and brought (their calabashes), and the spoon poured in food for them, and they lifted it and took it home. And the chief asked, 'Where did you get this thing?' And they said, 'We went to the stream and we met there the wife of So-and-so, and she said, Don't you see I am washing a spoon? We said, We have seen, and she said, Will you not salute it?

تَامَسَ غِيَلُسُوَا ؞ لَسُ مَامُتَرْ قَرْ ؞ قَتَبْ كُتَبَ

كُبْكَدَاكَ ؞ لَسُوقَنْكِ ؞ قَتَبْ لَسُو مَامُقَرْ ؞

شِبْشِبْتُو مَرْ ؞ لَسَرْ سُكَبْ ؞ وَرْنَامُكُمَّ ؞ اَكَبْ

مَسَرْ ؞ شِبْشِبْتُو مَرْ ؞ لَسَرْ مَامُتَمْرْ ؞ قَتَبْ كُبْ ؞

شِبْشِبْتُو مَرْ ؞ اِقْجِو ؞ لَسَرْ سُكَبْ ؞ شِبْشِبْتُو مَرْ

؞ اِفْمِرْ ؞ لَسَرْ مَادَارَا ؞ قَتَمِ قَغَ ؞ دُبَامَسَرْ ؞ قُدُورْ ؞

وَدِمْسَرْ ؞ لَسَنْجَ مَبِ ؞ دُوَا ؞ لَسَرْ سُكَدْ بَمَرْ ؞ لَسَكَدَاوُرْ

قَدْ بَامَسَرْ ؞ قُدُورْ ؞ لَسَكَرْ وُكِ ؞ لَسَكَكَيْ غِيدَا

لَسَرْكِمْ ؞ يِقَتْبِيسُرْ ؞ اَمَاكُكَلَسَامُوَا ؞ اَمِقَّرْ

لَسَرْ سُكَبْ ؞ وَاُمِ مُكَجِرْ ؞ مُكَاِبْشِرْ ؞ مَامُتَمْرْ

وَاَمْسَرْ ؞ لَسَرْ قَتَبْ بَكُغَنِمْ ؞ اِمَّاوُنْكِ ؞ مَادُوَاب

مُكَبْ ؞ مُنْغَنِمْ ؞ لَسَرْ قَتَبْ ؞ بَدَاكُغَيْنِنْتَ ؞

Mu-ka-che, Sannu [23] abuya. Ta che, Sannu kade. Sai mu-ka-yi shirū, mu-na-kalō, sai maātar nan ta che, Ba ku tanbaya sūnanta? Sai mu kūa, mu ka che, Kāka sūnanki? Ta che, Sunana Shibshibtō mani. Sai mu-ka-yi shirū, mu-na-dubanta, sai māatar nan ta che, Ku kāwō korainku, ku che, Shibshibtō mani in jia. Sai mu kūa mu-ka-che, Shibshibtō mani in jia, ta di-nga zubā muna tūō, ta chichika muna korai da tūō.' Sai sarki ya che, 'Ku je, ku kāwō ta, in gani.' Sai aka-tafi da fādāwa da dōgarai, aka-je, aka-tarda mutume nan, aka-che, 'Sarki ya che ka ba mu Shibshibtō mani, mu kāwō, shi gani.' Sai ya daukō ta dakansa, ya ba su. Shi na mai-bakin chiki

---

We said, Greetings, lady friend. And it said, Greetings to you. Next we were silent, we were gazing, when that woman said, Will you not ask its name? So we then said, What is your name? and it said, My name is Help me. Then we were silent (again), we were watching, when that woman said, Bring your calabashes and say, Help me that I may taste. And we too said, Help me that I may taste. And it kept pouring out food for us and filled up our calabashes with food.' Then the chief said, 'Go and bring it that I may see.' So they went off, the court officials and the chief's body-guard, and they went and met this person, and they said, 'The chief says, give us Help me, that we may bring it for him to see.' So he took it himself and gave them; he was black of heart

مكش لسنو ∴ ابي ∴ تش لسنو كجر ∴ لسر مكس

شرو ∴ فنا كلو ∴ لسر ما قرفر ∴ ما فتسر ∴ لسو

قنت ∴ لسر مو كو ∴ مكش كدك ∴ لسو فنك

تش لسو فلفر ∴ شبشبنو مر ∴ لسر مكر شروا

فنا دو منت ∴ لسر ما قنر قمر ∴ تش كلوو

كو نبك ∴ كش شبشبنو مر ∴ فجر ∴ لسر

مو كو ∴ مكش شبشبنو مر ∴ فجر ∴ قح

مخ دبا مر ∴ فغورو ∴ تشكا مر ∴ كغو رر

د فغورو ∴ لسر لسر كم يش ∴ كجر كلاووق

انغنم ∴ لسر اكتي ∴ د قبا داوا ∴ د دو غم مر

اكجر ∴ اكتر ء متجقر ∴ اكش لسر كم يش ∴

كبام ∴ شبشبنو مر ∴ مكدارو ∴ فشغنم ∴ لسر

يد و كو قا ∴ د كفلسر يبا لسر شفا قبكفشك

تش

Su-ka-karbe, su-ka-kai ma sarki, su-ka-che, 'Gā ta.'
Sarki ya che, 'Sannu, abuya,' sai ta amsa, sai ya che,
'Ku kāwō akushi.' Aka-kāwō akushi, ya che,
'Kāka sūnanki?' Ta che, 'Sūnana Shibshibtō mani.'
Sarki ya che, 'Shibshibtō mani.' Sai ta dinga zuba masa
tūō, ta chika masa akushi. Sai sarki
ya che, 'Wanan ya fi karfin gidan talaka.' Sai
sarki ya che akai ta gida. Aka-kai ta gida, ta-na-bai
gidan sarki abinchi. Shi kūa, wanda ke da māra,
shi-na-mutūa da yunwa. Ana-nan, ranan, maatansa,
wanda ta gwoda masa māra, ya dauke, ya bar ta,
sai ta je dāji, bidan abinchi. Sai ta gani tsumājīa,

They received (it) (from him), they brought (it) to the chief and said, 'Behold it.' The chief said, 'Hail, lady friend,' and it answered. And he said, 'Bring large wooden dishes,' and large wooden dishes were brought. Then he (the chief) said, 'What is your name?' and it said, 'My name is Help me.' And the chief said, 'Help me,' and it kept pouring out food and filled the wooden plates for him. And the chief said, 'This is too good a thing to be in a poor man's house.' So the chief ordered it to be brought to his house. It was brought to his house and it supplied the chief's house with food, but as for him who had the spoon (formerly) he was dying of hunger. Then one day his wife, the one who had shown him the spoon, when he had taken it and left her, went to the bush to look for food. And she saw a branch of a tree,

تَسَكَكُمْ بِيِّ ∴ تَسَكَكِيمَ سَرْكِمْ ∴ تَسَكَبْ شَغَلَتَ ∴

سَرْكِمْ يِثْ ∴ تَسَفْوَا ∴ أَبُمِّ ∴ تَسَوْتَمْ أَمْسَنْ تَسَرْ يِثْ ∴

كُكَلَاوُرُ ∴ أَكُشِمْ ∴ أَكَدَاوُرْ ∴ أَكُشِمْ ∴ يِثْ ∴

كَدَاكَ ∴ شُوفَنْكِ ∴ فَثْ سُوقَدَامُنْ ∴ شِبْشِبْشُومَ

سَرْكِمْ يِثْ ∴ شِبْشِبْشُومَ ∴ سَرْقَدِ فَخْ ∴ دُمَامَسَ

ثُخُوُرُوثْ فَثِكَدَامَسَنْ ∴ أَكُشِمْ ∴ تَسَرْ سَرْكِمْ ∴

يِثْ وَفَمْ نِيَدَ فِ كَمْ فِرْثْ غِدَ فَتَلَكَ ∴ تَسَرْ

سَرْكِمْ ∴ أَكُبِنْتِ غِدَا ∴ أَكُكُبِنْتِ غِدَا ∴ فَنَابَنْ يِثْ

فِدَ فَسَرْكِمْ ∴ أَبِنْفِثْ ∴ شِيكُوَ ∴ وَفَدَ بُكُدَ مَارَا

شِنَا مَتُو ∴ دِيمُو ∴ أَفَدَافَنْ وَفَمْ ∴ فَدَا فَتَسَ

وَفْدَ تَغُدَا أَمْسَنْ مَدَوَا ∴ يِدَّوْ بُكُو ∴ يِبَرْثْ ∴

تَسَرْ تَجِمْ دَاجِ بِدَ مَاتَ بِنْثِ ∴ تَسَرْ فَخِنْ ∴ طَمَا بِيَ

wadansu su-ka-che, 'kurfū,' ta gani chikin dāji. Ta che, 'Sannu.' Ta che, 'Sannu kade.' Maatar nan ta che, 'Kāka sūnanki?' Kurfū ta che, 'Sūnana Sharsharbō mani. Sai maatar nan ta che, 'Sharsharbō mani in jia.' Sai kurfū ya dinga feadinta, sharb! sharb! ta-na-gudu, ta-na-kūwa, ta-ma-che, 'Wāyō [24] nā tūba, nā bī ka, baa ni kārawa.' Kurfū kūa shi-na-dukanta, har mutāne su-ka-zō, (sk) su-ka-fāfēta. [25] Ta je gida; ta kirāwō mijinta; ta kai shi wurin bulāla; ta che, '[26] Kā gani, nā sāmu wani abu kuma mai-bāda abinchi.'

---

some say a whip; she saw it in the forest (bush). She said, 'Greetings,' and it said, 'Greetings to you.' And the wife said, 'What is your name?' and the whip said, 'My name is Whack me.' And the woman said, 'Whack me that I may feel.' Thereupon the whip kept flogging her, whack! whack! She was running away, she was yelling, she was saying, 'Alas, I am repentant, I shall follow you, I won't do it again.' But the whip flogged her until people came and rescued her. She went home and called her husband, and took him to where the whip was, and said, 'Have you seen, I have found another thing again for giving food.'

ادقمسن لسكب كرفو ∴ تمخنع ∴ ثكر داج

تمب سمنوا ∴ تمب لسمنو كجرن ∴ ماتمر قمر ∴

تمب كداك ∴ لسو قمك ∴ كمر فو تمب ∴

سو قداقمن ∴ لشمر شمر مجو مجن ∴ لسمر ماتمر قمر ∴

تمب لشمر شمر مجو مجن ∴ إفجمن ∴ لسمر كمر فو ∴

بيد قمغ ∴ فجد قمت ∴ لشرف ∴ لشرب ∴ قمد

قمد ∴ شتداكور ∴ قمتداش وبجو ∴ قمداشوقب

قدبيك ∴ بدانكدارو ∴ كمر فو كمو ∴ =

شنداد وكنت ∴ جمر قمتدابن ∴ لسكدرو ∴ اك

سكدافكت ∴ تمجمن غمدا ∴ تكيراور جبنت

تكيشن ورقبولال ∴ تمب كداغمنم ∴

قدسادموا ∴ ورقداب عجم ∴ مبدا دابنث

Sai ta tsaya daga nīsa, ta che, ‘Gā shi chan.’ Sai miji ya tafi
da hamzari, farm! farm! sai ya tarda bulāla, ta-na-
[27]-kunche. Ya che, ‘Sannu, abōkīna.’ Bulāla ya che,
‘Sannu kade.’ Shi-na-tsamāni, kō abin kirki ne.
Sai ya che, ‘Kāka sūnanki?’ Sai kurfū ya che,
‘Sunana Sharsharbō mani in jia.’ Sai
mutume nan ya che, ‘Sharsharbō mani in jia.’ Sai
bulāla ya dinga dūkansa, har ya gaji. Ya kō-
-mō, ya [28] kunta kurum. Mutume nan shi kuma
ya tafi gida, ya kunta, shi-na-nīshi. Maatarsa wa(n)da
shi ke sō, ta zō, ta-na-fadi, ‘Me ya fāru?’ Bai
tanka ba. Shi-na-kurum, har ya sāmu sauki.

Then she stood afar off, she said, ‘There it is over there.’ Then the husband went off in haste, tramp! tramp! until he met the whip; it was lying down. He said, ‘Hail, friend,’ and the whip said, ‘Hail to you.’ He was all the time thinking it was something good. Then he said, ‘What is your name?’ and the whip said, ‘My name is Whack me that I may feel.’ Then this man said, ‘Whack me that I may feel.’ Thereupon the whip kept beating him until it was tired. And the whip went back and lay quite still, and the man too went home and lay down. And the wife he loved came along and said, ‘What has happened?’ And he did not answer. He lay quiet until he got better.

لَسْ تَحْكُو ؞ دَ تَحِيمِيلَسْ ؞ قَتَبْ غَدَ لِشْ ؞ شَمْ ؞ لَسْ مِمْ يَتَوِ
نَ تَقْدُرِ ؞ فَدَمْ فَدَمْ ؞ لَسْ يَتَشْتَرِ دَ بُولَالَ ؞ قَنَدَ
كُنْشْ ؞ مَيِبْ ؞ لَسْنُوا ؞ أَبُو كِينَا ؞ بُولَالَ يَبْ ؞
لَسْنُو فَجِرْ ؞ شَنَا طَمَارِ ؞ كُوا أَمِنْكِمْ كِنِبُرْ ؞
لَسْ مَيِشْ ؞ كَدَكَ سُو تَشْكِ ؞ لَسْ كُمْ فُوا ؞ يَبْ
لُسُو فَدَافَ ؞ شَمْ شَمْ بُو قَمَ ؞ إِفْجِي ؞ لَسْ [redacted]
مُتَجِمْتَنْ ؞ مَيِبْ شَمْ شَمْ بُوجُو قَمَ ؞ إِفْجِي ؞ لَسْ
بُولَالَ ؞ مَيِ مْنَغْ ؞ دُو كَنْسَ شْ قَمْ يَكُعْج ؞ يَكُو
مُوا ؞ يَكُنْتَ ؞ كُمْ ؞ مُتَجِمْتَنْ ؞ شِيكُدَ ؞
يَتَوِ غَدَا ؞ يَكُنْتَ شِنَا فَيِلِشْ ؞ هَمْ قَمْ سَلِ ؞ وَفْدَ
شِكُسُوا ؞ قَمْرَا ؞ شَنَا قَدِ ؞ مِيقَاوِ ؞ بِسَّ
تَنْكَابَ ؞ شِنَا كُرُمْ ؞ حَمْ يَسَلَمُ ؞ سَوكِمْ

Sai ya tafi ya iske bulāla kunche. Sai ya di-
-nga kuntā. Shi-na-kuntō, har ya kai kusa
da ita. Sai ya zābura, ya taushe ta, ya kāwō gida,
ya sainya chikin runbu. Sai ya zamna kurum
har maatar nan da shi ke sō ta zō, ta che,
'Yau yunwa ni ke ji.' Sai ya che, 'Shiga chikin
runbū, ki gani me ke chiki.' Sai ta tāshi
maza maza, ta che, 'Me ka sāmu yau?' Ya che,
'Kedai shiga.' Sai ta che, 'In dauki koria?'
Ya che, 'ī.' Ta dauki koria, ta shiga chikin runbū.
Ya rufe, ya che, 'Me ki (ka) gani?' Sai ta che, 'Wani abu
nā gani mai-tsawō.' Ya che, 'Gaishe shi mana?' Ta che,

Then he went and came to where the whip was lying. Then he kept crouched down, he crouched down until he got near it, then he jumped and held it down, and took it home, and put it away in the grain store. Then he sat quietly until his favourite wife came. And she said, 'To-day I am feeling hungry.' Then he said, 'Go into the grain store and see what is inside.' Then she rose up in great haste, she said, 'What did you find to-day?' And he said, 'You yourself enter.' Then she said, 'Must I take a calabash?' He said, 'Yes.' She took a calabash and went into the grain store. He closed it. He said, 'What do you see?' And she said, 'Something I have seen which is long.' And he said, 'Greet it, cannot you?' She said,

لَسَنْ يَتَيْ ، مَيإِسْبَكِ مُولَانْ ، كُقْبْ ، لَسَنْ يَجِمْ
قْغَمْ كُنْتُوا ، لِشَنَ كُنْتُوا ، حَمْ يَكَمْ ، كُلَسَ
كَمإِقَ ، لَسَنْ يَغَ أُبَمْ ، يَقْتُوَلْبُتْمَتْ ، يَبَكَدَاوُ وُغِدَا
يَلَسَنْبَا قِكِمْ وُقْبُوا ، لَسَنْ يَقْدَ مُنْ ، كُمْ مْ ،
حَمْ مَا قَمْ قَمْ ، دِشَبْكَسُوا ، قَدُرْ ، قَتْبْ
يَخْ يُمُو ، قَجَكِ ، لَسَنْ يَتْ شِغْ ، ثِكِمْ
رُقْبُوا ، كِغَنِمْ ، مَبَكَشِكِمْ ، لَسَنْ قَنَاشِنْ
مَدَ مَدَ ، قَتْبْ مَبَكَسَّا مُوَايَّو ، يَتْبْ
بَكَدِ شِغَ ، لَسَنْ قَتْبْ ، إِقَمْ وَكِ كُمْ مَنْ ،
يَتْ إِي ، قَمْ وَكِ كُمْ نَ ، مَسِغَ تِكِمْ ، رُقْبُو
يَمْ قِنْ ، يَتْ مَكَكَغَنَمْ ، لَسَنْ قَتْ وَنِمَا بْ ،
قَلْغَنِمْ ، مَيْطُو ، يَتْ غَمِنْ بُسِشِمَنْ ، قَتْبْ

'Sannu da fūtāwa.' Ta che, 'Kāka sūnanka?' Ya che, 'Sunana Sharsharbō mani.' Ta che, 'Sharshar-bō mani in jia.' Sai bulāla ya dinga fīadinta, ta-na-kurūrūa. Mijinta da ya ji, sai ya sheka da gudu, ya yi dawa, maatarsa, wa(n)da ba shi sō, ita kuma sai ta fita, ta yi dawa, dōmin tsōrō. Ita kūa wachan, daket ta sāmu kafa, ta gudu. Su-ka-bar gida kangō. Da wuri māra da bulāla dāji su ke.

Mafārin zūansu gida ke nan.

[29] Kungurus kan kusu.

'I greet you (who are) resting,' (and) she said, 'What is your name?' It said, 'My name is Whack me,' and she said, 'Whack me that I may feel.' Thereupon the whip set about beating her, she was shouting. Her husband, when he heard, ran off to the forest, and his wife, the one he did not love, also ran out to the forest, through fear; and she also, the one who had entered the grain store, with difficulty she found a way of escape and ran off; and they left the house deserted. Long ago the spoon and the whip lived in the wilds, and this was the first time they made their appearance in the home. Off with the rat's head.

كُنْقَ سُو :. كَدَكَ ثَبْ تَ :. وَدَقَتْ فُو مُوشْنَسَ

شُمْ شُمْ ثَبْقَ :. مَيْ بُو شُمْ شَمْ :. كُفْقَدَ سُو ثْبَيْ

تَمُّ دَاءِ يَا ڢِ غَمُ يَدِ :. آلاَ مُوشُ سَنِ :. جِقَا :. مَيْ بُو

غُدُ :. كَشْبَيَسْ آ :. جِيَدُ تَفْمَجِ :. وَرُوُ رُكُمْ دَقَتَ

مَكُتَا :. وُسُشَ ادَبَ قْوَ نْسَرْ قَمَهَ :. وَرُ دِ يَمُّ

.: وُكُتُّا :. وَرُوُ دُمَّ وِدُ :. وَرُ دَمَتُّ :. قِمْجُقَ سَ

ادَغِبْكَسُ :. دُغُتَ :. اقَبُكُمُ دَسَقَ :. ثْبَكْدِ :. ثْمَّقَوَ

سَكُسَبِ ادَ :. اَلَّا بُودَ :. اوَدَمَ :. رُوُدَ شْوُغَنْكَ :.

مَجَكُ ادَغِ رُسْمُ وَرْغُقْوِ دَبَمَ

سُوقَنْكَ :. سُرْقَنْكُ

No. 6.

Wanan tātsūnīar wani sarki che

[1] Gātanan, gātanan, ta je, ta kōmō. Wani sarki ana-che da shi Kurungu-mūgun-kīfi, ya tsū--fa chikin sarauta. Da ya kusa mutūa, shi-na da dīa dayawa, sai ya tāra su, ya che, 'Idan [2] naa mutu me zaa ku giyāra makōkina da shi?' Baban dansa ya che, 'Idan [3] kā mutu naa giyāra makōkinka da zāki.' Kōwa ya fadi abinda zaa shi yi. Autansa ya che, 'Idan kā mutu, ina-yin makōkinka da [4] kūra.' Yau ana-nan ba adade ba sai ya mutu. Kōwa ya kāwō abinda ya che. Sauran babansu da auta. Sai auta ya tafi dāji, shi-na-yāwō, sai ya [5] chintō

This is a story about a certain chief. A tale, a tale. Let it go and let it return. A certain chief, by name Kurungu-the-bad-fish, grew old in his kingdom, and when he was near to death—he had many children—he called them together and said, 'If I were to die what would you all do to observe my funeral?' His eldest child said, 'When you are dead I shall mourn for you by (slaughtering) a lion.' Each one said what he would do. His youngest said, 'When you are dead I shall mourn for you by killing a hyena.' And it came to pass that not long after he died, and each brought what he said; only the eldest and the youngest remained (to fulfil the promise). Then the youngest went to the bush, he was walking, and he came across

وَقَمْرَنَا طُو فِيَّرْ وَنِ اَسْرِكِيشْ

غَمَاقَتَّنْ غَمَاقَتَّنْ ۞ تَجِي نِكُو سُو ۞ وَنِ اَسْرِكِم ۞

أَمَا شُعْ شِي ۞ كُرْ فَنْغُ ۞ مُوغُمْ كِيفِجِ ۞ بِيَا طُو

قَدْ ۞ قِكِمْ سَرْ وُقْتَ ۞ دَرِيكَسْ مُتُو ۞ شِنَادْ دِيَّيمْ ۞

دِ بَيُّو ۞ سَنْغُ عَتَنَا وَاسْ ۞ يِعِيشْ اِدَّنْ قَامُتُ ۞ بِمُدَاكِ

غِيَمْ ۞ مَكُو كِي   فَدَ شِي ۞ مَبَرْدَمُسْ ۞ يِعِيشْ

اِدَّنْ كَامُتُ ۞ فَاغْيَرْ مَكُوكِنْكَ ۞ دَزَاكِ

كُو وَا يِبْعِي اَبِنْغِ ۞ دَ أَشِسِّ ۞ اَوْ قَتَنْسِ يِشْ ۞

اِدَّنْ كَامُتُ ۞ اِقَا يِنْمَكُوكِنْكَ ۞ دَكُوَرَا ۞

يَّوْ اَفْلَقَّنْ ۞ بَادَدَ مُب ۞ سَنْ يِجُتُ ۞ كُوَرَا ۞

يَكَارُ ۞ اَبِنْغِ يِشْ ۞ سَوْرِ فِيبِسْ ۞ دَاَوْقَس

سَنْ اَوْقَمْ يِتَعِ دَاجِ ۞ شِنَا يَدَاوُ ۞ سَنْ يِتَنْتُوا

[6] sānia, ya kāwō. Su-ka-yanka, su-ka-yi salka, su-ka-dauki kan sānia da [7] kafāhu, (sk) su-ka-tūra chikin salka. Sai ya je ya kirāwō kūra. Ta zo, ya che, 'Mun yi [8] watanda, ba ka nan, mu-ka-ajie nāka.' Su-ka-goda masa burgāme, su-ka-che, 'Gā shi nan, shiga, ka dauka.' Sai kūrā ta kuna kai, ta shiga. Sai auta ya yi maza maza, ya rufe bākin burgāme, su-ka-damre kūra chiki, su-ka-ja kūra, su-ka-kai bisa [9] kabarin ubansu. Su-na-duka har kirgi ya pashe. Kūra ta sāmu [10] kafa, ta fita, ta gudu. Sai auta ya ji haushi, ya che, 'Naa kāma ta kuma.' Ana-nan, wata raana kuma ya sāmu

---

a cow and brought it back. They slaughtered it and made a skin bag of it, and they took the cow's head and feet and pushed them into the bag. Then he went and called the hyena. She came (and) he (the man) said, 'We divided up the meat (when) you were not there, (and) we set aside your share.' They showed her (lit. him) the bag, they said, 'There it is, go in and lift (the meat).' Then the hyena put in her head and entered. Then the youngest son immediately closed the mouth of the bag (and) they tied it up, the hyena inside, and they dragged the hyena and brought her above their father's grave. And they kept flogging her until the skin burst. The hyena found an exit, got out, and ran off. Then the youngest son got angry and said, 'I shall catch her again.' And so another day he found

ثُلُقِيَ ؞ يَكَلَاوُو ؞ سُكَيِّنْكَ ؞ سُكَنِ اَلَّلْكِنِ ؞

سُكَدَّرْكِ ؞ كَنْشَا قِيرَا ؞ دَكَبَلَهْ ؞ اسك

سُكَنْتُوَرُ ؞ قِكَنْ سَلْكُنْ ؞ سَنْ بِيجِى ؞ يَكَرَاوُو ؞ كُورَا

قَدُورُ ؞ يَبْ مُنْرُ وَتَنْقُدَ ؞ بِمَاكَشَّنْ ؞ قُكَاجِبِي ؞

قَدَاكَ ؞ سُكَقُرَا اَقَسَنْ ؞ مُرْغَدَامِبَ ؞ سُكَنْبُ

غَدَا اِشْتَقَّنْ ؞ شِقَنْ ؞ كَدَّرْكَ ؞ اَسَنْ كُورَا ؞

تُكَرْكَنْ ؞ قَتْشِغَ ؞ اَسَرْ اُوقَا لِيَقَّدْ هَدَ ؞

يَمُرْ قِنْ ؞ بَاكِنْ بُنْ غَدَامِكَ ؞ سُكَنْ جُمْرِمَنْ ؞

كُورَا ؞ ثِكِ ؞ سُكَجِبِي ؞ كُورَا ؞ سُكَكَنْ

بِسَنْ كَبِرْ نَا بِنْشَنْ سُنَا دُوكَ ؞ قَمْ كِرْغَ

يَقْبِشُ ؞ كُورَا ؞ قَلْسَدَمُ ؞ كَبَوَا ؞ تَبِقْتَ تَقُدُ

اَسَرْ اُوقَا ؞ يَجِي قَوْقِشِ ؞ يَبْ قَا اُكَدَمَا ؞

كُمَّ ؞ اَقَا قَمْ ؞ وَتَرَا اُقَمْ كُمَّ ؞ يَسَدَمُ ؞

sānia, ya kāwō, ya yanka, ya bidi [11] dawō, ya līke idānunsa da shi, ya tafi dāji, ya gani kūra, ya che, 'Kūra, mun yi watanda ba ki nan, mu-ka-neme ki mu-ka-gaji, mu kūa māsurikō alkawali ne, gama uwāyenmu, da zaa su mutūa, su-ka-che mu rika bāya, kōwa ya sāmu wani abu, shi bidi dan uwansa.' Kūra ya che, 'Gaskīa ne, amā wani mutum yā zō nan ya rūdē ni, hakanan ya kai ni, shi-na-sō shi kashe ni.' Sai auta ya che, '[12] Asha kūra mutum shii kira dan uwansa dōmin shi kashe?' Kūra ta che, 'Mu tafi.' Su-ka-kāma hainya, su-na-zūa, sai kūra ta tsaya

---

a cow, he brought it back and killed (it), he searched for porridge and covered his eye with it and went off to the forest. He saw the hyena and said, 'Hyena, we have divided up the meat in your absence, we looked for you until we were tired. And as for us, we are a people who keep a promise to our parents, and when they were about to die they said we must continually give (gifts), and whoever found anything let him seek his brother (to share with him).' The hyena said, 'That is quite true, but some one has come here and deceived me. It was thus he enticed me away and he was wanting to kill me.' Then the youngest son said, 'Come now, hyena, would a man call his brother to kill (him)?' The hyena answered, 'Let us go.' They took the road, they were coming, when the hyena stood still

ثَاقِيَنْ ؞ يَكَاوُو ؞ يِيَّنْكْ ؞ يِبِدِّ ؞ دُوو ؞ يِلِيقْكَشْ

إِدَّا أُقْنَسْ دْ شِمْ ؞ يِيتْبِحْدَاجْ ؞ يِيقْحِنْ كُورَا ؞ يِيثْ

كُورَاتْ مُتْنِّ وَتْقْدْ بَدَاكَقَّنْ ؞ مُكَبْحَكِ ؞ =

مُكَقْجْ ؞ مُوكُو ؞ مَاسَرْ كُو ؞ أَلْكَوْلِيتْقَنْ

غَمَدَ ؞ غُوَايِمْرْمُ ؞ دْذَأُسْ ؞ مُتُوا ؞ لُسْكْثْ ؞

مُرِكْ مَبَاتِّ ؞ كُورَا ؞ يِبَسَامُ ؞ وَرْقْنَامُ ؞ يِشِيجْ

دْنْغُجُقْسَنْ ؞ كُورَا ؞ يِيثْ غَسْكِيدَ قِّنْ ؞ أَمَّدَ

وَقُتُثْقْنْ يَدَاذْرِقَّنْ ؞ يِيقُرُودِمُسَنْ ؞ تَكَقَّنْ

يَكْيِيرْ ؞ لْشِنَالسُو ؞ لِشْكْشْبْمْ ؞ لَسَنْ أُوقْتُ

يِيثْ أَشَا كُورَاتْ مُتْنْ تِسْكِمَ ؞ مْ نُغُوقَّسَنْ

دُومِّنْ ؞ شِكْشْبِنْ نْكُورَا ؞ تَبْثْ مُتْبِجِ ؞ =

لُسْكَامَ حَقْتَنْ ؞ لُسْنَاذُرَّ ؞ لَسَنْ كُورَا ؞ تْتَطَنْ

ta che, 'Ai, jia wanda ya zō ya kirāye ni, kamanka shi ke, in ji bā kai bä ne.' Auta ya che, 'Mutume nan shi-na da [13] idānu gudā?' Kūra ya che, 'Mu tafi.' Su-ka-kāma hainya, su-na-tafia su-ka-kai gida. Sai auta ya goda masa wurin fāta sānia. Ya che, 'Shiga, akwai nāka chiki.' Sai kūra zaa shi kuna kai chiki, sai ya fitar ya che, 'Ai abōki, kad' ka zō ka yi mani kamar da dan uwa-nka ya yi mani.' Auta shi-na-tsaye. Sai ya che, 'Haba kūra, idan baa ka so [14] nāman ne, ka bari, [15] ka tafia(r)ka. Mutum shi kirāwō dan uwa-nsa dōmin shi chuche shi? Nāma na goda maka

---

and said, 'No, yesterday he who came to call me, like you was he, let me hear it was not you.' The youngest son said, 'This man, had he one eye?' The hyena said, 'Let us go on.' They took the road and were going on (and) they reached the house. Then the youngest son showed him (her) where the cow's hide was, and he said, 'Enter, your (share) is within.' Then the hyena, when he (she) was about to push in his (her) head, came out and said, 'No, friend, do not come and do to me as your brother did to me.' The youngest son was standing by, and he said, 'Come then, hyena, if it is that you do not want the meat, leave it, and go about your business. Does a man call his brother in order that he may do him harm? The meat I show you

تَبْ آءْ ؞ جِنّ وَفْدَ ؞ يَذُرْ ؞ يَكِرَ ابِيمِ ؞ كَمْنَكْ

شِكَ ؞ إِنْجِ مَاكَيْبَنْ ؞ أَوْقَايِشْ ؞ مُتُبَنّْ

شِنَادَ ؞ إِدَانُو ؞ غُدَا ؞ كُورَابِشْ مُنَّفِ

سُكَكَامَ قُشْنَ ؞ سُنَانَبِنَّ ؞ سُكَكَنْ غُدَا

لَسْ أَوْقَا بِغُدَ امَشَّ ؞ وُوَرْ ؞ قَلَتْ ثَا فِيمَ ؞

يَبْ شِغَ ؞ أَكُومِبْنَاكَ ثِكِمِ ؞ لَسَنْ كُورَا ؞

مَ اشِكُنْ كَمْ ؞ ثِكِمِ ؞ لَسْ يَجِمَنْ ؞ يَبْ أَيْ ؞

أَبُوكِمِ ؞ تَكَرْ كَذُرْ ؞ كَيَّقِنْ ؞ كَمَّنْ دَ دَمْغُو

مْكَ ؞ مَيَّقِمِ ؞ أَوْنَمْ شِقَا طِمِ ؞ لَسْ يَبْ

جَبَ كُورَا ؞ إِدَّنْ ؞ مَاكَسُو ؞ غَا مَنْبَنْ ؞

كَبَ ؞ كَتَقِيَّكَ ؞ مُتُمْ ؞ شِغَكِرَ اوْرَا ؞ دَمْغُو

فْلَسْ ؞ دُ وَقِمْ ؞ شَشِغُ بُشِّنْ ؞ قَامَ نُغْدَا مَكْ

in ba ka chi, ka bari, ka fita.' Sai kūra ya che, 'Aa ina-chi.' Sai ya tūra kai achiki, sai ya shiga. Kāmin shi daukō shi fitō, sai auta ya rufe kōfa, ya kāma bākin burgāme, ya rufe. Su-ka-tāru, su-ka-damre kūra, su-ka-ja, (sk) su-ka-kai bisa kabarin ubansu, [16] su-nā-dūka, su-ka-dūke ta har su-ka-pashe kirgi. Kūra ya sāmu kōfa, ya fita, ya gudu. Sai auta ya che, 'Naa [17] sāmō ta kuma.' Sai aka dede, kūra ta manche. Sai auta [18] ya sāmu bajinin sānia, ya kāwō. Su-ka-yanka, su-ka-fēde, su-ka-yi salka, su-ka-dauki katara na bāya, su-ka-sa

---

if you do not eat, leave it, and get out.' Then the hyena said, 'No, I am (going) to eat it.' So he (she) put his (her) head in and entered. As he (she) was going to lift the meat and then come out, then the youngest son seized the mouth of the bag and closed it. And they all came up and tied up the hyena and dragged it and brought it over their father's grave. They kept beating it, they beat it till the skin burst, and the hyena found an exit, and came out, and ran off. But the youngest son said, 'I will find and bring her back again.' Then some time passed and the hyena forgot. And the youngest son found a very large cow and brought it back. They slaughtered it, flayed it, and made a skin bag; they lifted a hind leg and put (it)

إِمْبَا كَحِثْ ∴ كَبِمْ بَجِتَ ∴ لَسُمْ كُوَرَا ∴ مِيثْ عَامَ ∴

إِمَاثْ ∴ لَسِنْ مَثُورَكَمْ ∴ أَنْكَمْ ∴ سَمْ مِيثَغْ ∴

كَامِرْ ∴ شَدُّوكُو ∴ شِبْثُوَا ∴ لَسْ أُومَرْ ∴ مِيرِفِي

كُوفَ ∴ يَكَامَ بَاكِرْ مِرْ غَامِنْ ∴ مِيرْفِي ∴ =

سُكَنْدَرْ ∴ سُكَدْ مَبَرْ ∴ كُوَرَا ∴ سُكَجَبْ ∴ لَسَكْ

سُكَكْ نَبِسْ ∴ كَبَمْ فَلَا مِنْسْ ∴ سُنَادُوكْ ∴

سُكَدُّوبَتْ ∴ حَمْ سُكَفِبْشُنْ ∴ كَرْغَ ∴ كُوَرَا

∴ مِبَسْلَامُ ∴ كُوفَ ∴ مِيبِقَتْ ∴ يَفُدْ سَمْ أُوقَلِ ∴

يَبْقَلَا سَلَامُ مُوتْ كَمّ ∴ سَمْ أَكَدَبِرْ ∴ كُوَرَا ∴

تَمَقْبْ ∴ سَمْ أُوقَمْ ∴ مِبَسَلَامُ ∴ بِجِنِرْ ثَامَفِيَا

يَكَاوُرْ ∴ سُكَيِّنْكَ ∴ سُكَبِجَبِرْ ∴ سُكَيِّ ∴

سَلَكَرْ ∴ سُكَدُّوكِ ∴ كَتَرْ ∴ قَبَابِي ∴ سُكَسْ

chikin burgāme, su-ka-yi tarkō. Sai auta
ya bidi dawō, ya tafi dāji, ya je kusa da rāme kūra.
Sai ya dauki dawō, ya līke idānunsa, dada
ba shi gani. Sai shi-na-kira, 'Inā wajen rāme(n)
kūra, gā shi, ankashe sānia, tun jia
aka-aje masa katara, bā agane shi ba.' Sai kūra
ya ji, shi-na chikin rāme. Sai ta fitō, ta che,
'Gā ni.' Sai kūra ya che, 'Ina [19] nāman shi ke?'
Sai auta ya mīka mata baban tsōka,
ya che, 'Kin gani shaida.' Sai kūra ya karbi,
ya hade nan da nan. Sai kūra ya che, 'Mu tafi
maza maza.' Sai kūra ya tuna, sai ya tsaya, ya che,

---

in the bag, and made a trap. Then the youngest son got some porridge, went to the bush, came near the hole where the hyena was, then took the (*dawo*) porridge, and covered up his eyes; then he could not see. Then he called, 'Where is the hyena's den? Look at this, a cow has been slaughtered since yesterday, they put on one side a leg for him (her), and he (she) is not to be seen.' Then the hyena heard, he (she) was in the hole, so out he (she) came and said, 'Here I am.' And the hyena said, 'Where is the meat?' Then the youngest son held out to her a large piece of meat and said, 'You see the sign (that what I say is true).' Then the hyena took it and swallowed it right off, and the hyena said, 'Let us go at once.' Then the hyena remembered, and he (she) pulled up, and said,

ثكر بن غدامس ؞ لسكس قمركوا ؞ سس أوتم

يبج دور ؞ يبقف داب ؞ يبجس كسن دوا امكورا

؞ لسن يبد وك ؞ دور ؞ يلبف ؞ إدا امنسن درم

بداشغنم ؞ لسن شنا كم ؞ إمّا وجن رابس

؞ كورا ؞ غاش ؞ أنكشن ؞ قد فيا ؞ تنجس

أكعجمس كتن ؞ بد غنبشي ؞ لسن كورا ؞

يبج ؞ شنا فكن ؞ وامس ؞ سن تبقتوا ؞ قب

غدو ؞ سن كورا ؞ يب إمّا قدامن ؞ شبكن ؞

سن أوتمن ؞ يميكا امت ؞ يبن هوك ؞ ے

يب كنغنم ؞ شيكم ؞ لسن كورا ؞ يكم ب ؞

يعجب قمدمن ؞ سن كورا ؞ يبا متجب

مغ مغ ؞ لسن كورا ؞ يثمن ؞ سن يكمن ؞ يب

'Abōkīna, wani dan uwanka, hakanan ya rūde ni, ya kai ni, shi-na-sō shi kashe ni.' Sai auta ya che, 'Haba kūra, kāka makāfō shi-ka-yi shi kashe wani?' Sai kūra ya che, 'Mu tafi.' Su-ka-kāma hainya, su-na-zūa, sai su-ka-kai wurin tarkō. Sai auta ya che, 'Kūra gā nāma nan.' Sai kūra ta gani katara mai-mai, kūra bai yi shāwara ba, sai ya zaabura, ya shiga, garin daukan nāma, bai san tarkō ba ne. Sai tarkō ya kāma shi. Sai kūra kūa shi-na-kūwa. Sai auta ya gudu, ya je gida, ya kirāwō yan uwansa. Su-ka-yi ta bugu kūra, har kūra ya galabaita. Su-ka-damre shi

---

'My friend, some one of your kindred, it was just thus he deceived me; he took me away and he wanted to kill me.' Then the youngest son said, 'Come now, hyena, how can a blind man manage to kill another person?' And the hyena said, 'Let us go on.' They took the road, they were coming, until they got to where the trap was. Then the youngest son said, 'Hyena, look at the meat there.' Then the hyena saw a very fat hind-quarter. The hyena, without a thought, leaped and went in, in order to lift the meat out; he (she) did not know it was a trap, till the trap caught him (her). Then the hyena began to shout, and the youngest son ran off and went home and called his brothers, (and) they flogged the hyena until the hyena became insensible. (And) they bound him (her)

أَبُوكِينَا ؞ وَرِفِ دَمْعُونْكِ ؞ فَكَتَّنْ ؞ يَرُوجُمُسِ

يَكِيمْ ؞ شِنَا سُو ؞ شِكَ شُبُمْ ؞ لَسَنْ أَوْقَا ؞ يَبْ

قَبْ كُورَا ؞ تَكَاكِ ؞ مَكَا فُوَا ؞ شِكَا مِ ؞ سَـ

شِكَشِمْ وَرِ ؞ لَسَنْ كُورَا ؞ يَبْ مُتَقِمْ ؞ سُكَامَ

فُنْ ؞ سُنَا دُرَ ؞ لَسَنْ سُكَكِنْ ؞ وُرِشْتَرْ كُوَا ؞

لَسَنْ أَوْقِنْ يَبَّ ؞ كُورَا ؞ غَمْ دَنْتَمْ فَنْ ؞ سَنْ كُورَا

تَفِيمْ ؞ كَتَمْ ؞ فَيْقَمْ ؞ كُورْ بِيمِّي ؞ تَادَوَرَبْ

؞ لَسَنْ يَدَ أَبُرَ ؞ يَشِغْ غَمْ فُدَرْكِ مَدَامَ ؞ يِنْسَنْ

تَرْكُوبِّنْ ؞ لَسَنْ فَنْ غُوَ ؞ يَكَا مَاشِنْ ؞ لَسَنْ

كُورَا كُوَّ ؞ شِنَا غُوَرُ ؞ لَسَنْ أَوْقَنْ ؞ يَغَدُ

يَبُجِنْ غَمْدَا ؞ يَكِرَا وُرُ ؞ يَنْغُوفَنْ سَنْ ؞ سُكِّنْ تَبِغْ

كُورَا ؞ قَرْكُورَا ؞ يَغَمَا بِيَتْ ؞ سُكَمْ صَبَرْ مَتَر

su-ka-ja, su-ka-kai gun kushewan ubansu,
su-ka-yanka, su-ka-fēde, su-ka-raba nāma, su-ka-chi.
Dada su-ka-che, 'Kōwa ya gerta makōki
ubanmu, saura babanmu.' Sai babansu ya dauki
makēra, ya kai dāji. [21] Shi-na-kīra. Sai zāki
ya zō, ya che, 'Abōkīna makēri in tafō
in yi maka zuga.' Ya che, 'Ī.' Sai zāki ya tafō, shi-nā-
-yi masa zuga. Ashe makēri ya yi wani abu,
ya bidō wani irin gainye, ya [22] danfara ga gū-
-tsunsa, sai ya dauki muntalaga, ya tūra
wuta. Sai ya che, zāki shi yi zuga. Zāki
shi-na-zuga har muntalaga ya yi ja. Sai

---

and dragged him (her), and brought him (her) to their father's grave, and (there) they cut (her throat), and skinned (her), and divided up the meat, and ate. Then they said, 'Each one has observed the funeral rites of our parent with the exception of our eldest brother.' Then their eldest brother lifted up an anvil, and took it to the bush; he was forging metal. Then the lion came, and said, 'Friend smith, let me come and work the bellows for you.' He said, 'Yes.' So the lion came and worked the bellows. Now of a truth the smith had done something, he had sought leaves of a certain kind and put (them) between his legs. Then he lifted the tongs and put (them) in the fire, and he told the lion to blow the bellows; and the lion blew them until the tongs were red hot. Then

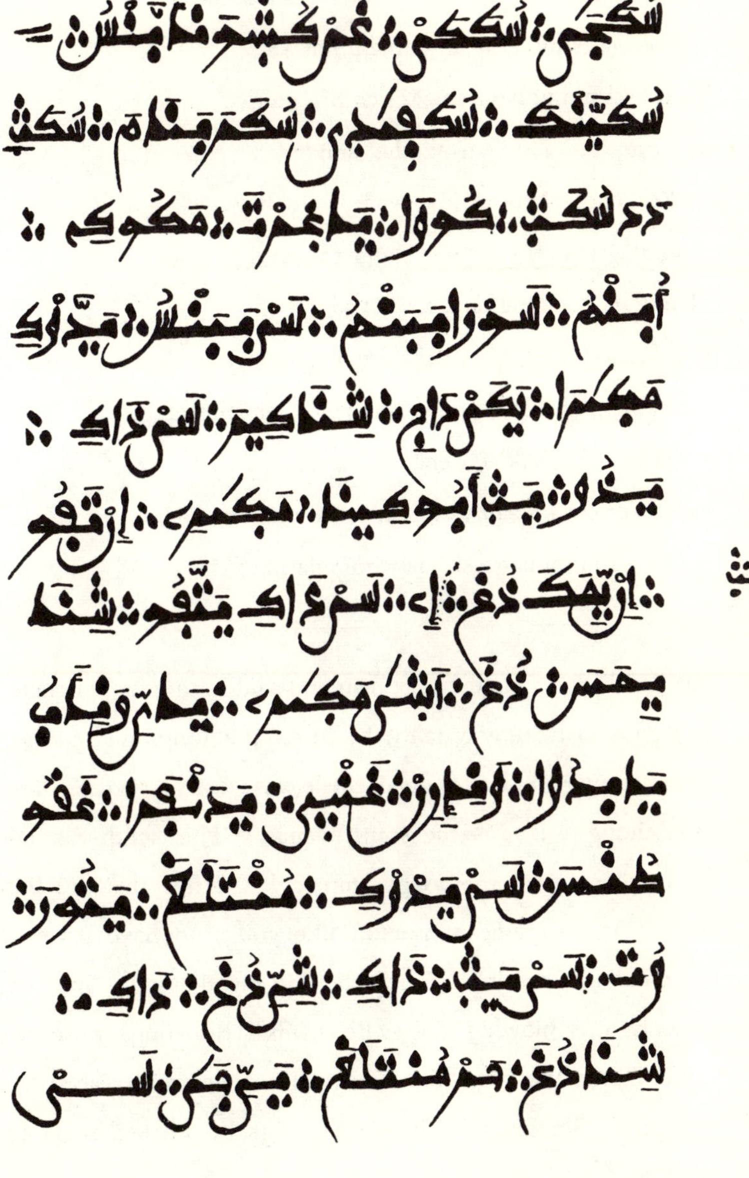

makēri ya tāshi, ya yi gōfō, ya che ma zāki,

'Abōkīna tsūlīāta ta-na-yi mani kai kai.'

Ya dauki muntalaga ya tūra chikin gainye. Gainye

na-kōnēwa. Zāki shi-na-che tsūlīar

makēri che. Makēri kūa ya [23] kyale, har

muntalaga ya yi sainye. Daga nan zāki ya che,

'Kai dan kankane nan, kai ka yi karfin

hali hakanan?' Sai zāki shi ma ya sainya

muntalaga chikin wuta, shi-na-zuga har muntalaga

ya yi ja. Sai zāki ya che, 'Abōkīna

dauki, ni ma ka sainya mani.' Sai makēri

ya dauki muntalaga shi-na-[24] rāgada ma zāki

---

the smith got up and bent down and said to the lion, 'Friend, my anus is itching'; (and) he lifted the tongs and pushed them among the leaves, (and) the leaves were set on fire. The lion thought it was the smith's anus. The smith too left them there until the tongs were cold. After this the lion said, 'An insignificant person like you, you have strength of mind to do this?' Then the lion put the tongs into the fire, he was blowing the bellows until the tongs were red hot. Then the lion said, 'Friend, lift (them) and place them for me.' So the smith lifted the tongs, he worked them up and down the lion's

مجمرى ∴ يتالش نمّى غوفو ∴ يب مغراك ∴

أبوكينا ∴ طوليدامن ∴ قنلاتيمن ∴ عيكم

يمّراك ∴ منتلخ ∴ يشورتكن غنيبن عنيبن

شفاكوفكوا ∴ ذراك شناب ∴ طوليرش

مجكمرى ڢ ∴ مجكمرى كوّ ∴ يكّبلي ∴ جر

منتلخ ∴ يمّسنّي ∴ دعمّر داك ∴ يب ∴ د

كمع منكنكبنّسر ∴ كمكو ∴ كرڢر

جلي ∴ مكمّر ∴ لسر ذراك ∴ شيمن ∴ يبلسنّي

منتلخ ∴ شكرومن ∴ شنادغ ∴ جر منتلخ

يمى يكن لسر ذراك ∴ ميب ∴ أبوكينا ∴

دراك ∴ نيمن ∴ كسنيامرن ∴ لسر مجكمرى

يمّراك ∴ منتلخ ∴ شنداراعمّامّراك

chikin shākira, har zāki ya sūma.
Sai makēri ya yi maza maza, ya tafi gida,
ya kirāwō kaninsa. Su-ka-zō, su-ka-ja,
su-ka-kai gida. Sai ya shiga gida
garin shi dēbō rūa, shi kāwō ma samāri.
Zāki na-kunche. Sai makēri ya dēbō
rūa, ya zō, mutāne sun tāru, su-na-kalō,
sai zāki ya falki, ya che, ' Abōkīna,
haka ka yi mani ? ' Sai makēri ya che,
' Nā gani kā galabaita, dōmin hakanan
na kāwō ka gida dōmin in zubā
maka rūa.' Sai zāki ya che, ' Karīa ne.'

---

anus until the lion fainted. Then the smith with all speed went home and summoned his younger brothers, (and) they came (and) they pulled (the lion) (and) brought it home. Then he entered the house to get some water to bring for the young men—the lion is lying still. Then the smith drew the water (and) came, (and) the people gathered round and looked on, then the lion came round from his faint and said, 'My friend, what are you doing to me?' And the smith said, 'I have seen you were weary, and so I brought you home to pour water on you.' But the lion said, 'You are a liar.'

ثكرشاكرا ؛ حمنداك ؛ يلسومن ؛

لسن مكجمي ؛ يتيمقمد ؛ يمتف غدا

يكراوو ؛ فتنس ؛ لسكدو ؛ لسكجو

لسكك ؛ غدا ؛ لسن يمشغ غدا ؛

غم فنشج مسبو ؛ زوا اشكاوو مسهاري

نداك ؛ نما كنبش ؛ لسن مكجمي ؛ يجبمبو

زوايدو ؛ منتامبل ؛ سشتادر ؛ لسناكلو

لسن نداك ؛ يقلك ؛ يبث أبوكيمنى

ممك كيمن لسن مكجمي يث ؛

قا غنم ؛ كاغما بميث ؛ دومن وككم

نكاووك ؛ غدا ؛ دومن ؛ ازدبما ؛

مك زوا ؛ لسن نداك ؛ يبث كمريابى

Sai zāki ya zaabura, ya tāke shi, ya fashe.
Mafārin [25] gizō gizō ke nan, da ya tāke shi,
ya fashe, sai ya yi kafāfu dayawa.
Mafārin tautau ke nan, dā makēri ne.
[26] Kungurus kan kūsu.

And the lion leaped and trampled him and tore (him). That was the origin of the spider; when he (the lion) trampled on him (the smith), he broke up, and made many feet. That was the beginning of the spider; formerly he was a smith. Off with the rat's head.

يَقِنْشِي ؞ يَنَّا بَكُلْشِ ؞ يَزَابِمَ ؞ كَدَاسَنْ

مَقَاوِزْ ؞ غُمَ ؞ غُدْوَ ؞ بَكُنْفَنْ ؞ يَنَّا بَكُمْشِ

بَقَشِنْبِ ؞ سَنْ يِمْتِي ؞ كَبَّا فُو ؞ يَوَّا ؞ =

مَقَارِزْ ؞ قَوْ قَوْ ؞ بَكُنْفَنْ ؞ امَكِّبْرِ يِنْبِي

كُنْفُرْسَ ؞ كُنْفُوسَ ؞

No. 7.

Wanan tātsūnīar marāyū che.

[1] Gātanan, gātanan, ta je, ta kōmō. Wani mutum
ke da [2] mātansa guda bīū. Ya mutu, ya bar su. Guda
daia chikin mātan ta sāmu chīwō. Ta gani
ta kusa mutūa. Sai ta che ma kīshiyanta, 'Dada
kin gani chīwō nan ba shi bari na, gā dīa
ta [3] nā bar taulafi garēki, dōmin Ala da anabi
ki dūba mani ita da ke(a)u.' Yau, mache ta mutu,
aka-bisna ta, su-na-nan da yārinya. Sai kulum
ta-na-gwoda mata wahala, har ranan yārinya,
chīwō ya kāma ta. Ta-na-[4] kunche ; [5] kīshia
uwa tata ta che, 'Tāshi ki tafi raafi.'

This is the story about orphans. A story, a story. Let it go, let it come. A certain man had wives, two in number. He died and left them. One among the wives fell ill. She saw she was near to death, so she said to the second wife, 'Now you have seen this illness will not leave me. There is my daughter, I have left her as a trust to you; for the sake of Allah and the prophets look after her well for me.' So the woman died and was buried, and they were left with the maid (her child). Now always they were showing her cruelty, until one day a sickness took hold of the maiden. She was lying down. Her step-mother said, 'Get up, (and) go to the stream.'

رَمْنَ قَمَا طُوفِيَمْ هَرَامِيُوبْ ∴

تَمَا قَمْنَ ∴ تَمَا قَنَمْ تَحِرْ نَكُومُو ∴ وَنِفَنَمْ
بِكَ دَمَا قَنْسَ ∴ غَدَ امِيُو ∴ مِيحَتْ مِيَمْرَسْ ∴ غَدَا
تَمَ ∴ نِكِمْ مَا قَنْ تَقَسَادَمْ ∴ تِيُو ∴ مَكَنِمْ ∴ دَ
تَمَا كَسَ مَتُو ∴ آسَمْ تَبْتَكِيشِيَتْ ∴ دَدَرَ ∴
كِنْعَنِمْ ∴ فِيُو وَمَنْ ∴ مَاشِبِرْ مِيَرَ ∴ غَادِ دِيَا
تَمَا قَوْلَجَمْ ∴ غَمْرَكِ ∴ دُوقِمْ ∴ أَلَ ∴ دَأَمْبَ تَمَابَرْ
كِدِ رَبَا مَرْ ∴ إِنَّ ∴ رَبَكُو ∴ مِيُومَبْ ∴ نَفَتْ
أَكِبُسْتَرَاتْ ∴ سَنَا قَمْ ∴ دِيَا رِفَتِ ∴ آسَ كُلَمْ
تَنَا غُدَ امَتْ ∴ وَقَلَ ∴ قَرْ رَمَنْ ∴ مِيَا رِفَنَ ∴
فِيُو ∴ نِيَكَا قَلَاقَ ∴ تَقَا كُنْتْ ∴ كِيمِيشِنَ ∴
غُوَ اقَتَ ∴ قَبْ ∴ تَاشِ كِنَفِ ∴ وَأَفِمْ ∴

Yārinya [6] ta tāshi, ta-na-nīshi, ta dauki
dan maburmi, ta kāma hainya. Ta tafi raafi,
ta dauko rūa, ta kāwō, ta che, '[7] Uma sabke ni.'
Sai kīshiar uwa tata ta che, 'Ba ki gani ina-[8]da-
-ka ba ne, sai nā gama?' Ta yi surfe, ta kāre,
ta-na-bākache, yārinya na-tasye. Yārinya
ta che, 'Uma sabke ni.' Sai kīshiar uwa tata
ta che, 'Ba ki gani ina-bākache ba ne sai nā gama?'
Yārinya na-tsaye, har ta gama, har ta wanke,
ba ta kula da yārinya ba. Yārinya ta che, 'Uma sabke ni.'
Ta che, 'Ba ki gani nā zuba hatsi turmi ba,
sai nā gama daka?' Yārinya nā-tsaye

The maid got up, she was groaning, she lifted a small calabash, (and) took the road. She went to the stream (and) drew water; she took it back (and) said, 'Mother, lift the calabash down for me.' But her step-mother said, 'Do you not see I am pounding? Not now, when I have finished.' She finished husking the grain, she was winnowing, the maiden was standing by. The maiden said, 'Mother, lift down the calabash for me.' But her step-mother said, 'Do you not see I am winnowing? (Not now), when I have finished.' The maiden stood by till she had finished, until she had washed; she paid no attention to the maiden. The maiden said, 'Mother, help me down (with the water-pot).' She said, 'Do you not see I am pouring grain into the mortar? (Not now), but when I have finished pounding.' The maiden kept standing by

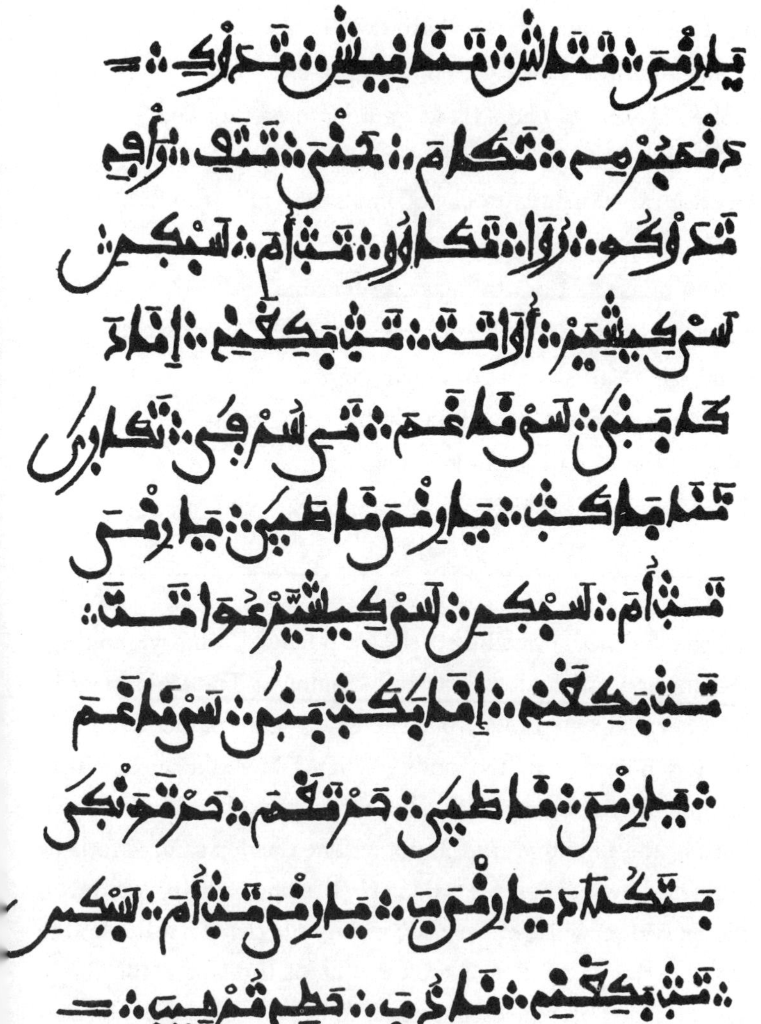

har ta gama daka; ta yi ribidi, ta yi tankade, ta kāre, yārinya nā-tsaye. Yārinya ta che, 'Uma sabke ni.' Sai ta che, 'Ba ki gani ina-nasa fura ba, sai nā kāre?' Yārinya ta-na-tsaye har ta gama [9] nasa fura. Yārinya ta che, 'Uma sabke ni.' Sai ta che, 'In je garin sabke ki, fura ta [10] tsinbire, sai fura tā tafasa.' Fura ta tafasa, ta [11] tsāme, har ta kirba, ta dunkula, ta gama, ba ta che ma yārinya kōmi ba. Sai iska ya zō kamar gūgūa. Ya dauke yārinya, ya tafi da ita, ba agane ta ba. Iska ya kai ta dāji, bābu kōwa sai ita kadai. Ta-na-yāwō chikin dāji, sai ta gani buka. Sai ta je.

---

till she finished pounding; she re-pounded, she winnowed, she finished, the maiden was still standing. The maiden said, 'Mother, help me down,' but she said, 'Do you not see I am putting porridge in the pot? When I have finished.' The maiden kept standing by till she (the step-mother) had finished putting the porridge (in the pot). The maiden said, 'Mother, help me down,' but she said, 'If (I) come to help you down the porridge will get burned; (wait) till the porridge boils.' The porridge boiled, she took it out of the water, till (then) she pounded it, squeezed it, and finished. She did not say anything to the maid, till the wind came like a whirlwind; it lifted the maiden and went off with her (and) she was not seen. The wind took her to the forest (bush), there was no one but she alone. She was roaming in the forest till she saw a grass hut. Then she went (up to it).

تم تغم دك : قسّ وجد : تي تنكجن :

تكابرن ميلوفم : قماطين : ميلوفم قتبا أم :

لسنبكسن لسى قتبمكغنم : إقامس فراب :

لسن قداكاون ميلوفم : قتقاطين : قم تنغم

فسفرا : ميلوفم : قتبا أم : لسنبكسن : لسن قتب

إفجن غم فلسبكم : فرامى : قطنبمكن لسى

فرا : نقامتبس : فرا متنفسن قطامبن : =

تسم قيكمن : تمد نكسا : تنغم : بتنشميارنى

كدو ميمن : لسن إسك : ميغدو : كمن غو غد :

ميد وبكن ميلوفم : ميتنف : دإك : ماغبنشب :

إلسك ميكنيد دابج : بابـ : كدوا : لسن إتـ كدنن :

تشد ميد ون : نكردابج : لسن قتغنم : نبك : لسن تنون

Ta lēka, ta iske katara da kare ke chiki.
Sai ta kōma, sai katara ta che, ' Us! us! ', sai kare
ya che, ' Wai ki kōmō.' Yārinya ta kōmō,
sai katara ta che, ' Us! us! ', sai kare ya che, ' Wai ki shigō.'
Yārinya ta shiga buka, ta rusuna ta-na-gurfane,
sai katara ta che, ' Us! us!, sai kare ya che, ' Wai kin iya
tūō ? ' Yārinya ta che, ' Ī.' Sai su-ka-ba ta shinkā-
-fa kwāra guda, su-ka-che ta dafa. Ta dauki
shinkāfa kwāra guda. Ba ta yi gardama ba,
ta nasa chikin turmi, ta-na-daka, kā́min ta daka
ta kāre, shinkāfa t.. chika turmi.
Ta susuka shinkāfa ta kāre, ta sheke.

She peeped in, (and) met a thigh-bone and a dog inside. Then she drew back, but the thigh-bone said, ' Us! us! ', and the dog said, ' He says you are to come back.' The maiden came back, and the thigh-bone said, ' Us! us! ', and the dog said, ' He says you are to enter.' The maiden entered the hut, and bowed down and prostrated herself, and the thigh-bone said, ' Us! us! ', and the dog said, ' He says, Can you (cook) food ? ' And the maiden said, ' Yes.' So they gave her rice, one grain, and said she was to cook it. She picked up the single grain of rice. She did not grumble, she put it in the mortar and pounded, and when she had finished pounding, the rice filled the mortar. She dry pounded the rice and finished, and poured it from a height to let the wind blow away the chaff (*sheke*).

تبلفس قنا إسجكن ∴ كتر ∴ كبرن ∴ بخكي ∴

لسر تكوتم ∴ لسر كتر ∴ قب أسر أسن ∴ لسر كبرن

يب ∴ ور يكي كومو ا ∴ يا وقم ∴ تكومو ا ∴

لسر كتر تب ∴ أسر أسن ∴ لسر كبرن ∴ يب وريكي شخو

يا ورقم ∴ قنشخ بك ∴ قتر سغن ∴ قنا غمر قا ابن

لسر كتر ∴ قب أسر أسن ∴ لسر كبرن يب ∴ وريكي

قدور ∴ يا وقن قب إي ∴ لسر لسكبا ق ∴ شنكا

قن ∴ كوارن غدا ∴ لسكب تعرق ∴ قدرك

شنكا قن ∴ كوارن غدا ∴ بتن غمر دقم ∴

قنلس نيكر غمر مي ∴ قنا دك ∴ كا مير قدك

∴ تكا برن ∴ شنكا قن ∴ قشك غمر مي ∴

قلسك ∴ شنكا قن ∴ تكابرن ∴ قبشهكن

Ta je raafi, ta wanke, ta kāwō gida, ta [12] sāsanwa,
ta zuba shinkāfa, kaṇda ajima shinkāfa
ta chika tukunia. Sai katara ta che, 'Us! us!', sai kare
ya che, 'Wai kin iya mia?' Yārinya ta che, 'Ī, nā iya.'
Katara ta che, 'Us! us!', sai kare ya tāshi, ya je
kan jibji, ya tōnō wani tsōfō kashi,
ya ba yārinya. Ta karbi, ta sainya tukunia.
Kāmin ajima kadan, sai nāma ya chika tukunia.
Sai nāma ya nuna, ta zuba gishiri da daudawa, ta zuba
kāyan mia duka. Mia ya nīna, ta shīde tukunia,
ta tūka tūō, ta kwāche, ta sainya ma
katara malmala gōma, ta sainya ma kare

She went to the stream and washed (it); she brought (it) back home, she set (the pot) on the fire, she poured in the rice and in a short time the rice filled the pot. Then the thigh-bone said, 'Us! us!', and the dog said, 'He says are you able (to make) soup?' The maiden said, 'Yes, I can.' The thigh-bone said, 'Us! us!', so the dog got up and went to a small refuse heap, (and) scraped up an old bone, and gave it to the maiden. She received it and put it in the pot. When a little while had passed, the meat filled the pot. When the meat was ready, she poured in salt and (*daudawa*) spice, (and) she put in all kinds of soup spices. When the soup was ready she took the pot off the fire, she served out the food and divided it up. Ten helpings she set aside for the thigh-bone, for the dog she set aside

تجراقي ⁖ قونبكن ⁖ تكاووغدا ⁖ تسا اسنو ⁖

قمغب يشنكاقن ⁖ كند اقجم ⁖ يشنكاقن ⁖ مـ

تيشك ⁖ تكنيا ⁖ تسوكتم قشب ⁖ اسر اسن ⁖ تسن كبرن

ميشب ورنكنكن ⁖ مين ⁖ ميارقن ⁖ قشب اء ⁖ قاعمن ⁖ =

كتم قشب ⁖ اسر اسن ⁖ تسن كجرن ⁖ ميقا يشن ⁖ بجسن

كنجبجم ⁖ ميشوقد ⁖ ونظوقو ⁖ كيشم ⁖

ميا ميارقن ⁖ تكمب ⁖ تسنبن ⁖ قكنيا ⁖ =

كامن ⁖ اقجم كغرن ⁖ تسقادم ⁖ ميشك تكنيا

تسن قادم ميقوق ⁖ قتغب غيشر ⁖ دغودوا ⁖ قتدب

كاميقمن ⁖ دك ⁖ ميمن ميبنين ⁖ قشيجرن تكنيا

⁖ تشوك ⁖ قشوو ⁖ تكواشبن ⁖ قتسقيابم

كتم ⁖ قلقلن ⁖ غوقم ⁖ قتسنيام ⁖ كبرن

malmala tara, ta sainya ma kanta malmala bīū.
Su-ka-chi, su-ka-kōshi. Tō, dōmin hakanan
ne, idan bākō yā zō garēka, ka girmama shi,
ka ba shi abinchi shi chi, saanan ka [13] jarabi
hālinsa, ka gani mūgū ne, kō nagari ne.
Yau, shi ke nan tāshin zanche, su-ka-kwāna,
gari yā wāye, sai katara ta che, 'Us! us!', sai
kare ya che ma yārinya, 'Wai kin iya fura?' Ta che,
'Ī.' Katara ta che, 'Us! us!' Sai kare ya tāshi,
ya je, ya daukō kwāra hatsi guda daia,
ya kāwō, ya bā ta. Ta karbi ta sainya chikin
turmi, ta zuba rūa, ta dauki tabaria,

---

nine helpings, (and) she set out for herself two. They ate (and) were filled. So it is, because of this, if a stranger has come to you, honour him, give him food to eat. Meanwhile you study his nature, you see if (it) is bad or good. To return to the story. They went to sleep. At dawn the thigh-bone said, 'Us! us!', and the dog said to the maiden, 'He says, Can you make "fura" cakes?' She said, 'Yes.' The thigh-bone said, 'Us! us!' Then the dog got up (and) came (and) lifted one grain of corn; he brought it and gave her. She received it (and) put it in the mortar; she poured in water, she lifted the pestle,

هَلْمَلَى تَمَرِ ؞ قَسَنْيَامَ ؞ كُنْتَ هَلْمَلِ مِبِيُو

؞ سَكَيِ ؞ لُسَكَكُو يِشِم ؞ قُو ؞ دُو مِرْ قَكَنْ

بُمَ ؞ إِكَّوِ ؞ مَا كُواُ ؞ يَا دُ و غَمِ يَكَ ؞ كَيِغْرْ مَمَا يِشِم

كَبَا يِشِ ؞ أَمِنْتِ ؞ يِشِ ؞ تَسَعَنَّ ؞ كَجَرِ ؞

قَا لِنْسَ كَفِنِم مُو غُو بَنْ ؞ كُو نَفِرْ بِن

؞ يُو يِشِي كَبُنَّ ؞ قَا يِشِ ؞ رُفْشِ ؞ لُسَكَكُوا وِ ؞

غَمِر ؞ مِيُو ايكِ ؞ تَسْ كَتَمَ قَثِ ؞ أُسِ أَسِ تَسِ

كَبُرَ ؞ مِيشْقَيَا رِقُمَ ؞ زَرْ بِكَنْعِنَ ؞ قُمَرا ؞ قَتِ

إِي ؞ كَتَمَ قَتَثِ ؞ أَسِ أُسِ تَسْ كَبُرَ مِقَا يِشِ

يَجَن ؞ يَدَّ وُكُوا ؞ كُوا وَقِطِم ؞ غُدَا دَرِ ؞

يَكَا وُرِ ؞ مِيَا قَ ؞ قَكَرِبِ ؞ قَسَنْيَا ؞ يِكِمِ

قُرْمِي ؞ قَنْغَبَ ؞ زُوَا ؞ قَدَّوُكِ ؞ قَبَرْيَا ؞ =

ta-na-daka ; kāmin ta surfe, hatsi ya yi
yawa. Ta kwāche, ta bākache, ta kai raafi,
ta wanke, ta kōmō, ta daka, ta kwāche,
ta bākache, ta kōmō, ta zuba, ta ribde, ta kwā-
-che, ta chibra, ta nasa tukunia, har ya tafasa,
ta sabke, ta tsāme, ta zuba turmi,
ta kirba, ta kwāche, ta dunkula, ta bai
wa katara dunkuli uku, ta ba kare
dunkuli bīū. Dada gari ya wāye
katara ta che, 'Us! us!', sai kare ya che,
'Wai kii tafi gida?' Ta che, [14] 'Naa tafi ama
ban san hainya ba.' Sai katara ta che, 'Us! us!',

---

she was pounding; as she (wet) pounded, the corn became much. She took it out, she winnowed, she took it to the water, she washed it, she returned, she pounded, she took it out, she winnowed, she returned, (and) poured (it in again). She pounded it very finely, she took it out, rolled it into cakes, and put it in the pot until it boiled. She took it off (the fire), set it down, poured it into the mortar, pounded, took it out, rolled it up into balls, and gave to the thigh-bone three balls, to the dog she gave two. When it was dawn the thigh-bone said, 'Us! us!', and the dog said, 'He says, Are you going home?' She said, 'I will go, but I do not know the way.' Then the thigh-bone said, 'Us! us!',

تَنَادَكِ ؞ كَدَامِنْ ؞ قَسْرِفِي ؞ قَطِمِ ؞ يَاسِّ

؞ مِيوَّ ؞ تَكُوَاشِي ؞ تَبَاكَبْ ؞ تَكُنْ رَاوِ

تَوِنْبَكِي ؞ تَكُومُوا ؞ قَدَكِ ؞ تَكُوَاشِي

قَبَاكَبْ ؞ تَكُومَ ؞ تَدُبَ قَرِمَبْجِرَ ؞ تَكُوَا

شِي ؞ قَخَيْبَرِ ؞ قَنَلَسَ ؞ تُكُنْفِيَا ؞ قَمْ يَتَقَسَ

؞ قَلَسَنْبَكِي ؞ قَطَامِي ؞ تَدُبَ قُرْمِمِ ؞ ═

تَكِرْفِ ؞ تَكُوَاشِي ؞ قَدَنْكَلَا ؞ قَبَنْ

وَكُنَّ ؞ دَنْكُرِ ؞ أَكُ ؞ قَبَاكَبَرِ ؞

دَنْكَلِ ؞ مِبِيُو ؞ دَدَغَمِ ؞ مِيوَاپِي ؞

كَنَرَقَبْ ؞ أَنْرَاشِ ؞ لَسَنْ كَمَ ؞ مَيْبْ ؞

وَبِكْنَتَفِ غِدَا ؞ قَبْ فَمَا قَبِقِ ؞ أَمَّا

بِنْلَسَنْ قَوِ ؞ لَسَنْ كُنَّ ؞ قَبْ أَنْرَاسِ

sai kare ya tāshi; ya je, ya kāwō bāyi māsu-keau, ya kāwō shānu, da tumāki, dāwāki da kāji, da rākuma da dawāki, angarmu, da jiminu da rīguna, kōmi duka na dūnīa, kare ya kāwō ya bai wa yārinya. Ya che, 'Ga shi, katara ta che, in ba ki, ki yi guzūri, wai ta salame ki, ki tafi gida.' Sai yārinya ta che, 'Ban san hainya ba.' Sai kare ya gaia ma katara, sai katara ta che, 'Us! us!' Sai kare ya che, 'Wai mu tafi in gwoda maki hainya.' Sai kare ya wuche gaba, yārinya ta hau rākumi, ana-jan rākumi.

---

and the dog rose up; he went and brought slaves, beautiful ones, he brought cattle and sheep, horses and fowls, camels and war-horses, and ostriches, and robes, everything in the world, the dog brought and gave to the maiden. He said, 'There they are, the thigh-bone says I must give you (them); you will make them the provision for your journey. And he says he gives you leave to set out, and go to your home.' But the maiden said, 'I do not know the way.' So the dog told the thigh-bone, and the thigh-bone said, 'Us! us!' And the dog said, 'He says let us set out, (and) I must show you the way.' So the dog passed on in front, the maiden mounted a camel, the camel was led.

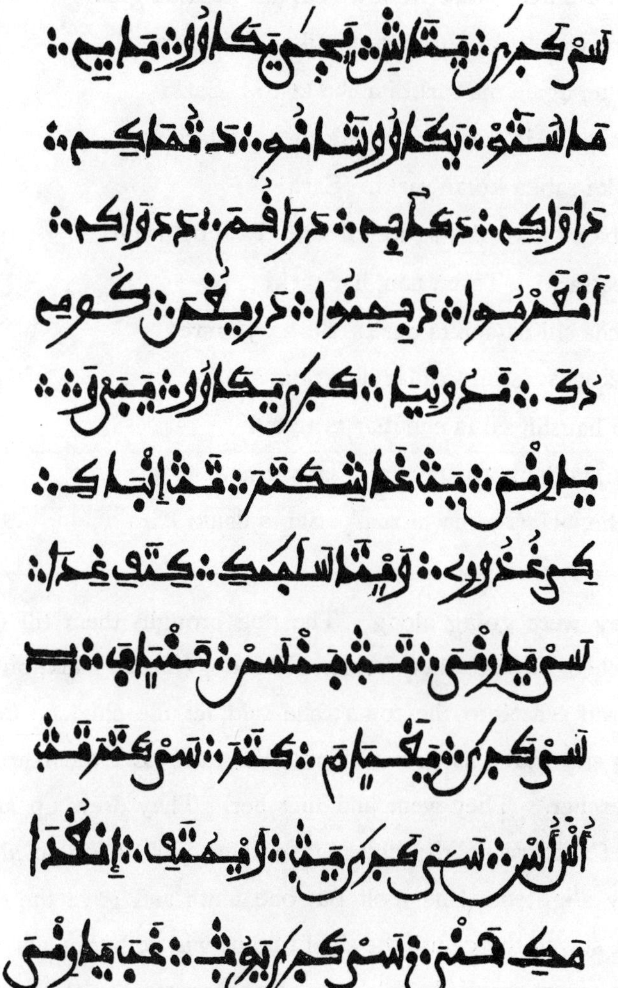

Su-na-tafia. Kare ya kāwō su, har kusa da gida.
Kare ya kōmā. Ita kūa, ta aiki chikin gari
ta che, agaia ma sarki ita che ta zō. Sarki
ya che, 'Aje atarbō ta.' Aka-je, aka-tarbō ta.
Su-ka-sabka kōfan sarki. Sarki
ya ba su masabki, su-ka-sabka. Ta fi da ushuri,
ta ba sarki. Ta-na nan, har sarki
ya che shi-na-son ta aure. Su-ka-yi aure.
Ita kūa, wachan kīshiar uwa tata,
ta ji haushi, sai ta che dīar ta ta tafi
raafi, ta daukō mata rūa. Sai yārinya
ta che, 'Uma ni ba ni zūa.' Sai ta dauki kara

They were going along. The dog brought them till (they reached) close to (her) home. The dog turned back, but she herself sent into the town; she said, let the chief be told it was she who was come. The chief said, 'Let them go and meet her.' They went and met her. They drew up at the chief's doorway, the chief gave them permission to alight, they alighted. She took out one tenth and gave the chief. She stayed there until the chief said he wished her in marriage. They were married. She also, that step-mother of hers, (her late father's second wife) was envious, so she told her own daughter to go to the stream to draw water for her. But the little girl said, 'Mother, I am not going.' But she (the mother) lifted a reed

سنا تبي ∴ كبرن بيكا اورس ∴ حر كسر غد ا ∴

كبرن بيكوم ∴ اِتكو ∴ تأبك ∴ فيكرغر

قسبأ أغيا مسركم ∴ اِقصب قدو ∴ آسركي ∴

يسبأ أجكي ∴ أقسر موقا ∴ أكجي ∴ أكتر بجوق

∴ سكسبك ∴ كوقر سركي ∴ سركم ∴

يماس ∴ مسبكم ∴ سكسبك ∴ قيع عشر

∴ قبا سركم ∴ قسفا قمر ∴ قم سركم ∴

يسب يشنا سفخ أورن ∴ سكم أورس

اِتكو ∴ رقمر ∴ كيشير عوا قتا ∴

تجم قوشم ∴ سوقسب ميم قا ∴ قتجم

راقيقم وكو مت روا ∴ سوميار فم ∴

قسبأم ∴ فيمبا فخو ∴ سوقسر وكي ∴ كرا

ta kōrē ta, ta tafi raafi tīlas. Yau yārinya ta je raafi, ta dauko rūa, ta kāwō, ta iske uwa tata, ta-na-daka, ta che, ' Uma sabke ni.' Sai uwa tata ta che, ' Ina surfe, sai nā gama.' Ta gama surfe, yārinya ta che, ' Uma sabke ni.' Sai ta che, ' Zaa ni bākache ne, sai nā gama.' Ta gama bākache. Yārinya ta che, ' Uma sabke ni.' Ta che, ' Zaa ni daka ne, sai nā gama.' Kanda ta gama daka, sai ta nemi yārinya kasa da bisa, ba ta gane ta ba, iska yā dauke ta, ya kai dāji. Ya yar, ta-na nan, ta-na-yāwō chikin dāji, sai ta gani buka. Ta je ta lēka buka, sai ta gani

---

and drove her, (and) she went to the stream by compulsion. Now the girl went to the stream, drew water, and took (it) home. She came across her mother as she was pounding; she said, ' Mother, help me down (with the pot).' But her mother said, ' I am pounding, (wait) till I have finished.' She finished pounding, and the girl said, ' Mother, help me down.' But she answered, ' I am about to winnow, (wait) till I have finished.' She finished winnowing (and) the girl said, ' Mother, help me down (with the pot).' She replied, I am just going to pound—when I have finished.' When she had finished pounding then she sought the girl low and high; she did not see her, the wind has (had) lifted her (and) taken her to the bush. It cast her there, she was roaming in the forest, when she saw a grass hut. She went and peeped in the hut, and she saw

تَكُوبَكَتَ ∴ تَمَتَّفِ رَاوْجِ ∴ قِيلَسْ بِيَخُو ∴ يِيَارْفَسَ

∴ قَجِي رَاوْجِ ∴ قَسَّ وُكُوزُوَا ∴ تَكَدَاوُ ∴ قَا إِسْبَكَ

غُوَاقَتَ ∴ تَقَادَكَ ∴ قَبُّ أُمْ ∴ تَسْبَكِمْ ∴ =

لَسْ غُوَاقَتَ ∴ قَبُّ إِقَدَاسُرُوكَ ∴ لَسْ قَاغَمْ

قَغَمْ سُسُرْوكَ ∴ بِيَادَرْفِي قَبُّ ∴ أُمْ لَسْبَكَمْ

∴ لَسْ قَبُّ دَاأُقِبَاكُشْبُو ∴ لَسْ قَاغَمْ ∴ قَغَمْ

بَاكَشْبُ ∴ بِيَاوْفَمْ قَبُّ ∴ أُمْ لَسْبَكَمْ ∴ قَبُّ

دَاأُقِمْ كَدَاقِبَمْ ∴ لَسْ قَاغَمْ ∴ كَنْدَ قَكَمْ

دَكَ ∴ لَسْ قَبِيَمْ ∴ بِيَارْفَمْ ∴ كَلَسْ ∴ عِ بِسَ

∴ بَتَكَبُشَبَ ∴ إِسْكَ ∴ بِيَادَّ وُبُكَمْتَ ∴ بِيَكِنْ

دَاءِ ∴ بِيَبِّرْ ∴ قَمَنْدَا قَمَّرْ ∴ قَنْدَا بِيَاوُ ∴ تِكِرْ دَاجِ

لَسْ قَغَنِمْ بُكَ ∴ قَجِي ∴ قَبِلِيوُ بُكَ ∴ لَسْ قَغَنِمْ

katara da kare. Sai ta koma, sai katara
ta che, 'Us! us!' Kare ya che, 'Wai ki zo.' Sai ta zo
ta che, 'Gā ni.' Katara ta che, 'Us! us!' Kare ya che, (wk)
'Wai ki zamna.' Sai ta zamna ta che, 'Mu dai alhairi
katara da magana, wani abu ne Us! us?' Sai su-ka-[16] kyale.
Aka-jima katara ta che, 'Us! us!' Sai kare ya che,
'Wai kin iya tūō?' Sai ta che, 'Ai ana-mugunya
shēkara, makwarwa tā ga dashe. Katara kuma,
har ita da mai-gaio; nā iya, kū kuma
hatsi ke garēku har ku na-tanbaya wai aniya
tūō.' Su-ka-kyale, kare ya tāshi, ya dau-
-ko kwāra shinkāfa guda daia

---

a thigh-bone and a dog. Then she drew back, and the thigh-bone said, 'Us! us!' The dog said, 'He says you are to come.' So she came and said, 'Here I am.' The thigh-bone said, 'Us! us!' The dog said, 'He says you are to sit down.' So she sat down, (and) said, 'Mercy on us, a thigh-bone that talks. What sort of a thing is Us! us?' But they gave no answer. A short time after the thigh-bone said, 'Us!' us!' Then the dog said, 'He says, Can you (cook) food?' And she said, 'Ah, it's a bad year when the partridge has seen them planting out the young trees (instead of sowing, when it could eat the seed). A thigh-bone, too, even it has an interpreter. I am able, you, I suppose, have the grain, when you are asking if people can cook food.' They gave no answer, (but) the dog got up; he lifted one single grain of rice

كـتتر ، ذكجري ، تسن تكوم ، تسن كتتر ،

تتث أسر أسر كجري بث ، وريكذو ، تسن تمذور ، ـ

تمث غدر ، كتتر قتث ، أسر أسر ، كجري بث وريكـ

وريكذ مهتر ، تسن تمذ مهر ، قتث مهو بن ، الخيبر

كتتر ذ مغمر ، وفـأ مجنى ، أسر أسر ، تسمو سكجلى

أكجمر ، كتتر قجث أسر أسر ، تسن كجري بث ، ـ

أريكلكم قمذور ، تسن قتث ، أى أمل مغمسو ، د

بسكحر ، قكمرورا ، قمل غدبشى ، كتتر كحم

، قمر اقد ، ذ ميقخيبو ، قمل عى ، كحوكم ،

قطم ، بكمجريك ، قمر كمد تسنبر ، وبجيحس

، شخو رو ، سكجلى ، كجري ، قند البشر بيجمو

كحو ، كحوار ، شسكل اقمر ، غداكر بكـ

ya ba ta. Ta che, 'Gāsa, yau zaa ni gani
kaman da shinkāfa, kwāra guda daia,
ta ke yin tūō.' Kare ya che, 'Kedai yi hakanan,'
Ta dauki shinkāfa, ta nasa turmi,
ta-na-daka. Kanda ajima kadan, shinkāfa
ta yi yawa. Ta chāshe, ta kwāshe, ta shekē,
ta zuba rūa, ta dafa. Kanda
ta gama dafūa shinkāfa ta chika
tukunia. Ta-na-māmāki. Kare ya daukō
wani shekarare kashi, ya kāwö, ya ba ta.
Sai ta che, 'Kāka zaa ni yi da shi,
wanga shekarare kashi?' Kare ya che,

(and) gave her. 'What's this?' she said, 'to-day I am about to see how one single grain of rice makes food.' The dog replied, 'As for you, make it thus.' She lifted the rice and put it in the mortar, she was pounding, and after a little while the rice became much. She dry pounded it, took it out, poured it out so as to blow away the chaff, poured on water, cooked it. By the time she had finished cooking it the rice filled the pot. She was amazed. The dog lifted up a year-old bone, brought it, and gave her. Then she said, 'What am I to do with it, this is a year-old bone?' The dog replied,

يبات ∴ قب غداس ∴ ميوكداون ∴ غنيم ∴ ك

كمر دشنكا ابقن ∴ كواو ∴ غداعرن ∴

تبيير شغوو ∴ كمرن ∴ ميث بكدرن ∴ يمكقن

تدوك ∴ شنكا بقن ∴ قنسن ∴ شرمي ∴

تنادك ∴ كندأجم ∴ ككرن ∴ شنكا ابقن

تن ميو ∴ تنابشى ∴ تكوابشن ∴ تبنجكن

تغبوق ∴ قونجكن ∴ تقرق ∴ كندم ∴

تغحم دبوا ∴ شنكا بقن ∴ منيك ∴

تكنيا ∴ قندمامداك ∴ كمرن مدركو

∴ ونبشكر ركمشى ∴ يكداو ∴ ميبات

تسن قنب ∴ كداك ∴ دأوجن دنشم ∴

ونغ ∴ بشكرره كشم ∴ كمرن يث ∴

'Kedai yi kakanan.' Ta che, 'In ji ku māsu-
-sidabaru ne, [17] kashēdi, bābu rūāna mā-
-yū su chainye ni.' Kare na kurum, bai che
kōmi ba. Ta wanke kashi, ta nasa
tukunia. Kāmin ajima, tukunia ta chika
da nāma. Yārinya ta-na-māmāki. Sai ta tūka
tūō, ta kwāche, ta sabke mia, ta sainya ma
katara malmala uku, kare malmala bīū.
Sai kare ya yi fushi, dōmin ya gani
nāta dayawa, nāsu kadan kadan. Sai ya che,
'Haba.' Garin shi che, 'Haba,' sai ya che, 'Hab hab,'
dōmin da bai gaia ma katara ba. Da wuri kare bafāde ne

'As for you, make it thus.' She said, 'Are you supposed to be conjurers? I warn you; it is not my business that wizards should eat me.' The dog remained silent; not a thing did he say. She washed the bone and put it in the pot, and in a short time the pot was full of meat. The girl was amazed, but she stirred the food, she took it out (and) set the soup down. She put aside for the thigh-bone three helpings, for the dog two. But the dog was angry because he saw her share was large, theirs very small, and he said, 'What's this?' When he would have said, 'Haba,' he could only say, 'Hab hab,' because he had not told the thigh-bone first before he spoke. Formerly the dog was a minister at court

بَعدِين يَمَكَنْتَ تَجَاْفِجِ ؞ كُومَاسْ

سِعِ بَمبَرْبَمُ ؞ كُبَشْمِحِ ؞ بَطَابُ وُوَاأَفُمْ ؞ مَا

يِوْ ؞ سُتَشَنْبِيمِ ؞ كِجِرَ ؞ نَاأَكُرُمْ ؞ بِيبْ

كُومِيبَ ؞ تَوِنْكُبِ ؞ كِيشِمِ ؞ نَعَسَ

تُكُنْيَا ؞ نَكَمِنْ أَجِحَمِ ؞ تُكُنْيَا ؞ تَاثِكِ ؞

دِنَاتَمِ ؞ يَاوِنِيْ ؞ تَنَامَامَاكِ ؞ سِنِ تَنْتُوكِ

تُوُرُوْ ؞ تَكُوَاشُنِ ؞ تَسْبِكَ جِمِّ ؞ تَسْبِيَامِ ؞

كُتَمَ مَلَمَلِي ؞ أَكُ ؞ كُجِرِ ؞ مَلَمَلِي ؞ يِيُو ؞

سِنْكُجِرِ ؞ يَمُّ فِشِمِ ؞ دُومِنِ ؞ مَيَاغِيْمِ ؞

نَامَاتَ دِيَّو ؞ مَالُسِ كَدَّ رِكَدَّرْشِ ؞ سِنْ يَبِبْ

تَبَ ؞ غِمِ فِشِبْ حَبَ ؞ سِنْ يَبِبْ حَبْ حَبِ ؞

دُوقِّرِ ؞ عُ بِنِعْمَ ؞ كُتَرَابِ ؞ دِوُوْ ؞ كُجِرِ ؞ بَقَابِ مَنْبَر

magana shi ke yi kamar mutum, da ya yi fushi
gaban sarki, shi ya sa shi ke yin 'Hab,
hab', idan ya tāshi zaa shi yin fada.
Dōmin hakanan ne yārō ba shi
fushi wurin da baba shi ke.
Yau, su-ka-chi abinchinsu, su-ka-kwāna.
Gari ya wāye katara ta che, 'Us! us!'
Dada kare bai iya ya yi magāna ba.
Sai ya je, ya kāwō makāfi mutāne,
da kutāre, da makāfi dawāki,
da gurgun jāki, da ragōgi,
rīguna da wanduna aka-ba ta, kare ya gwoda mata

---

and used to talk like a person, when (on this day) he got in a temper in front of the king, he condemned him to say 'Hab! hab!' if he rose up to quarrel. And the moral of this is, a youth must not lose his temper in the presence of an elder. Now they had eaten their food and slept. At dawn the thigh-bone said, 'Us! us!' Then the dog was not able to speak, but he went and brought blind men, and lepers, and blind horses, and lame asses, and sheep, robes and trousers were brought to her, (and) the dog showed her

مَغَرْ شَكُمّ ؞ كَمَرْ مُتَنْ ؞ دَيمّ فِشِم ؞

غُمَرْ سَمرِكِم ؞ لِشِم يَسَنْ ؞ شَكُمّيرْ قَبْ

تَمْ ؞ إِدَنْ ؞ يمقاش ؞ دَ أَشِيِّنْكَم ؞

دومِنْ ؞ تَكَنَّرْ فُمْ ؞ ميمُرْ ؞ مُداش

فُشِم ؞ وُرفَدِ مبم ؞ لُشِكَمْ =

ميحْ ؞ سُكشِ ؞ أَبِمشَنْسَنْ ؞ لَسَكَوَان

غُمِ يمِيوَابِمَن ؞ كَتَمْ قَمَشْ أَسْ أَسَنْ ؞

دَدَ ؞ عَجَرْ مَيِكَمْ ؞ ميماتي مَغَنَا قَ ؞

سَنْ فِجَمْ ؞ بَكَاوُرْ ؞ مَكَاقِم مُتَابِسْ

دُكَتَاوُرْ ؞ دَمَكَاقِمْ دُوَاكِم ؞

دُغَمْ غُمْ ؞ قَدكِم ؞ دَرْغُوغِم ؞

بِرِمُغَمْ ؞ دُوُفَدرَنْ ؞ أَكَبَدَاقَ ؞ كَمَرْ بَغُدَاقَمْ

hainya. Ya kāwō ta kusa da gida, ya kōma. Sai katara ya kōre shi, sai ya kōmō maza maza, ya chika da su, ya bi su har su-ka-kāwō gida. Mafārin kare shi zō gida ke nan, da wurin dawa shi ke. Tō, tāshin zanche, da su-ka-kāwō kusa da gida, sai ta aika kuturu guda daia chikin mutānenta, shi na bisa makāfō dōki, wai shi je shi gaya ma sarki tā zō. Sarki shi bari atarbe ta. Sarki ya sa galadima da mutāne dayawa aka-je, aka-tarbe su. Da su-ka-zō fagashi, sai dwai ya chika gari.

---

the way. He brought her to near (her) home and turned back. But the thigh-bone drove him away, so he came back very quickly and joined them, and followed them until they reached the house. That is the first time the dog came to the house, formerly he was in the bush. Well, to continue, when they had got near the house, then she (the girl) sent one leper from among her retinue. He sat on a blind horse and his message was to tell the chief she has come. The chief allowed her to be met. The chief made the galadima and many people to go and meet them. When they reached the open space in front of the chief's house, then a stink filled the town.

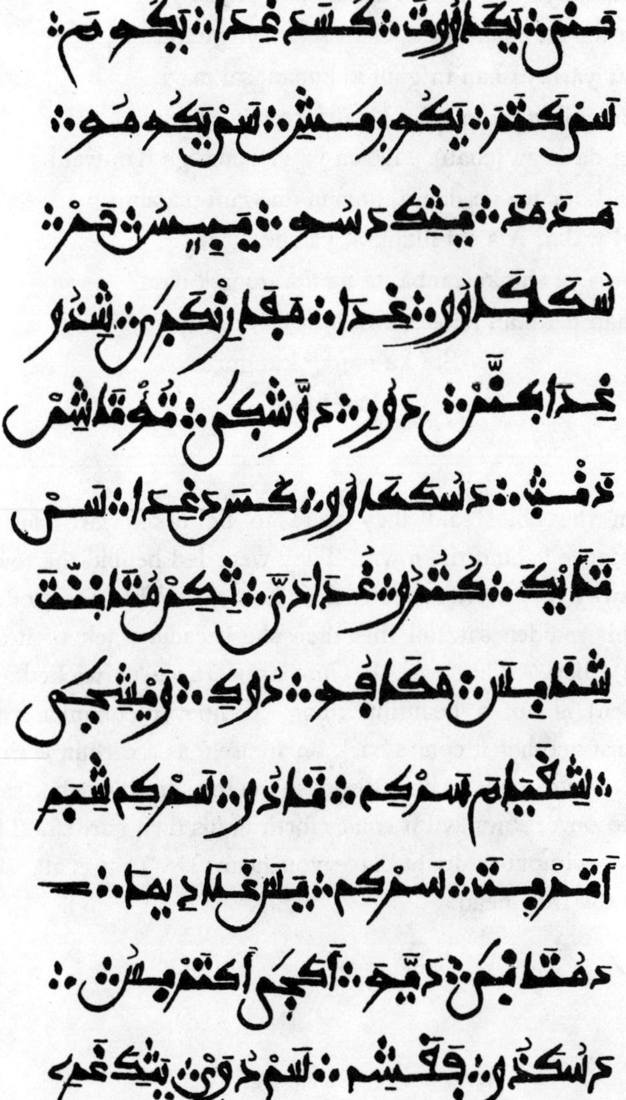

Sai sarki ya che akōma da su chan bayan gari.
Aka-kai su bayan gari, chan su-ka-yi gidāje su.
Uwar yārinya nan ta gani kakanan, sai ta yi
bakin chikin, ta mutu. Mafāri ke nan zanba,
ba ta da keau (chau). Kōwa ya yi zanba ga dan wani
ta-na-kōmāwa ga dansa, kaman da wani mālami
ya yi wāka, Ala shi jikainsa, ya che,
'Kōwa ya shibka zanba, ta na fita gōna [18] nasa.'
Wanan hakikan bābu wāwa kun jia?'

Shi ke nan, [19] kungurus
kan kusu.

Then the chief said they were to be taken far back to a distance behind the town. They were led behind the town, far away they were to make their houses. When the mother of this maiden saw all this, then she became black of heart, (and) died. That was the first appearance of wickedness, (which) is not a beautiful thing. Whoever commits a sin against another it comes back on himself, as a certain learned man sung, may Allah dispense mercy on him, he says, 'Whosoever sows evil it comes forth in his own garden. That is true without a doubt, have you heard?' That is all. Off with the rat's head.

لسن لسن بكم ؞ ميب أكوتم ع لسو ؞ شمن بلمين غم

أككيبس ؞ بلمين غم ؞ قمر سككي ؞ غداجس

عموزيار فيبنن ؞ تقغنم ؞ حككمن ؞ اسو تين ؞ =

بكنشك ؞ تفوف ؞ مبار بكمنن ؞ ع نب

؞ مباف دقو ؞ كوورا ؞ بيى دفب ؞ غد فون ؞

تنكوماورا ؞ غد فمن كمن عرو فمالم ؞

بيىواك ؞ أأنشجكيس ؞ ميبش ؞

كووا ؞ يشبك ؞ دفب ؞ تنا وقنا ؞ غوفم قسه

وفمن ؞ قحيفا ؞ بابوراو ؞ كنجيا ؞

شبكنن ؞ فنغر سن

كنركوسن ؞

No. 8.

Wanan tātsūnīar [1] mayā che.

[2] Gātanan, gātanan, ta je, ta kōmō. Wata tsōfūa ta ke da yāyanta, budūri tara, sai [3] ta je dōka dāji ta zamna. Sai wadansu yāra, samāri, su tara, su-ka-tāshi daka gari-nsu, su-ka-tafi gidan mayā, wurin budūri. Su-ka-je. Budūri su-ka-ba su rūa, kōwa budūransa ta ba shi rūa ya sha. Sai karaminsu, karamar budūri ta kāwō rua, ta ba shi, sai ya ki sha. Dare ya yi, kōwa budūransa ta yi tūō, ta ba shi. Su-ka-chi. Autan budūri ta yi tūō, ta kāwō ma autan samāri, sai ya ki chi. Aka che, 'Kāka, da ka zō kōwa ya chi abinchi, sai kai daia ka ki chi?' Ya che, 'Idan

---

This is a story about a witch. A story, a story. Let it go, let it come. A certain old woman had children, nine girls, and she went far into the bush and lived (there). Now some boys, youths, there were nine of them too, set out from their village and went to the house of the witch, where the girls were. They came. The girls gave them water, each had a maid who gave him water to drink. Now the youngest (among the boys) the youngest maid brought water to (him) and gave him, but he refused to drink. When night came each of (the young men's) maids made food and gave him; (and) they ate. The youngest of the maidens made food and brought it to the youngest of the youths, but he refused to eat. They said, 'How is it when you come every one eats food, but you alone refuse to eat?' He said, 'If

وَمِنْ قَالُو فِيَنْ مَيَا بْشِى

قَدَ انْتَغَنْ عَدَ انْتَغَنْ تَجِكِ تَكُومُوا ∴ وَنْتَلُوبَوَا ∴ تَبْلَكَ ∴

يَدَ مِيغَنْتَ ∴ بُدُرِي تَمْرَ ∴ اَسُنْ قَجِمْ ∴ دُوكَدَاجِ ∴ مَدَ مُسَنْ

اَسُنْ وَدَ مُلَسْ ∴ يَدَ وَا ∴ اَسَدَارِي ∴ اَسُوقَمَرَ ∴ سُكَنْتَا اِشِنْ ∴ دَكَفَمِ

فُسَنْ ∴ سُكَنْتَجِمْ ∴ نِعُ مَنْقِيَا ∴ وُرْ مُبُدُورِي ∴ شُكَجُسِى

بُدُورِي ∴ شُكَبَلِسُرْ وَا ∴ كُووَا ∴ بُدُرُ وُمُسَنْ

قَبَا اِشِنْ رُوَا ∴ مِيشِى ∴ اَسُنْ كَمِ يِغَسْ ∴ كَتَرِمْ

بُدُورِي ∴ تَكَاوُرُوَا ∴ قَبَا اِشِنْ ∴ سَرِيكِشْ ∴ دَبِرَا

يِّسِي ∴ كُووَا ∴ بُدُرُ وُمُسَنْ ∴ تَنِ قُوُرُ ∴ قَبَا اِشِنْ

سُكَنْشِ ∴ اَوُ قَمَرْ ∴ بُدَارِي ∴ قَتَنِ قُوُرُ ∴ تَكَاوُرُ ∴

مَاوُ قَمَرْ سَدَارِي ∴ اَسُنْ يَكِشِ ∴ اَكَبُ ∴ كَدَاكَ ∴ دَكَدُو

كُووَا ∴ بِمَاشِ اَمِنْشِ ∴ اَسُوكَمِ دَمَنِ ∴ نَعُكِشِ ∴ يِبَ اِدَرُ

samāri su-ka zō gidan budūri, su-na-chin abinchi, saanan sun zama samārin banza.' Aka che, 'Gaskīa ne.' [4] Wakatin kwāna ya zō, sai kōwa duka budrua tasa ta yi masa shinfida, su-ka-kwanta, su-na-kwāna. Autan samāri [5] ya tāshi, ya [6] kunche bantu nan waninsu, ya damra ma budūri. Ya fida rigunansu, ya sainya ma budūri, ya dauki fatalōli budūri, ya damra ma [7] mazan, ya dauki zannuan [8] mātan, ya damra masu. Aka-jima, ana-kwāna, sai tsōfūa nan ta zō. Idan ta lālaba, ta gani mai-rīga da bante. Sai ta yanke, hakanan har ta yanke dīanta duka, ta kōma, ta kwanta. Sai auta kūa shi-na-ganinta, bai yi kwāna ba. Ya tāshi, ya gina

---

young men come to the house of maidens and eat food, then they have become worthless young men.' And they said, 'That is true.' The time for sleep came, when for each and all his maiden prepared his couch, and they lay down and were sleeping. The youngest of the boys got up and unfastened the others' waist-cloths and tied them on the maidens. He took off their cloaks and put them on the maidens, he lifted the kerchiefs of the maidens and tied them on the boys. He took away the dresses of the girls and tied them on (the boys). A short time passed, they were asleep, when this old woman came. When she felt about with her hand, she discovered who had cloaks and who waist-cloths. Then she cut (their throats), and thus she did till she had cut off (the heads) of all her daughters; (then) she returned and lay down. But the baby of the family also had seen her, he had not slept. He got up, dug

تَجَارِ ءٌ تُكَغُو ءٌ غَدَّوْ [redacted] و مُدُوِ ءٌ تُقَاشِرَ أَمْنَتِ

تَغَفَّنْ ءٌ تُنْدَمْ ءٌ تَقَادُو فَبَنْدَا ءٌ أَكَبْ غَسْكَيِلَفَكُ

وَفِتِّن كُوَامُ ءٌ يَدُوَا ءٌ تَنْكُوَانْدَكْ ءٌ بُدَ زَوَاقَسَ

تَيِقَسْ شِنْبِدَ ءٌ تُكَكُنْتَا ءٌ تُقَنَاكُوَامُ ءٌ أَزَقَمَ

تَحَادِ ءٌ يَقَّاشِ ءٌ يَكُنْبُ ءٌ بُنْتُقَّنْ وَفِّقَّنْ ءٌ

يَدْ فَمْ فَبُدُوِ ءٌ يَبِدِ رِيغُنَّنْ ءٌ يَسَنْفِيَا فَبُدِ

يَدَارِكِ ءٌ بُتَاوَلِمْ ءٌ بُدُرِ ءٌ يَدْ فَمْ فَمَّغَرُنْ يَدَّرْكَ

دَفْنُو فُمَاقَمْ ءٌ يَدَّ فَرْ فَسَنْ أَكِجَمْ أَفَاكُوَامُ

تَنْطُو فُو فَّنْمْ ءٌ تَدُوَاشْ إِدَّنْ تَلَالَبَ ءٌ قَفِنْمْ

فَبِرِ يَغُو ءٌ دَمْ بِنْتُبُنْ ءٌ تَنْقَيِنْكُمْ ءٌ فَكَنَّمْ ءٌ قَمْ فَيِنْكُمْ

دِيَفْنَتْ دُكَ ءٌ تَكُوَمْ ءٌ تَكُنْتَمْ ءٌ تَنْ أَوْقَمْ كُوَ ءٌ =

شِنَاغِفْنَتَ ءٌ بَيَمَّ كُوَافَاعَ ءٌ يَتَاشِرْ يَبِغَسْ

rāmē tun daga [9] dākin da su ke kunche har dākin
uwansu. Sai auta ya tāda waninsa daga kwāna.
Su-ka-shiga chikin rāme, su-ka-tafi gida, su-ka-bar dīanta
kunche, [10] yankaki. Da gari ya wāye, tsōfūa ta zō.
Ta na murna, [11] zaa ta chin nāma, sai ta iske dīanta yankaki.
Sai ta chizi hannu, dōmin haushi, sai ta [12] kyale,
ta che, 'Naa rāma.' Wata rāna sai ta tafi chikin garin.
Ta zama [13] magarīa, sai yāra, mutun gōma sha bīar
su-ka-hau, su-na-zamne. Sai ta chire da su,
ta tafi gidanta da su. Uwayen yāra
su-na-kūka. Auta ya zō ya che, 'Ku bar kūka,
naa kāwō maku dīanku.' Ya tafi dāji, ya gani
sāniar tsōfūa nan, sai ya shiga chikin chikinta.

---

a hole from the house where they were lying to their mother's house. Then the baby of the family wakened the others from sleep. They entered the hole and went home and left her daughters lying (with their throats) cut. When day dawned the old woman came. She was rejoicing (because) she was about to eat meat, then she came across her daughters (with their throats) cut; then she ate her hand from vexation. Then she left off, and said, 'I shall be revenged.' Another day she went into the town (of the young men). (And) she turned herself into a *magaria* tree, then the boys, fifteen in number, climbed up and were sitting there. But she tore up (the tree) with them and went off to her house with them. The boys' parents were lamenting. The baby of the family came and said, 'Leave off crying, I shall bring you your children.' He went off to the bush, (and) he saw this old woman's cow, then he went inside its belly.

رابِس ؞ تَنْغَمْ غَدَ اِكِنْ ؞ دُ لِسْكِي ؞ كَنْبْ ؞ حَمْ دَ اِكِنْ

عُوفَنْسُ ؞ سَنْ آوْ تَا يِتَلَ دَ وَفِنْسَنْ ؞ دَ غَكُوا فَمِي

سَكِيشَعَ ؞ ثِكِسْ رَابِسْ ؞ سَكَتَفِيمِ غَدَا ؞ سَكَبِيرْ ؞ دِ يِسْتَ

كُنْبْ ؞ يَنْكَكِي ؞ دَ غَمِ عَبَوَايِسْ ؞ طُوفُوا اَمُدُرْ ؞

قَنَا فَمْرْ ؞ دَ اَقْتِشْ ؞ قَدَمْ ؞ سَنْ قَدِ اَسْكِي ؞ دِ يِقَنْتَ يِنْكِمْ

؞ سَنْ تَشِيخِ ؞ حَفْنُوا ؞ دُ وُوسْ قَوْشِمْ ؞ سَنْ تَنَكَّلُو

قَسْبَا ؞ قَدُوَاسْ ؞ اَرْقَمْ اَقَلْ ؞ سَنْ قَتَفِمْ ؞ ثِكِسْ غَمِرْ ؞

قَدَمْ ؞ مَغْرِبِي ؞ سَنْ يِدَوَا ؞ فُشْرْ غُومْ ؞ شَادِيِرْ

؞ سَكَحُوْ ؞ لَسَنَا دَ فَنْبُ ؞ سَنْ قَتِشِبْرُ نْ دَ سُوا ؞

تَسَتَفِ غَمْ فَنْتَ ؞ دُ لِسُوا ؞ غُوَايِمْ ؞ يِدَوَا ؞ =

سَنَا كُوكَمْ ؞ آوْ قَدَ يِدُوَا ؞ يِيشْ كَبِرْ كُوكَمْ

فَكَدَ اَوُرْكَ ؞ دِ يِقَنْكَ ؞ يِقَنَا فِمْ دَ اِمْ ؞ يِقَخِمْ

قَدَ فِيَرْ ؞ طُوفُو فَرْتَ سَنْ يِقِيشَعَ ؞ ثِكَشِكَمْتَ

Da sānia ta kōmō gida, ta yi kamar mai-chiki.
Sai tsōfūa ta che sāniar nan tāwa, 'Idan
ki haifu namiji, [14] naa yanka ki, idan ki haifi
mache, naa bar ki.' Ananan, ranan, sai ta haifi
mache. Ashe auta ne, ya zama dan sānia.
Su-na nan, sai auta, idan tsōfūa tā yi
wanke kōrai, sai ya tuma, shi fāda achiki,
shi farfasa. Ranan ta wanke kōrainta,
ta shainya, sai [15] maraki sānia ta tuma, ta fāda
achiki, ta farfasa. Sai tsōfūa ta yi fushi,
ta che yāra nan su duka su tāshi, su tafi,
su kāmō shi, su yanka. Sai yāra
su-ka-tāshi, su ka bi maraka. Maraka ta shēka

When the cow came home, it was as if in calf. And the old woman said (to) this cow of hers, 'If you give birth to a son, I shall cut your throat; if you give birth to a daughter I shall leave you alone.' And it came to pass that one day the cow gave birth to a daughter. Now of a truth it was the baby of the family, he had turned into the child of a cow. They were living like this, when the baby of the family (who was now a calf), if the old woman washed her calabashes, jumped and fell among them and smashed them. One day she washed her calabashes and put them in the sun to dry, then the cow's calf jumped and fell on them and smashed them. And the old woman got in a rage, and said to these boys that they must all rise up, and go and catch and bring it, and cut (its throat). So the boys rose up (and) followed the calf. The calf ran off

دَ قَدَ فِيَا ؞ تَكْوَمُوَا ؞ نَجِدَرَا ؞ تَسِ كَمَرْ بَيْشِكِ

سَنْ طُوَ فُجَوَا ؞ تَشَّبْ شَيَا فِيبَرْ قَّنْ ؞ قَدَوَّا ؞ إِدَّرْنْ

كِ كَمْيَفْ نَجِمَ ؞ فَدْ أُبَنْكَ كَمْ ؞ إِدَّرْ كَمْنَعِ

مَبْ قَدْ أُبَمْ بَرْكِ ؞ أَقَّا مَقَرْ رَقَّمْ ؞ سَنْ قَحْيِبِ

مَبْ ؞ آبَشِ أُوْ فَقْ بَجِ ؞ يَدَّمْ ؞ دَفْشَا فِيَا ؞

سَنَ قَمَّعْ ؞ سَنْ أُوْ قَمُرْ ؞ إِدَّرْنْ طُوَ فُجَوَا ؞ قَدَّرْ

رَوَكُوَّ بَكْرَ كُوَّمَنْ سَنْ يَسْتُمْ بِشَبَ دَرَ ؞ آكِلِّتْ ؞

شَبْقَمْ فَبْسَ ؞ رَقَّمْ تَحَ فَحَكْبَ ؞ كُوَرْتَ

قَشْفِيَا ؞ سَنْ مَرَكِ قَشْفِيَا ؞ قَتْقَمْ ؞ قَبَادَرْ ؞

آكِمْ ؞ قَقْمْ فَبْسَ ؞ سَنْدُ وَفُجَوَا ؞ قَمْ فَبْشِمَ

قَمْبْ ؞ يَدَوْ قَّمْ ؞ نَسُوَ دُكْ ؞ نَسْتَا أَشْ نَسْقِجِمْ

نَسْكَا مُوَ لِيْمَ ؞ [redacted] نَسَيْنَكْ ؞ سَنْ يَدَوَا ؞ =

نَسْكَتَا أَشْ نَسْكِبَ مَرْكَمْ ؞ مَرْكَمْ ؞ قَتْبَشْكَ

har chikin gari, yāra su-ka-bi ta. Sai maraka ta zama mutun, ashe auta ne. Sai ya che, 'Kōwa shi zō shi kāma dansa.' Sai kōwa ya fitō, ya kāma dansa, auta kūa sai ya tafi gidansu. Sai ta che, 'Naa kāma shi kuma.' Sai ta zama Bihilāta, ta dauki nōnō, ta kāwō chikin gari. Aka-che, kar kōwa shi dūba chikin nōnō, sai baban wan auta ya dūba, sai idānunsa ya fāda. Sai ta dauki nōnō ta, ta zama gūgūa, ta tafi da shi. Sai ya zō da wuri, ba shi gida. Aka che, 'Wata Bihilāta ta zō da nōnō, ta dauki idānu wanmu, ta tafi da su.' Sai auta ya che,

---

till (it came) right into the town; the boys followed it. Then the calf turned into a person, truly it was (he who was) the baby of the family. And he said, 'Let each come and catch his son.' So each one came out and caught his son, and the baby of the family he also went home. Now she (the old witch) said, 'I will catch him again.' So she turned into a Fulani woman, (and) took some milk, (and) brought it into the town. It was said that no one was to look into the milk. But one of the baby of the family's elder brothers looked in, and his eyes fell out. Then she took her milk, turned into a whirlwind, (and) went off with him. Then he (the baby of the family) came early, (and found his elder brother) was not at home. And they said, 'A certain Fulani woman came with milk and lifted the eyes of our elder brother and went off with them.' And the baby of the family said,

قمْ ثِكمْ كمِ ے :: يَطوَا :: لُسكِيتِّ :: لسْ مَمكمَ ::

تَغَمْ مُتَنْ :: أَبشَ أَوْقَدافُمْ :: لَسْ يَبُ كُووَا ::

يِشُغْ وَاِشكَامْ :: دَفْلَسْ لَسْ كُوَاوَا يَجُتوَا ::

يَكَامْ :: دَفْسَنْ أَوْقَدَاكُوَا :: لَسْ يَتَيِ غَدَفْلَنْ

سْ تَبْ فَدَأكَاهَدَ شُكُمَّ :: لَسْ تَدَمْ يَمِلَامَتْ ::

تَدَّ أَرْكِ :: فُوفُوَا :: تَكَاوُ ثِكُمْ غَمِ ے :: أَكَبْ

كُمْ كُووَا :: شُكَوُبَ :: ثِكُمْ نُوفُوَا :: لَسْ يَبَّنْ

وُنْدَاوْتَمْ :: يَدُ وُبَ :: لَسْ إِدَ افُنْلَسْ يَقَبَادَ ::

لَسْ تَدَوْكِ نُوفُوفُ :: تَغَمْ :: غُوغُوَ :: تَتَيِ

دَشُمْ :: لَسْ يَدُوُ :: دَوُ رِمَا شُغْدَا :: أَكَبْوُتَ ::

بَعِلَاقَ :: تَدُوَا :: دَفُوَافُو تَدَّرْكِ :: إِدَافُو

وَفُمْ :: تَتَيِ دَسُوَا :: لَسْ أَوْتَمْ :: يَثْ

'Naa karbō su.' Sai ya damra zane da fatala, ya tafi gidan tsōfūa. Da ta gane shi, ya yi kama da auta dīanta, sai ta che, 'Marhabi, marhabi.' Da auta shi kūa sai ya rika kūka, shi-na-kūka, shi-na-fadi, 'Laalātatu samāri sun zō, sun yi mani zanba, sun kashe mani wani.' Tsō-fūa kūa ta-na-che autan dīanta ne, sai ta che, 'Bari kūka auta, ai mu ma, [16] muu rāma.' Ta che, 'Ai ni ma, ga idānu babansu, [17] nā kāwō.' Sai auta ta che, 'Ba ni in gani [18] uma nāma in yi wāsa da su.' Sai tsōfuā ta dau-ki, ta ba shi, ba ta san shi ba ne. Shi-na-wāsa da su sai ta che, 'Zamna ki dūba gida, zaa ni raafi in kōmō.' Ta dauki tūlū, ta bāda bāya.

'I shall get them back.' So he fastened on a (girl's) dress and head kerchief, (and) went to the old woman's house. When she saw him, he was like her (own) youngest daughter, and she said, 'Welcome, welcome.' And the baby of the family he also began to cry, he was weeping and said, 'Bad boys came and sinned against me, they killed my elder sisters.' The old woman too was saying, 'It is the youngest of my daughters.' And she said, 'Cease crying, youngest of my children, as for us, we shall be revenged.' She said, 'As for me, see the eyes of the eldest of them I have brought.' And the baby of the family said, 'Give me that I may see, mother, the meat (eyes), (and) that I may play with them.' So the old woman took them, and gave him, she did not know it was he. He was playing with them, when she said, 'Sit and look after the house; I am going to the stream and shall return.' She lifted up the water-pot (and) turned her back.

نَأكَمْبِوَ لُسِ لَسِمْ قِيدِ مْمَ طَيْبُنِ : دَمْ فِتَلِي : مِتَقِي غَمَّ أَنِ :

طُوبُجُوا : دَمْقَبْشِنِ يِبَا يَكَمِى : دَاوقَادِمِنَةَ :

سُومْتَبْ مَمْ حَبِ : مَمْ حَبِ دَاوقَا : شِيكُو : كَسْتِرقِيرِكِ :

كُوكَى : شِنَا كُوكَى : شِنَاقِجِى : لَالَاقْتُوَا : أَسمَارِي

: لُسْنَزُو : لُسْنِيقِمُو : دَفِبِ : لُسْنَكْبَشِقِمُو : اوفِي : طُو

بُوَا كُوَا : قَنَافِ : اوقَتِمْ دِينِيقَتِبِي : امْرقَتِبْ : نَبِمْ كُوكَى

اوقَتِي : آ : فُومُوَى : سُوزَامْ : تَبْ أَعْمِيقِيَقِي : غَدَا إِدَا افُو :

بَبْنَشْ : فَاكَدَاو : لَسْرَاوقَدِ : قَتَبْ بَادَفِي : اوفَنِمْ

: أمْ : قَامُو : إِمِي وَاسَكِى : دَ لُسُو : امْرطُوبُجُوَا : قَدَوُ

كِ : قَبَدَاشِ : بَتَلَسْنَشِيجَبِي : شِنَا وَاسَكِي : عَمْ لُسُوَا

امْرقَتِبْ : دَمَتْمَى : كَدُو بَغَدَا : دَافِي : وَاجِمْ : =

إِنْكُومُوَا : تَدَّوكِ : قُولُوَا : قَتَبْ اد بَاعِي : =

Sai auta ya tāshi, ya shēka da idānun wansu, ya tafi da shi, ya bai wansu. Sai tsōfūa ta kōmō, ta che, 'Ina auta?' Ba ta gani auta ba, sai ta sabke rūa. Aka jima, sai yārinya ta zō, tsōfūa ta che, 'Kāwō idānu, mu dafa.' Yārinya ta che, 'Ai ba ki ba ni idānu ba.' Sai ta che, '[19] La ila autansu ne ya zō ya rūde ni, ina-che ke che, ama bābu laifi naa kāma shi.' Ta kyale. Wata rāna auta ya tafi dāji, shi-na-farauta, sai ya gamu da tsōfūa. Ta kāma shi, ta kai gidanta, ta sainya rāme, ta rufe sai ta tafi raafi. Ta bar dīanta karama, ta che ta jiran auta kada shi gudu.

Then the baby of the family rose up, and ran off with his brother's eyes; he went with it (them) (and) gave his elder brother. Then the old woman returned (from the stream) (and) said, 'Where is (my) youngest child?' She did not see her youngest child, and she set down the water. After a little while then the maiden came, and the old woman said, 'Bring the eyes that we may cook (them).' The maiden said, 'No, you did not give me any eyes.' And she said, '*La ila* it is the youngest of their family, he came and deceived me; I said (thought) it was you, but it cannot be helped, I shall catch him.' She ceased. Another day the baby of the family went to the bush. He was hunting when he met the old woman. She caught him, (and) took him to her house, put him in a hole, (and) covered (him) up, while she went to the stream. She left her youngest daughter and told her to wait and watch the baby of the family lest he ran away.

سِ أومني ؞ يتناقش يبشك ؞ ءإم أفنو فسو

يتفادشم ؞ يتجيفة ؞ وفسش لسن طوبجوا ؞ =

تكوموا ؞ تشا إمي أومني ؞ بتغنيم ؞ أوقداب

؞ لسن تسبكي زورا ؞ أكجم لسن يدورمن ؞ قدوا ؞

طوفجوا قشب ؞ يكدوو ؞ إدافو ؞ مدق ؞

يدورموقشب ؞ أ ؞ بكجاو ؞ إدافو مبن لسن قشب ؞

لا إلمي ؞ أوقنسبني ؞ يغدوا ؞ يبروجمس ؞ إنداب

بجش ؞ أمداباب ؞ ليفم ؞ ما أكلمداش تبجلو

؞ ومراقمي ؞ أومني يتقيدام ؞ لشا قبر ومت ؞ لمسى

يقحم ؞ ء طوبجوا ؞ تكلماش ؞ تكنغدمة

تلفيدرامون تزبجي ؞ لسن تقيم راوجم ؞ قبر

ديمنة كتمون ؞ قبقبجرن أومدا ؞ يكرثيقد

Sai ta tafi raafi. Sai auta dianta ta je wurin auta wanda ke chikin rāme, ta che, 'Auta me ka ke chi?' Sai shi kua ya che, 'Mīkō [20] hannu(n)ki in ba ki, abinda ni ke chi.' Sai ta mīka hannu. Sai auta ya kāma hannunta ya ja ta, ya nasa rāme. Ta-na--chiki, ta-na-kūka. Auta ya rufe ta, kaman da uw(a)--nta ta rufe shi, ya dauki zane da fatala, ya damra. Shi-na nan, shi-na-wāsa, har tsōfūa ta zō. Ta che, 'In ji auta bai gudu ba.' Sai ya che, 'Shi-na-nan, bai gudu ba.' Ta dafa ruan zāfi, ya tafasa ta dauki ta che, 'Dan nema yau [21] shii gani.' Sai ta je wurin rāme, ta zuba, sai yārinya, da da ji zāfi

---

Then she went off to the stream. Then her (the witch's) youngest daughter came to the place where the baby of the family was in the pit (and) she said, 'Oh, baby of the family, what are you eating.' And he said, 'Stretch out your hand and I will give you what I am eating.' So she put out her hand, but the baby of the family seized her hand, (and) pulled her, (and) cast her into the pit; she was inside, she was crying. The baby of the family covered her up as her mother had covered him. He took (her) dress and kerchief and tied them on. He remained there, and was playing about until the old woman came. She said, 'Let me hear that the baby of the family has not run away,' and he replied, 'He is here, he has not run away.' She boiled hot water, it boiled, she took it up, and she said, 'Son of a profligate, to-day he will see.' Then she went to the hole and poured in (the water), and the maiden, when she felt the heat

لسن متّي راجه ؛ لسن اوقد ديمت ؛ تجو ور مد اومتن

وفد بكيكز ؛ رامو ؛ متب اومتن مككبي ؛

لسن شيكو ؛ ييب ميكوا فنتوك ؛ إنبا كـ ؛

أمنعر نكبي ؛ لسن تميك حنوا ؛ لسن اومتن ؛

يكدام ؛ فنتوف ؛ يجات ؛ يغلس رامو ؛ تقد

ثكي ؛ تقاكوكن اومتن يمربت ؛ ككمر ءمو

فنت ؛ فرحش ن يمدرك طبن ؛ ءم بتلن ؛

ميم مر ؛ شنا قمر ؛ شنا والسن ؛ حم طوبوا ؛

تمدوا ؛ تبت إنجم اوقو ؛ ينغدب ؛ لسن يب ؛

شنا قمر ؛ ميتغدب ؛ مءف وفمدا إفم ؛ ييتبس

تمرك ؛ قتب ء فبقن ؛ ميو شنغنم ؛ لسن تجى

وومفر امون ؛ نفعب ؛ لسن يادوفمن ؛ ء قبج نداقم ؛

ta-na-kūwa, ta-na-fadi, 'Uma ni che, uma ni che.' Auta shi-na-fadi, 'Karīa ka ke yi. Ala shi tsari uma ta haife ka, Ala tsare ta ta haife ka.' Hakanan har ta mutu. Ta dauko, ta [22] sasāre, ta nasa tukunia, ta dafa. Yārinya ta nina, ta sainya daudawa da gishiri, ta shīde tukunia, ta tsāme nāma, ta che, 'Auta tafō, kedai mu chi dan nema.' Sai ya che, 'Aa ni ba ni chi, yanzu kedai chi, ki kōshi.' Ta-na-ham! ham! har ta kusa chinye nāma. Sai ta rage, ta che. 'Gā nāki auta.' Auta ya che, 'Uma, idan ba ki kō-shi ba, ki chainye duka,' sai ta dauki saura, ta chi. Ta rage kankane, ta aje, ta che, 'Gā nāki.'

---

kept shouting out, and saying, 'Mother, it is I, mother, it is I.' He, the baby of the family, said, 'It is a lie you are telling. May Allah guard mother from giving birth to such as you, may Allah guard her from giving birth to such as you,' and so on till she died. She (the old woman) lifted her out, cut (her) up in small pieces, put her in a pot and cooked her. When the girl was cooked she put in *daudawa* spice and salt, took the pot off the fire, took out the meat and said, 'Youngest daughter, come forward. You alone will eat the son of the profligate woman.' But he said, 'No, as for me I shall not eat, now you yourself eat and be filled.' She was crunching, crunch! crunch! until she had almost eaten (all) the meat. Then she ceased, and said, 'There is your share, little daughter.' The baby of the family replied, 'Mother, if you are not full eat up all,' and she (the old woman) took up what was left and ate. She left a small piece, put it aside, and said, 'There is yours.'

تناكور ؞ تناقجي ؞ أم فيبشي ؞ أم فيبيغ ؞ أوتمي

شناقجي ؞ كم ياكجي ؞ أاشطم أم ؞ تعنبعك ؞

أاطبمتا ؞ تعنبعكي ؞ فككنم تكنن ؞ قم قمت

تدوكوا ؞ تسلسابرس ؞ تقنلس ؞ تكفنيا ؞ تعرق ؞

يلوفن ؞ تفيمن ؞ تسفن ؞ دزودوا ؞ دغشيري ؞

تشيجسو ؞ تكنيا ؞ تطابو ؞ قدام ؞ تتب اوتمن ؞

تفجوا ؞ بكعن ؞ مثد فبمن ؞ لسن ميب ؞ تماع ؞

فم بدافث ؞ بيثغ ؞ بكعي ؞ فككوشن ؞ تند

تفقفم ؞ تم تكسن ؞ فثپلي قدام ؞ لسن قم فبي ؞

تبه ؞ غدانداك ؞ أوتمن ؞ أوتمي يتب ؞ ألم إكرو ؞ تيكو

شب ؞ يكثپين ؞ دك ؞ لسفد وك ؞ لسورا ؞ تثي

تم غمن ؞ كنغنبي ؞ تفآجي ؞ قث غداداك ؞

Sai auta ya che, 'Yau kin chainye dīanki duka, sauran ki chi kainki.' Sai ya yāda zane, ya che, 'Kin gane ni, ni ne auta, ba ki chi na.' Sai ya shēka, ya tafō gida, ya gaya ma mutānen gidansu, ya che, 'Mu gudu.' Sai garin duka
[23] ya tāshi, su-ka-gudu. Da su-ka-tafi, sai baban wansu
[24] ya che yā yāda tākalminsa, ya che shi kōma, shi [25] daukō. Auta ya che, kar ka kōma. [26] Ya che, yaa kōma. Auta ya che, 'Bari ni in kōma.' Auta ya kōma, ya je, ya shiga dāki. Sai ta rufe shi, ya hau bisan dāki, ya kāma tanka. Sai ya che mata, 'Idan ki-na-sō ki chainye ni, sai ki būde mani idānu, in ji tsōrō, in fādō, ki kāma ni.' Sai ta tāda kainta bisa, ta bubūde

---

And he who was the youngest of the family said, 'To-day you have eaten up all your daughters, and there only remains for you to eat yourself.' Then he threw aside the cloak (and) said, 'Do you see it is I, the baby of my family, you did not eat me.' Then he ran off, and went home and told the people of his town (saying) 'Flee'. And the whole town rose up and fled. When they had gone, then their elder brother said he has dropped his slipper; he said he would turn back and get it. The baby of the family said, 'Do not go back,' (but) he said he would return (for it). The baby of the family said, 'Allow me to return.' The baby of the family returned, he went and entered the house. And she (the old woman) came and closed (the door); he climbed on to the top of the house and caught hold of a beam. Then he said to her (the old witch), 'If you are wanting to eat me up, you have only to open your eyes at me when I shall be afraid and fall down (on you) (and) you will catch me.' Then she raised her head, and opened very widely

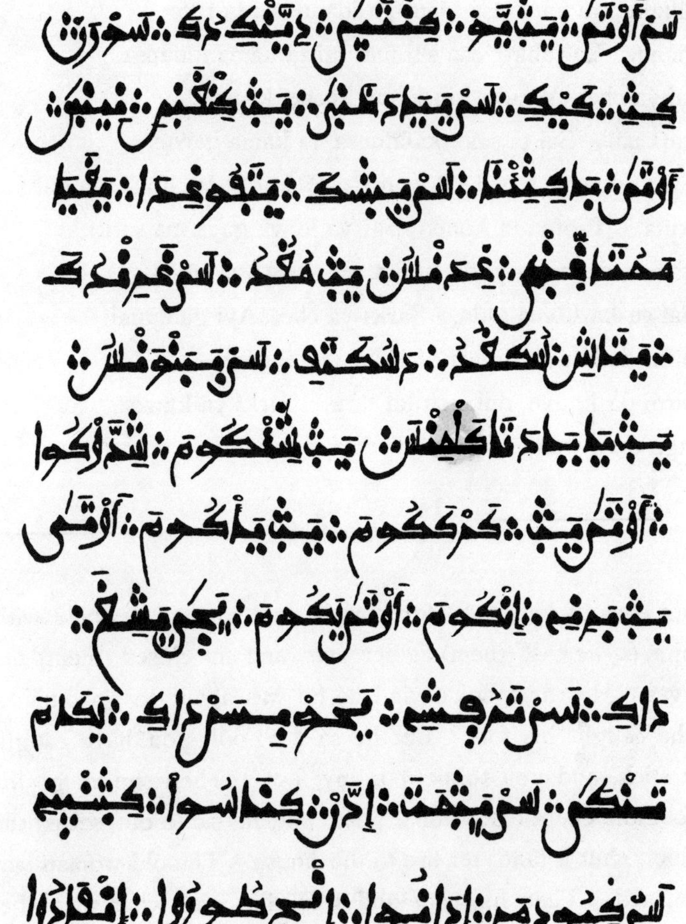

masa idānū. Shi kūa, akwai [27] tunka wurinsa nikake, sai ya wātsa mata ga idānu, sai ta rufe idānu. Ya sabkō, zāa shi fita, sai ta kāma kafansa, sai ya che, 'Wāwa, kin kāma itāche, ki-na-che kafa na.' Sai ta sake kafafunsa, ta kāma itāche. Sai ya fita ya kāma [28] kyaure, ya [29] kuble ya chūna ma dāki wuta. Tsōfūa ta kōne. Sai ya je, ya gaya ma sarki, kaman da su ka yi da tsōfūa, ya che, 'Mu kōma gida.' Sai su-ka-kōma gida. Sarki ya che, 'Ayi gangami birni da kauye su tāru.' Aka-yi gangami birni da kauye, duka su-ka-tāru. Sarki ya kāwō rīga dari, wandō dari, sānia dari, dōki dari,

---

her eyes at him. As for him, he had ground peppers with him, so he cast (them) at her eyes, and she closed (them) the eyes. He came down, and as he was about to go outside, she caught his foot. But he said, 'Fool, you have caught a stick, and you think it is my foot.' Then she let go his foot and caught hold of a post; and he came out, seized the door, shut it (and) set fire to the house. The old woman was burned. Then he went and told the chief what they (he) had done with the old woman, (and) he said, 'Let us return home.' So they returned home. And the chief said, 'Let the drums be beaten in town and village and let them assemble.' Drums were beaten in town and village and every one assembled. And the chief brought one hundred cloaks, one hundred trousers, one hundred cattle, one hundred horses,

مَسَرِإِ افُو ٝ شِيكُوَّ ٝ أَكُونِ ٝ شْنكُن ٝ اُرِفَسِن

نِكَكُن ٝ اَسِن مِيَوَا اَطَامَتَ ٝ غَمِإِ اِ افُوَا ٝ اَسِن تَرِفِي

إِ اِ افُوَا ٝ مِيَسَبكُوَا ٝ دِ أُشِبِتَن ٝ اَسِن تَكَامَ كَبنَس

ٝ اَسِن مِبَ وَاوَا ٝ كِنكَامَ ٝ إِتَابَ ٝ كِنَابَ ٝ =

كَبَا افُنَ ٝ اَسِن تَسَبَجُن كَبَا فِنَس تَكَامَ ٝ إِتَابَ

سِن مِبِتَ ٝ يكَامَ فُرُن ٝ مِكَبَلِي ٝ مِيتُو فِهِدَاكِ

وُتَمُن ٝ طُوفُوَا اتكُوفُن ٝ اَسِن تَجِن مِنغِيَا مَسَرِكِم ٝ

كَمَرِ سَكِّن ٝ دِ طُو فُوَا ٝ مِيبَ مَكُوتَم ٝ غَدَا

اَسِن سَكَكُوتَم ٝ غَدَا ٝ اَسِرِكِم ٝ مِبَ أَيِّ فَغَفَغِم

مِيرِ فِم ٝ دِ كُوبِّن ٝ سَتَاوُ ٝ أَكَيِّ غَفَغِم ٝ

مِرِ فِم دِ كُوبِّن ٝ دِكَ ٝ سَكَنَاوُ ٝ اَسِرِكِم ٝ يكَاوَاوُ

وِبِغُوعِ رِي ٝ وُنَدِ وَاعِ رِي ٝ شَافِيَا دِ رِي ٝ دُوكِ دِ رِي ٝ

kōmi duka na dūnīa dari dari. [30] Ya che yā ba shi
rabin gari, abin nan da aka tāra duka sarki ya che yā baiwa
auta. Sai auta ya che, 'Sarki, gari, idan ba shi
da [31] tsari, banza ne, ka bari agina birni, tun mutāne
ba su wātse ba.' Sarki ya che, 'Bābu wanda ya iya ginin
birni.' Auta ya che, 'Ni naa gina, kai kadai ka taimake ni
da mutāne.' Sarki ya amsa, sai auta ya gina birni.
Mafārin ginin birni ke nan, auta ya fāra, kōwa
ya gani. [32] Kungurus kan kūsu.

---

of everything in the world one hundred of each. He said he gave him half his town (and) all the things which had been brought, the chief said he gave to the baby of the family. And the baby of the family said, 'Chief, a town, if it has not a protection, is worthless. Let a wall be built before the people have dispersed.' And the chief said, 'There is no one able to build a walled town.' And the baby of the family said, 'I shall build it; do you only give me assistance with the men.' The chief consented, so the baby of the family built a walled town. And that was the origin of walled towns, the baby of the family began that every one might see. Off with the rat's head.

بِيثِ يَدَابَاشِنْ ؞ كَرِي كَرِي ؞ قَدَرِ افِيَا ؞ نْدِكِ كُوَمِيمِ

بِيثِ يَابِيوُ ؞ اَسْرِكِمِ ؞ اَكِتَارَ نْدِكِ ؞ اَمِتَّنْ نْدَ ؞ وَنْكُفِرِ

يَدَاشِ ؞ اِدَّنْ ؞ غَمِ ؞ اَسْرِكِمِ ؞ بِيثِ اَوْقَنِ اَسِرِ اَوْقَنِ اَ

مُثْمْقُتَّمَ ؞ مِرُقِمِ اَغِمِ كِبِرِ ؞ بِنْغِرَاهِيمُ ؞ نْطِمِ

غِمُّنْ ؞ مِكَّنْ اَوْنْغُ ؞ بِيثِ بِابُ ؞ اَسْرِكِمِ ؞ بِسْوَابِبُ

كِتِبُقِجِمْ ؞ كِنِكِمِ ؞ غِمْ نَا ؞ فِمِنْنَا ؞ بِيثِ اَوْقَنِ ؞ بِرُفِمِ

بِرُفِ بِغِفَ ؞ اَوْقَنِ اَسِرِ ؞ مُسِنِ ؞ يَمِ ؞ اَسْرِكِمِ ؞ اَبِنِ مِتَّعَدَ

كُوَاِ ؞ يَيْدِوُ ؞ اَوْمْثِ ؞ بِكِتَّنْ ؞ مِرُفِمِ ؞ غِمُّنْ ؞ مْبِقَاوُنْ

كِنِكُوشِ ؞ فِنْكُوَلِسِ ؞ يِفِنِيهِ

No. 9.

Wanan tātsūnīar [1] mālami che.

Wani mālami ya tāshi zūa Maka, dōmin shi dada lādansa shi yi yawa. Shi-na da kwarangaman gōdīansa. Ya hau, ya je tsakan dōkar dāji, sai ya gani [2] kūra. [3] Gōdīar tā gaji, sai kūra ta che, 'Mālam ina [4] zaa ka?' Mālami ya che, 'Zaa ni haji.' 'Me ya fāru?' Ya che, 'Gōdīa ta che ta gaza.' Ta che, 'Ita ke nan?' Kūra ta che, 'Ba ni ita, in yanke, in chainye, ka hau ni, mu tafi.' Mālami ya che, 'Hakanan?' Ta che, 'I.' Mālam ya che, 'Kar ki rūdē ni.' Ta che, '[5] Asha mālam, dōmin [6] nā gani ba ta iya tafia, dōmin hakanan ne; ni kūa, idan ka hau ni, yanzu yanzu naa kai ka Maka.' Mālam ya che, 'Bābu laifi, kāma, ki chainye.' Kūra

---

This is a story about a learned man. A certain doctor of learning set out to go to Mecca in order to add to his rewards hereafter that they might be many. He had a very thin mare. He mounted, (and) went deep into the forest when he saw a hyena. The mare was weary and the hyena said, 'Doctor, where are you going?' The doctor said, 'I am going the pilgrimage.' 'What is the matter?' (said the hyena). He said, 'It is the mare, she is weary.' She (the hyena) said, 'Is that it?' the hyena said, 'Give her (the mare) to me, I shall kill her, and eat her up. You will mount me and we shall set out.' The doctor said, 'So?' She (the hyena) said, 'Yes.' The doctor said, 'You must not deceive me.' She replied, 'Come now, Doctor, because I have seen she was unable to go on, it is because of that, (I speak thus) I for my part, if you mount me, this instant will I carry you to Mecca.' The doctor said, 'All right, catch (the mare) and eat (it) up.' The hyena

وَفَمْ تَاطُبُوتُمِيرْ ؞ مَدَاَلِمِيثْ

وَفِحَدَالِمِ ؞ يِبَتَاشِنْ دُرْوْ ؞ فَكَ ؞ دُوِمِنْ شِتَّدَ ؞ آلَادَمْنْسْ

شِيْيِبُوَ ؞ شِنْدَتُكُمْ نْكَمِنْ ؞ غُودِيَتِفْسْنْ فِحَوُ ؞ يَحُسْ

طَكُمْ دُوكُمْ دَاجِ ؞ اَلسِ يَتَغِنِمْ كُورَا ؞ غُودِيَمْ ؞ تَاغَمِ

اَسُوكُورَا ؞ تَبْ مَدَالَمْ ؞ اِقَادَاَكَ ؞ مَدَالِمِ ؞ يِبْ دَارُشْ

فِجِ ؞ بِيَقَادُوْ ؞ يِبْ غُودِيمِ تَاقُبْ ؞ تَغُدُ ؞ تَبْ اِتِكُنْسْ

ؠكُورَاتَبْ ؞ بِدَاوَاتَ ؞ اِفِيْنْكُسْ ؞ اِفْشْيِنِ ؞ كُحُونْ

مَتُوفِ ؞ هَدَالِمِ ؞ يِبْ حَكَتَنْ ؞ تَبْ اِيَ ؞ مَدَالَمْ يِبْ

؞ كُمْ كُمْ دُوجِ مَنْ ؞ تَبْ آشْ مَدَالَمْ ؞ دُوِمِنْ ؞ فَدَغِنِ ؞

بَاتَحِنَّ ؞ تَبِجُونْ دُوِمِّرْ حَكَتُرْفِيُونْ نِيكُحُوَ ؞ =

اِدَّنْ كُحُونْ مِنْغُمِنْغُ ؞ فَدْكِنِيكَ ؞ فَكَ ؞ ـــ

مَدَالِمِ ؞ يِبْ بِدَاوُ اَلِنْفِ ؞ كَدَاَمَنْ وُكَتْشِيِنْ كُورَا

[7] ta kāma gōdīa, ta yāge, ta dībi nāma,
ta kai gida. Su ka chi da dīanta, su-ka-chainye nāma,
ta ki zakūa. Mālami ya zamna, ya gaji, bai gani
kūra tā zō ba. Ananan, sai [8] karen buki
ya zō, ya tarda mālam shi-na-zamne, karen buki
ya che, 'Mālam me ya fāru?' Mālami ya che, '[9] Nā tasō
daga gidana, zaa ni Maka, gōdīata ta gaji,
ina zamna, kūra ta tarshe ni, ta che, me ya fāru,
na che mata, Zaa ni Maka ne, gōdīata ta gaji,
shi ya sa ina zamne nan. Kūra ta che, Ai wanan
ba ta iya kai ka Maka, ba ni ita in chainye,
in ji dādi, in kāra [10] karfī, in kai ka Maka.

---

seized the mare, tore it up, picked up the meat (and) took it home. She ate it with her cubs (children), they ate up (all) the meat; (then) she refused to return. The doctor sat down (and) got tired (of waiting), he did not see that the hyena has (had) come back. Things were like this, when a jackal came and met the doctor sitting there. The jackal said, 'Doctor, what has happened?' The doctor said, 'I have set out from my home going to Mecca, my mare got tired, I was sitting down, the hyena came across me and asked what was the matter, and I said, I am going to Mecca, my mare got tired, and that is the cause of my sitting here. And the hyena said, Oh, this thing can never take you to Mecca. Give her to me to eat that I may feel joy, and increase my strength, so that I may carry you to Mecca.

تكدم غودميا ؞ تيا نجس قديمب ؞ قادم ؞

تكن غدا ؞ سككش ؞ كد مينتا ؞ سكتشي فادم ؞

تك زقوا ؞ مدالم ؞ يبد مس ؞ يغج ؞ ببغينم

؞ بجوا ؞ قدا ذوب ؞ أقاقس ؞ لس كب فبو ؞

مدو ؞ ميتنر د مدالم ؞ لشفد ذمبن ؞ كب فبو ؞

يبش مدالم ؞ مبكار ؞ مدالم يبش قدا قدا سوا ؞

د غيدا قس ؞ د أنتك ؞ غودمياق ؞ قغج ؞

إقاد مبن ؞ كورا ؞ قتنر بشم ؞ قبش مبكار ؞

قبقند ؞ د أنتك كبن ؞ غودمياق ؞ قغج ؞ =

يبيس ؞ إقاد مبنس كورا ؞ قب إز وقس

بدا قيح ؞ كيك ؞ قك ؞ بطارت ؞ إقشين

أنجداد ؞ إنكار ؞ كم قج ؞ إنكيك قك

Nī kūa na che, Kūra kar ki rūdē ni, ki chainye mani
gōdīata, saanan ki gudu, ban gane ki ba. Ta che,
Ina ake yin hakanan, da gaskīa na ke fadi, bābu karīa
achiki. Ni kūa ina che gaskīa ne, na che ta kāma.
Shi ke nan, kūra ta tafi, har yau ban gane ta ba.'
Sai karen buki ya che, '[11] Kyale mālam [12] naa kāwō maka ita,
yanzu.' Ya dauki sirdi da kāfu, da linzāme, da ragama,
da kayāmai, da bulāla, ya tafi, ya sāmu tsōka nāma,
ya tafi da shi. Shi-na-tafia, shi-na-yāda kayan dōki
guda guda, har ya kai kusa da bākin rāminta, ya aje
kāfu, ya wuche, ya je bākin rāmenta, ya tsaya,
ya yi salama. Su-ka-kyale, da wuri kūa kūra tā gaya ma

I then said, Hyena, you must not deceive me, eat up my mare for me, and then run away, (and) I shall not see you again. She replied, Where do they do that sort of thing? it is the truth I told you, there is no lie in it, then I said (thought) it was true, (and) told her to catch (the mare). That is all, the hyena went off; till to-day I have not seen her.' And the jackal said, 'Leave off, Doctor, I will bring her to you now.' He lifted the saddle and saddle-cloth and bit and halter and spurs and whip and went off, and he got a lump of meat and took it. As he went he was dropping the horse furniture one by one until he got near the mouth of the hole (where the hyena) was. He put aside the saddle-cloth and passed on, and came to the mouth of her hole, and stood, and announced his arrival. No answer, for previous to this the hyena has told

نيكو ∴ قب كورا ∴ كركم ودمن ∴ كشيقمن ∴
غود يادق ∴ هعقن ∴ يكغد ∴ بتغبكيب ∴ قب
إما أكبين قكقن ∴ دغسكيا مكبقي ∴ بابكزيكى
أنكم ∴ نيكو ∴ إقاف غسكيا بقي ∴ مب تكادم
يشيكن كورا ∴ شقي حم يحوا ∴ بتقبشي ∴
لسن كم فمبو ∴ يشبكلمن ∴ مدالم ∴ فدأكا روقك ∴ إف
يفد ∴ يدوك ∴ يسردى ∴ دكافوا ∴ دلغا بمن ∴ دوغمى
∴ دكيامن ∴ دبولال ∴ يتقي ∴ يسادم ∴ طوكنادم
يتفدشم ∴ يشنا قبو ∴ يشنا ياد ∴ كايمن ∴ دوك
غدا غدا ∴ حزيكن ∴ كسر دماكنرا منتا ∴ ياب
كافوا ∴ تيوف ∴ يجي ماكن ∴ وا منتا ∴ بطرن ∴
بيق لسلم ∴ سكجلى ∴ دوري كو ∴ كورا ∴ قد غيادم

dīanta ta che, 'Kōwa ya zō nan, shi-na-nema na, ku che ba ni nan.' Da dila ya yi salama, sai su ka che, 'Ba ta nan.' Dila ya che, 'Tir Ala wada maras arziki ana-neman mutāne da arziki tsīa ta-na-hana su, ga wani sānia yā mutu, [13] mamāya, [14] nā zō dōmin in kirāye ta, in gwodu mata, sai ku che, ba ta nan, bari in kōma.' Sai kūra ta che, 'Wa ke nema na?' Dila ya che, 'Ni ke nemanki, wata sānia ta mutu, māmāya, na yankō baba tsōka, nā kāwō maki, dōmin ki gani shi ne, yāranga su ka che, ba ki nan.' Sai kūra ta che, '[15] La ila, kā ga lalatatu, ina-kwāna, ana-bida na, ku che ba ni nan.' Sai kūra ta fitō.

---

her children saying, 'Whoever comes here looking for me, you mus say I am not here.' So when the jackal hailed, they said, 'She is nc here.' And the jackal said, 'Allah curse her, she has no luck; me are sought for that they may get something good, and bad luck prevent them from getting it. See, a cow has died, a very fat one, I have com to call her and show her, and you say, she is not here. Let me return Then the hyena said, 'Who is seeking me?' The jackal said, 'I ar seeking you. Some cow died, a very fat one, I cut off a big lum and have brought it to you, but these boys are saying you are nc here.' And the hyena said, 'There is no God but Allah! yo have seen, worthless fellows. I was asleep and was sought for, (and you say I am not here.' So the hyena came out.

دِيَمْتَ ∴ مَتَبْ كَحُورَا ∴ يَنْدُو وَقَّمْ ∴ لِشَنَا بَجَلَقَمْ ∴ كُبْ بَلِنِفَمْ

دِدَلَا ∴ بِيَوْ لَسَكَمْ ∴ لَسَنْ لُسَكُبْ ∴ بَدَ قَنْفَمْ ∴ دِلَامِبْ ∴ قِمْ أَرْوَدَمْ

مَرْسَنْ ∴ أَرْزِفِمْ ∴ أَمَا بَحَمْ مَتَدَ قَبَمْ ∴ دَ أَرْزِفِمْ ∴ طِيَبَا

تَمَدَ قَنَدَا لَسَنْ ∴ نَعَدَ وَرِنْشَ دَفِيَا ∴ مِيَدَاسَثْ ∴ مَحَدَ يَمْ ∴

تَمَدُ وَا ∴ دُ وِمَّرْ ∴ إِنْكَرَا مِيَتْ ∴ إِمْغُدَا مَتْ ∴

لَسَنْ كُبْ ∴ بَدَا تَمَّنْ ∴ بِمْ إِنْكُوَمْ ∴ لَسَمْ كُورَا ∴

تَمَبْ ∴ وَرَا كِبْنَدَا قَمْ ∴ دِلَامِيَبْ ∴ نِيبِكِنْبَنْكِ

وَمَتَّ فِيَا ∴ تَمُفَّثْ ∴ مَمَّدَا يَمْ ∴ فِيِنْكُوَا ∴ بَبْ

طُوبَهْ ∴ تَكَدَ وَرَقِكِ ∴ دُ وِمْ رَكِ خِنِمْ ∴ لِشِيبَنْ

يَادَ وِرْفَعْ ∴ شَكِبْ بَدَا كِنَّمْ ∴ لَسَنْ كُورَا ∴ تَبْ

لَا إِلَنْ ∴ هَدَاغْ ∴ لَا لَا أَمْتُو ∴ إِمَدَا كُوَا قَمْ ∴

آقَدَ بِمْ أَمَنْ ∴ كُبْ بَلِفَمْ ∴ لَسَنْ كُورَا قِبْتُو ∴

Sai ta fitō ta che, 'Gā ni.' Dila ya che, 'Amshi, dandana.' Ta karbi, ta hade, ba ta bai dīanta. Ta che, 'Mu tafi.' Su-ka-kāma hainya, su-na-tafia, kūra ta-na-gaba gaba, dila na bāya. Sai ta che, 'Kai ba ka iya tāfia, hau ni, mu tafi maza maza.' Dila ya hau ta, su-na-tafia, su-ka-iske mashimfidi. Dila ya che, 'Bari in shifida abinga ga bāyanki, gāshin bāyanki shi-na--sūkāna.' Sai ta che, 'Yi maza maza mu tafi.' Dila ya dauki, ya shimfida, ya hau, su-na-tafia. Su-ka-iske linzāme, sai dila ya che, 'Bari in dauki abinan in sa maki bāki, kō naa ji dadi--n rikō.' Ta che, 'Sa maza maza mu tafi.' Dila ya sainya mata

---

When she came out she said, 'Here I am.' The jackal said, 'Take (it), taste.' She received (the meat), swallowed it; she did not give to her children. She said, 'Let us be off.' They took the road, they were going along; the hyena was in front a long way, the jackal behind. Then she said, 'You cannot walk, mount me (and) let us get along quickly.' The jackal mounted her, they were going along; they come across the saddle-cloth. The jackal said, 'Let me spread this thing on your back, the hair on your back is getting ruffled.' And she said, 'Do it quickly and let us get on.' The jackal lifted and spread it. He mounted, they were going along. They came across the bit, when the jackal said, 'Let me lift up this thing and put it in your mouth; perhaps it will be better for me to hold.' She said, 'Put it on quickly and let us get on.' The jackal put on

لَسِنْ تَبِجِتُوا . مَقَبْ غَمَافِهِ ∴ دِ لَايَيْبْ آمَشِنْ ∴ دِ مْدِمْ مَسْ

نَكْرِبْ ∴ تَعَجِرِ ∴ بِتَبِمْ دِيِّفْتَ ∴ قَبْ فَتَوِ ∴

سُعَكَامْ ∴ قَمْتَنِ ∴ سُنَدَ افَيِقِّ ∴ كُورَا ∴ فَتَاغَبْ

قَمَبْ ∴ دِلَافَبَاتِ ∴ لَسِمْ قَتَبْ ∴ كَمْ يَدَاكَ عَمْ تَبِقِّ

قَكُونِ ∴ مُقَيِ مَمْ مَغَ ∴ دِلَايَحَوْتْ ∴ سُنَدَ افَبِقِ

سُكَاسْبَكِنْ ∴ مِيشِنْبِجِ ∴ دِلَايَيْبْ ∴ بِجَاقِشِجِ

آبِمْغِ ∴ غَمْبَايِنْكِ ∴ غَمَاشِنْبَايِنْكِ ∴ اِشَنَا

سُوعَدَامْنِ ∴ لَسِنْ قَبْ يِّحَمَغَ ∴ مُتَبِمْ ∴

دِلَايَدْ وَرِكِ ∴ يِشْبِجِدَا ∴ يَحَوْ ∴ لَسَنَدَاقَبِقِ

سُكَاسْبَكِنْ ∴ لِنَرَامِسْ ∴ لَسِنْ دِلَايَيْبْ ∴ بِجَامِدْ وَرِكِ

آبِسِنِّ ∴ اِفْلَامَكِ ∴ بِدَاكِمْ ∴ كُومَدَاجِ ∴ دَادِ

فُرِكُوا ∴ قَبْ سَدَامَغَ ∴ مُتَبِمْ ∴ دِلَايَسِنْيَا مَقَا

lizāme, ya hau. Su-na-tafia, su-ka-iske kayāmai. Ya sabka, ya dauki kayāmai, ya sainya a-kafa, ya hau. Su-na-tafia, su-ka-kusa da mālami, sai kūra ta che, 'Kar mu bi nan. Dila ya che, 'Gurin da [16] nāman shi ke ke nan.' Kūra ta che, 'Mu karkata wajen haka.' Su-ka-karkata wani wuri da dila ya sani, sun kai dai dai da mālami, sai ya karkata lizāme zūa wurin mālami, ya kafa mata kaimi. Sai kūra ta zaabura, ta-na-che, 'Uu, uu.' Ba su zāme ba, sai wurin mālami. Dila ya zāme gaban mālami, ya sabka, ya che, 'Malam gā mabachinka, tāshi, ka hau, kar ka sabka, sai ka kai wurinda zaa ka.

---

the bit (and) mounted. They were going along; they came across the spurs. He dismounted, picked up the spurs, (and) put them on his feet, (and) mounted. They were going along, they were near the doctor, when the hyena said, 'You must not take this way.' The jackal replied, 'This is where the meat is.' The hyena said, 'Let us make a détour thus.' They have turned off another way, which the jackal knew, and got opposite to where the doctor was, when he turned the bit towards where the doctor was and struck her with the spurs. Then the hyena sprang forward, saying, 'Uu, uu.' They did not pull up till (they reached) where the doctor was. The jackal pulled up in front of the doctor, dismounted, and said, 'Doctor, behold your debtor. Rise up, mount, and do not get off until you reach where you are going.

لقرابتي . يحو لسنا تيوي . لسكل النكجو . فيبا مني

يسنبك . يدروك فيبا مني . يسفيا اكق .

يحو لسنا تيوي . سككسن . د مدا اهم . اسن

كحورا امتبنكرفيسنر . د لا يبنا . اهم فك مدامنن

شبك بجتن نحورا امتبنعنر كتا . وهوك

لسكنر كتا مورحوري . [redacted] د لا ييسر .

لسنحكن هكيحم ورد م مدا اهم . اسن يكنر كتا اقرابتي

كون وفحد اهم . يكبا امت . فنيهم . اسن كحورا

. عقر ابدم . تمناف . عجوعم . عموعم . بفقع ابب

اسن ورفحدا اهم . د لا يقرابتي . عجبر مدا اهم .

يفنبك . يبث مدا اهم . غدا مبتنك . مداشن .

كهم . كنر كامنبك . اسن كاكنن . ورفعد اك

Idan kā sabka, kō rūa, kar ka che akai ta raafi.' Mālami ya che, '[17] Nā ji.' Mālami ya hau, bai sabka ba har ya kai Maka. Saanan ya sabka, ya ba yāra rikō, ya che, 'Kar ku hau, kar ku kai ta raafi.' Mālami ya shiga masalāchi, su-na-sala. Sai yāra su-ka-hau, su-ka-tafi da ita raafi. Da su-ka-fita bāyan gari, sai su-ka-yi sukūa. Kūra ta dauke su, ta shiga dawa da su, ta-na-gudu, har ta kāshe su, ta [18] tafianta. Mālami ya fitō masalāchi, bai gani yāra ba, bai gani kūra ba.

Shi ke nan, [19] kungurus kan kūsu.

If you dismount, even at the water, do not say she is to be taken to the stream.' The doctor replied, 'I have heard.' The doctor mounted, (and) did not get down till he had reached Mecca. Then he dismounted and gave (the hyena) to (some) boys to hold, saying, 'You must not mount, you must not take her to the stream.' The doctor entered the mosque, they were praying. Then the boys mounted, (and) went off with her to the stream. When they got behind the town then they galloped. The hyena carried them off, and entered the bush with them, and ran until she threw them and went her own way. (Then) the doctor came out of the mosque; he did not see the boys, he did not see the hyena. That is all. Off with the rat's head.

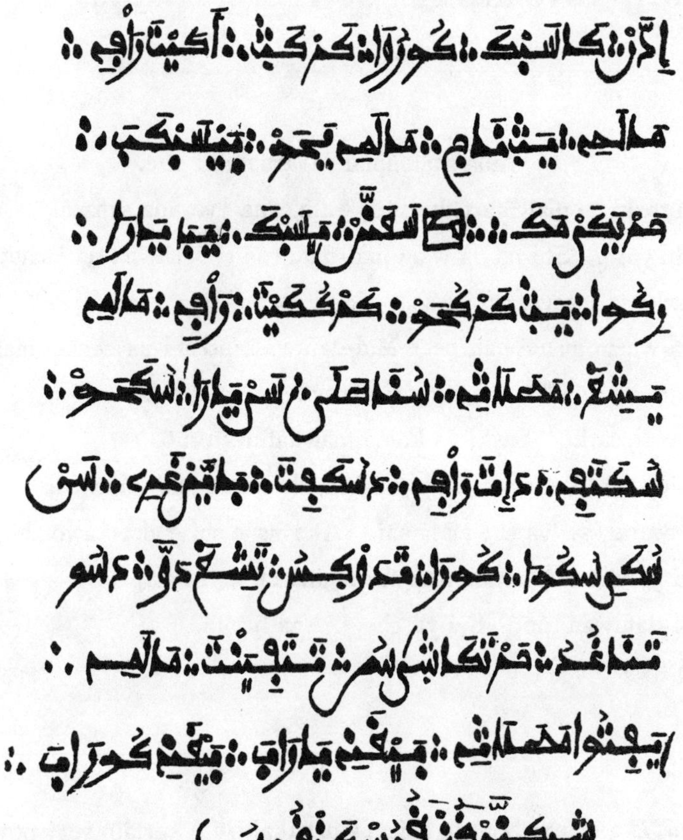

No. 10.

Wanan tātsūnīar [1] Garnakaki che.

Wani sarki ne mai-[2]karfī kwarai, wata rāna [3] ya fida sansani zaa shi yāki. Shi-na da wani mai-dafuwan tūō, shi-na da [4] maatansa, shi sarki nan, wada shi ke sō. Kōmi na sarki shi-na wurin maata nan ne. Mai-dafuwan tūō shi-na-neman maa--ta nan, ita kūa [5] ta-na-sō(n)sa, har wata rāna aka-kwar--mata ma sarki. Sarki ya kāma mai-dafuwan tūō, ya sainya shi kurkuku. Shi, sarkin, shi-na-sō mai-dafuwa nan kwarai, sai ya che afida shi. Aka-fishe shi, [6] aka-kāwō shi. Sarki ya che, 'Ama idan ka bar maata ta, ka kōma, ka-na-dafuwan tūō.' Sai ya che, '[7] Naa bar ta.' Ashe karīa ne.

This is a story about (a chief) Garnakaki. A certain very powerful chief one day struck camp to go to war. He had a certain cook, (and) he had a wife, this chief, whom he loved. Everything the chief had was in this wife's possession. The cook was after this woman, and she also loved him, until one day the chief was secretly informed. The chief seized the cook (and) put him in prison. Now he, the chief, was very fond of the cook, so he said he was to be taken out. He was taken out and brought forward. The chief said, 'In spite of all if you give up my wife, you may return and continue cooking food.' And he said, 'I shall leave her.' Truly it was a lie.

رفن تاطو فيّيغ غم تعفيث ::

وافسركين ميكزوف همرن وتمراقى :: يبيك سغسن ::

واشتياك :: لشناد ولمينيد فوقتوور :: شناد ماتغسن

شيمسركنّت ودّشكمسوا :: كوبيه تسركم ::

شنا وفما فتنغي :: مينج فوقتوور :: شنا بعتما

تفن اتكو :: فنا سوا :: نن همر وتمراقى :: اكيكم

قنا فستركم :: تسركم يكا [redacted] م :: همنيد فوقتوور

يلشتيا اشكم كك :: شيمسركم لشنا سو :: مينيد فو

نركم نن تسن ينت افود تشم :: اكفبشن اكحاوو نش

سركم :: يب امد ادّر كبم ماقات :: ككو م ::

كنا دفو فتوّو :: اسن يبت فما ابرت

ابشر كم يا ابّى

Shi-na nan, shi-na-dafa ma sarki tūō. Ashe su-na-
-tāre da [8] maatar nan, su-na-yi ma sarki [9] tānadi,
har su-ka-karbō māgani, su-ka-sainya wa sarki
achikin abinchi. Sarki ya chi, ya mutu. Maatar nan
ta dība kāyan sarki dayawa, da kurdin sar-
-ki dayawa, ta ba shi daga bōye, bābu
wanda ya sani, har aka gama kōmi duka. Saanan
ta fita, ta aure shi. Mafāri ke nan
aka-che, 'Sō mai-sonka, rabu da makīyinka,
kar shi ba ka māgani, ka chi, ka mutu.'
[10] Kungurus kan kūsu.

Time went on, (and) he was cooking food for the chief. Of a truth they were together, (he) and this woman, (and) they were sinning against the chief, until (one day) they got medicine, (and) put it in the chief's food. The chief ate and died. This woman took possession of much of the chief's property and much of the chief's money. She gave him (the cook) (them) secretly (and) no one knew, until they had finished taking everything. Then she came forward and married him. That was the origin of the saying, 'Love him who loves you, leave him who hates you, lest he give you medicine to eat (and) you die.' Off with the rat's head.

شَنَا فَمْ ؞ شَنَا دِ قَا فَسَمْ كِم ؞ فُحُوْوُ ؞ أَبْشَى سَنَا

تَدَاوُرِشْ دِ مَا فَتَرْ فَمَّ شَنَا يَمَسَنْ كِمْ ؞ تَمَا قَدِ ى ؞

قَمْ سُكَكَمْ بُجُوا ؞ قَا غَنِم ؞ سَكَسْكَ سَنِيْدَا وَانَتَرْكِم ؞

أَشْكِنَا أَسِنْفِ ؞ آسَرْكِم ؞ يِيِنْ يَمْت ؞ مَا أَمْ مَتَّرْ ؞

تَدِيمِيَبَ ؞ كَا يِّيْرْ سَرْكِم ؞ دِيِّيَوَ ؞ دَكَمْ كِ نَسَرْ

كِم ؞ دِيِّيَوَ ؞ قَبَدَا لِشْ دَ غَمُبُوبِي ؞ مَابُ بَ ؞

وَفْدِ يِسَسْ قَمْ أَكَ غَمْ ؞ كُوبِمِيدِكَ ؞ أَسَعَقَّنْ

قَبِعَتَ ؞ قَا أَوُرَّ ؞ [redacted] ش مَجَادِي ؞ بَجَمَّنْ ؞

أَكَبْ ؞ أَسُوَ مَيْسَنْكَ ؞ زَبِدَ مَكَيِّنْكَ ؞

كَمْ شَبَاكَ ؞ قَا غَنِم ؞ كَشْ كَحُتَ ؞ ـــ

فُنْقُمْ سُنْ ؞ كَمْ كُوسُنْ ؞

No. 11.

Wanan tātsūniar samāri che.

Wadansu samāri su-ka-tafi kauye wurin
budūri. Su-ka-je, su-ka-iske raafi, hainya bābu
rūa, rūa iyāka idānun sau. Su-ka-wuche.
Su-ka-isa gurin budūri, su-ka-je, su-ka-gaishe su,
su-ka-daukō su. Su-ka-zō wurin raafi, su-ka i-
-shẹ, ya-chika da rūa. Sai su-ka-che, 'Af ai
mun wuche rūanga, bai kai haka ba.' Su-ka-che,
'Kāka ke nan?' Daia chikinsu ya che, 'Mu kōma.'
Saura su-ka-che, 'Aa ba mu kōmāwa.'
Su kūa, su uku ne, da dan sarkin kō-
-kūa, da dan sarkin mahalba, da dan limāmi.

This tale is about (some) youths. Certain young men went to an outlying village where some young girls were. They went on, and came to a stream; there was (practically) no water on the road; the water came (only) up to their ankles. They passed on. They came to where the maidens were, and came and greeted them, and carried them off. They came to the stream and found it full up with water. (Then) they said, 'Ah (when) we passed this water it was not so,' and they said, 'How is this?' One among them said, 'Let us turn back.' The rest said, 'No, we do not go back.' Now they were three, the king of wrestlers, the king of bowmen, and the king of prayer.

وَاَمْرُ قَنَاطُو فِيْنِيمْ اَسْحَارِي شْ

وَاَمُسُ ⁘ اَسْحَارِي ⁘ سُكَنْتِجِمْ ⁘ سَكُوبِيَ ⁘ اُورُونْ

بُمُورِي ⁘ سُكَجِيَ ⁘ سُكَاِ اَسْكَبِيَ ⁘ وَاُوِمْ حَنُمْ ⁘ بَابْ

رُوَا ⁘ رُوَا ⁘ اِيَّا كُمْ ⁘ اِدَا اَفُمْ ⁘ اَسْجُو ⁘ سُكُوشْ ⁘

سُكَاِ اَسْ ⁘ غَمْ فَبُمُورِي ⁘ سُكَجِيَ ⁘ سُكَغِيبُسْ ⁘

سُكَمْ وُكُوسُشْ سُكَمْ وَا ⁘ وُرُفُمْ اُوِمْ ⁘ سُكَاِ

شْبِيَ ⁘ بِيَاشِكَ ⁘ دَرُوَا ⁘ اَسْنُ سُكَشْ ⁘ اَاَفْ اَتِ ⁘

مُنُوشْ ⁘ وُرُفُغْ ⁘ جِيجِمْ ⁘ مَكَبْ ⁘ سُكَشِبْ

تَكَاكَ ⁘ بَجُنْ ⁘ دَتَوْ ⁘ شِكَغُشْ ⁘ بِيَشْمُكُوتَمْ ⁘

اَسْجُوَرَا ⁘ سُكَشْ ⁘ نَعَاعْ ⁘ قِبَا ⁘ مُكُوقَدَا وَا ⁘

اَسْوُكُو ⁘ اَسْوُاُكَجُنْ مُنْ ⁘ دَدَفْنُمْ يَكُنْ ⁘ كُو ⁘

كُوَّ ⁘ دَدَفْسَرْيَكُنْ ⁘ مَعَلُبُلَى ⁘ دَدَفْلِيرِيَهَامْ ⁘

Su-ka-che, 'Kōwa shi yi dabāra gidansu, ta fishe shi.'
Su-ka-che, 'Dan limāmi shi fāra.' Sai [1] ya yi adua,
ya tōfa ga sandarsa, ya buga rūa, rūa ya tsāge,
da shi da budūra tasa su-ka-wuche. Sai rūa ya kōma wada shi ke.
Sai dan sarkin mahalba ya zazage kibau nasa
daga chikin [2] kori, ya jēra su bisa rūa, tun daga
wanan ganga har wanan ganga, ya kōmō, ya dau-
-ki budūra tasa. Su-ka-tāka kan kibau,
su-ka-wuche. Sai ya kōmō, ya tsinche kabausa.
Sauran dan sarkin kōkūa. Shi kūa
ya bidi wada zaa shi yi, ya rasa. Shi bi nan, shi rasa
gurin bi, shi yi wanan dabāra, shi rasa, har ya gaji.

(And) they said, 'Let each try and get out of the difficulty by resorting to his own particular skill.' They said, 'Let the one who is strong in prayer commence.' So he prostrated himself, spat on his staff (and) struck the water; (and) the water opened, and he with his maiden passed over. Then the water returned to where it was. Next the prince of bowmen drew out his arrows from his quiver, he set them in a line on the water, from one bank to another, he returned and lifted up his maiden. They stepped on the arrows, (and) passed over. Then he came back, (and) picked up his arrows. There remained the king of wrestlers. He too sought for what he should do; he could not find a way. He tried this way, (and) failed, he made that plan (and) failed, until he was weary.

لَسِكَبُ كَحُوَرَا : شَيِّعِ بَدَا وَسِغِ عَ فَسُنْ : تَجِبُشِ

سُكَبُ : ءِم فَلِيَا بِجَامِ : شَبَادَوْ : آسُمْ يَمّ آدُءَمِ :

يُشُوقْ : غِمْسَنْءِمْرِلَسُ مِيبُغُوَرَا : رُوَرَا بِيَطْغِمِي

ءِلِشِمْ ءِمْ بُدُ زُوَرَا قُسَفَرْشِ آسِي وُرَا بِيكُومَمْ : وَءِ شِيبَكَسْ

آسِي ءِمْ فُلْسِمْ كِمْنْ : مَعَلْبُنْ مِيءَمْ ءِمْ غِمِي : كِبُوفُلْسُنْ

ءَمْ غِشِكُمْ : كُمْرِ : بِيجِمْ أَلْسُنْ بِسُرُوَرَا : مُنْمُءَمْ غِمْ

وَفُنْ غَمْنْغُوْ : قَمْ وَفُنْ غَمْنْغَى : يَكُو مُوَا : بِيَدُّوْ

كِ : بُمْ زُوَرَا قُسُنْ لَسُكْنَادَك : كَنْكِبُو : ١ =

لَسَكُوبُ : آسِي يَكُو مُوَا : يَطِشُبُ : كَبُوكَسْ

لَسُو وَنْ ءِ فُلْسِرْ كِمْنْ : كَحُوكُو : شِيكُوَّ :

بِيبِجِ : وَءِ ءَمْ أَشِي : بِيمُ مِنْ : شِبِمُنْ : لِشِمُرْسُ :

غُمِ فُبِ : لِشِي وَقَمْ : ءِ بَدَا وَ : لِشِمُرْسُ : قَمْ يَغْجَمْ

Sai ya yi fushi, ya kāma budrua tasa, da kō-
-kūa ya nada mata hardīa, su-ka-tuma, su-ka-yi
bisa, ba su fādi ba, sai bākin ganga. Tō,
chikinsu wa ya fi dan uwansa? Idan ba-ka-san wanda
ya fi ba, shi ke nan. [3] Kungurus kan kūsu.

Then he got in a rage, (and) seized his maiden, and with a wrestling trick twisted his leg round hers (and) they jumped, (and) rose in the air, (and) did not fall, except on the edge of the (far) bank. Now among them who was better than another? If you do not know who was least, there you are. Off with the rat's head.

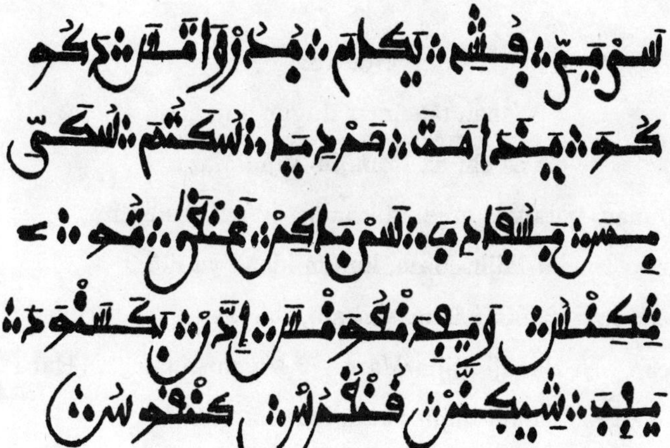

No. 12.

Wanan tātsūnīar dugun dāji che,

da shi da Namijin-Mijin-Maza.

[1] Gātanan, gātanan, ta je, ta kōmō. Wani mutun ne, sūnansa Namiji-Mijin-Maza, kulum idan [2] ya fitō dāji shi kan daukō itāche, shi tafō, shi yas, shi che, 'Ni Namiji-Mijin-Maza.' [3] Maatarsa ta che, 'Haba bari fadi kai namiji-mijin-maza, idan ka gani namiji-mijin-maza, [4] kaa gudu.' Sai shi che, 'Karīa ne.' Yau hakanan hakanan kulum, idan [5] yā kāwō itāche, sai shi yas da karfī, shi che, 'Ni Namiji-Mijin-Maza.' [6] Maatar ta che, 'Haba bari fadi hakanan, idan [7] kā gani

---

This story is about a forest giant, about him and a man called, A-Man-among-Men. A story, a story. Let it go, let it come. There was a certain man by name, A-Man-among-Men, always when he came from the bush he used to lift up a tree (and) come, (and) throw (it down), and say, 'I am A-Man-among-Men.' His wife said, 'Come now, leave off saying you are a-man-among-men; if you saw a-man-among-men you would run.' But he said, 'It is a lie.' Now it was always so, if he has brought in wood, then he would throw it down with force, (and) say, 'I am A-Man-among-Men.' The wife said, 'Come now, leave off saying so; if you have seen

وَقَّمْ قَمَا صُوفِيَّيْ ؞ دُ غَفْدَ اجَبْ

دَشِمْ ؞ دَنَبِجْ ؞ مِجَنْفَدَا

قَمَا تَنَّ قَمَا قَنَّ قَبِجُ ؞ تَكُومُوا ؞ وَنِفُتَفْبَلْ
بُسُو فَنْلَسَ ؞ نَبِجْ مِجَنْفَدَا ؞ كُلُمْ ؞ إِدَّنْ ؞ يَبِقُوا ؞
دَاجْ ؞ شِكَفْدَ وُكُوا ؞ إِلقَادَبْ ؞ شِتَقُبُوا ؞ شِيَشْ
شِشَبْ فِيبِنَجْ ؞ مِجَنْفَعَ ا ؞ قَدَاقُتَرْلَسْ ؞ قَبْ قَبَّ ؞
بَمْ قِجِ ؞ كَنِنِمِجْ ؞ مِجَنْفَدَا ؞ إِدَّنْ ؞ كَقَنِمْ ؞
نَبِجْ ؞ مِجَنْفَدَا ؞ كُدْ اُغُدُ ؞ آسْ شِشَبْ ؞ قُدْ يَدَابِي
يَبُو قَكَنَّ قَكَنَّ شْ كُلُمْ ؞ إِدَّنْ ؞ يَدَكَدُ وُإِقَدَبْ
لَسْ شِيبَشْ دَكَرْ قِجْ ؞ شِشَبْ ؞ فِيبَنِجْ ؞ مِجَنْفَدَا
؞ قَدَاقُتَرْ ؞ قَبْ قَبَّ ؞ بَمْ قِجِ قَكَنَّ ؞ إِدَّنْ ؞ كَدَاعَنِمْ ؞

namiji-mijin-maza, kaa gudu.' Sai shi che, 'Karīa ne.' Yau
ranan maatarsa ta tafi raafi, ta je gurin wata rījīa;
[8] wasakin rījīan mutun gōma ke jāwō shi.
Ta je, ta rasa rūa, sai ta kōma. Zaa ta gida, ta gamu
da wata mache, ta che, 'Ina zaa ki da kworīa, bābu rūa?'
Ta che, 'Nā je, nā gani gūga nan, ba ni iya jansa,
shi ya sa ina-kōmāwa gida.' Sai maatar nan,
da ke da yārō nan, ta che, 'Mu kōma ki sāmu.'
Ta che, 'Tō.' Sai su-ka-kōma tāre wurin rījīa.
Maatar nan, da ke da yārō, ta che yārō shi dauki
wasaki, shi dēbō rūa, [9] yāron kūa kankane ne,
bai wuche gōyō ba. Sai ya dauki gūga
nan da nan, ya nasa rījīa, ya jāwō rūa. Su-ka-chika

---

a man-among-men, you would run.' But he said, 'It is a lie.' Now one day his wife went to the stream. She came to a certain well; the well bucket, ten men were (necessary to) draw it up. She came, (but) had to do without the water, so she turned back. She was going home, when she met another woman (who) said, 'Where are you going with a calabash, with no water?' She said, 'I have come and seen a bucket there. I could not draw it; that is what caused me to turn back home.' And this (second) woman, who had this (a) son, said, 'Let us return that you may find (water).' She said, 'All right.' So they returned together to the well. This woman, who had the son, told the boy to lift the bucket and draw water. Now the boy was small, not past the age when he was carried on his mother's back. Then he lifted the bucket then and there, and put it in the well, (and) drew up the water. They filled

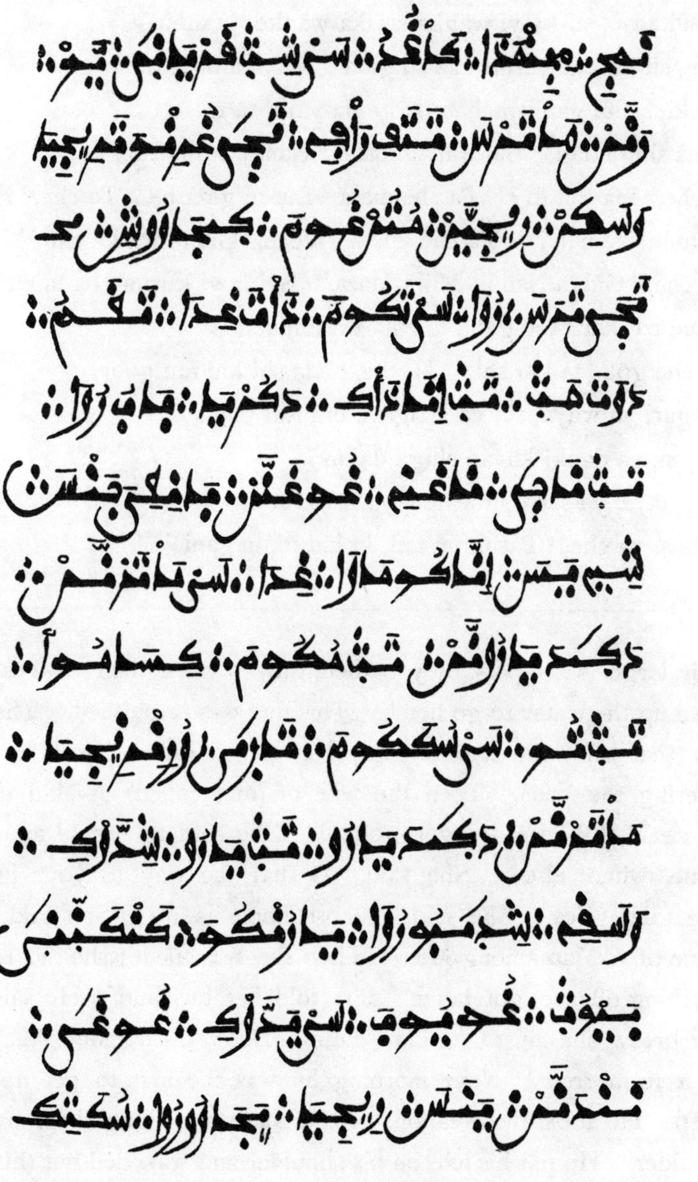

masukansu, su-ka-yi wanka, su-ka-wanke [10] zannua--nsu, su-ka-dauki rūa, zaa su gida. Wanan ta-na-mā--māki, sai ta gani wachan da ke da yārō, tā rātse, ta na shiga dāji. Sai wanan maatar Namiji-Mijin-Maza ta che, 'Ina zaa ki?' Ta che mata, 'Zaa ni gida ne.' Ta che, 'Hainya gidanku ke nan?' Ta che, 'I.' Ta che, 'Gidan wa ke nan?' Ta che, 'Gidan Namiji-Mijin-Maza.' Sai ta yi kurum, ba ta che kōme ba, har ta je gida, ta gaia wa mijinta. Ya che gōbe ta kai shi. Ta che, 'Ala shi kai mu gōbe.' Da gari ya wāye, shi ya [11] rigāye ta tāshi daga kwāna, ya dauki kāyan shiga dājinsa. Ya rātaya, ya saba gātarinsa, ya tāshe ta daga kwāna, ya che, 'Tāshi mu tafi, ki kai ni, in gani

---

their large water-pots, they bathed, they washed their clothes, they lifted up the water to go home. This one was astonished. Then she saw that one who had the boy has turned off the path and was entering the bush. Then the wife of (him called) A-Man-among-Men said, 'Where are you going?' She said to her, 'I am going home, where else?' She said, 'Is that the way to your home?' She said, 'Yes.' She said, 'Whose home is it?' She said, 'The home of A-Man-among-Men.' Then she was silent; she did not say anything till she got home. She told her husband. He said that to-morrow she must take him (there). She replied, 'May Allah give us a to-morrow.' Next morning he was the first to get up from sleep. He took the weapons of the chase and slung them over his shoulder. He put his axe on his shoulder and wakened her (his wife) from sleep. He said, 'Get up, let us go. Take me that I may see,

مسكنس نسكين .. ونكن .. نسكو فجكي .. طلنو

فمس نسكد وك .. ووا .. دا سغدا .. ونم قنا امه

قاك .. تسن قغيم .. وقم .. دبكد بيه زو .. قدوا جس

تقدا شقو دام .. سن وقن ما قن نيم .. بجنقدا ..

تبا اقادا ك .. تب مد .. دا غدا امي .. تبا حنى

غد نك .. يكن تبا ي .. تبا غد قوا بكن

تبا غد قنيم .. بجنقدا .. سن قم كرم .. بتب

كو قب .. حم تجي غدا .. قيادوا .. بجنت ..

يبا غو بي .. تكيش .. تبا ان شكيم غو بي

.. دغمي .. يوابي .. شم يم غا يبت .. قداشن دغ

كو امي .. يم وك .. كا يتشكو .. دا جسن ..

يم اقيا .. يلسم .. غا قم قلن .. يتا بشت .. دغ

كو امي .. يب قاشن متبي .. يكيبن ازغنم

in gani Namiji-Mijin-Maza.' Ta tāshi, ta dauki masakinta, ta wuche gaba. Shi-na-binta har su-ka-kai, bākin rījīa. Su-ka-yi katar kūa. Su na zūa, maatar Namiji-Mijin-Maza ta zō, da ita da danta. Su-ka-gaishe ta, sai maatar wanan ta goda masa gūga, ta che, 'Dauki ka dēbō mani rūa.'
Sai ya je, ya dauki gūga, da fushi, ya nasa
chikiṇ rījīa, sai gūga ta ja shi, zaa shi fāda rījīa,
sai yārō kankane, ya kāma shi, da shi da guga,
ya fisgō, ya yas waje. Sai yārō ya dauki gū-
-ga, ya sainya chikin rījīa, ya dēbō rūa. Su-ka-chika tūlunansu. Maatarsa ta che, 'Kā che ka-na-zūa ka gani Namiji-Mijin-Maza, kā gani maatarsa ke nan, da dansa, idan ka-na-zūa, ku je tāre, ni ba ni zūa.' Uwar yārō ta che,

---

that I may see the (one called) A-Man-among-Men.' She got up, lifted her large water-pot, and passed on in front. He was following her until they got to the edge of the well. Now they found what they sought indeed. (As) they were coming, the wife of A-Man-among-Men came up, both she and her son. They greeted her, and the wife of this one showed him the bucket (and) said, 'Lift it and draw water for me.' So he went and lifted the bucket in a rage and let it down the well; but the bucket pulled him, (and) he would have fallen into the well, when the little boy seized him, both him and the bucket, and drew (out) and threw them on one side. Then the boy lifted up the bucket, put it in the well, drew water, and filled their water-pots. His wife said, 'You have said you are going to see him called A-Man-among-Men. You have seen this is his wife and son. If you still want to go you can go together. As for me, I am not going.' The boy's mother said,

إِرِنْ فِيَّ ∴ نِمِجِ ∴ مُحَمَّدَا ∴ قَتَاشِ ∴ قَدَرُوكِ مَسَكِنْتَا ∴

تَوُفْ ∴ عَبَ شِنَا مِنْتَا ∴ حَرْ لُسَكِكَنْ ∴ بَدَا كِنْرِ يِجِيَا ∴

سَكِي كُنْتَرْكُو ∴ لَسَفَدَ دُوَرَ ∴ مَدَاقُرْ نِمِجِ ∴ مُحَمَّدَا ∴ قَدَرُوا ∴

دَإِتَ دَ دَمْقَ ∴ لَسَكَفِيشَتَ ∴ لَسْ مَدَاقُرْ فَقَّرْ ∴ قَدَرَا

مَسَنْ ∴ غُوغُو ∴ قَبْ دَرُوكِ ∴ عَجَ مَجُوقَنْ ∴ وُرَا ∴

لَسْ يَجِي يَدُوكِ ∴ غُو غُو ∴ دَ فِشِمْ ∴ يَنَّسَنْ ∴ =

ثِكِنْ رِجِيَا ∴ لَسْ غُو غُو ∴ تُجَاشِنْ دَأَيْنْ قَادَرْ ∴ رِجِيَا

لَسْ يَدَاوُرْ ∴ فَنْفُبِي ∴ يَكَ مَدَاشِنْ دَشِيدْ غُو غُو ∴

يِبِنْ غُوَا ∴ يِيَّشْ وَرَجِي ∴ لَسْ يَدَاوُرْ شِيَدُّوكِ ∴ غُو

غُو ∴ يِسَنِيَا ∴ ثِكِنْ رِيجِيَا ∴ يَجِ مَجُوقُرَا ∴ لَسَكِنِكَ

تُولُقَسَنْ مَدَاقُرْسَ ∴ قَبْ كَدَا فُ ∴ كَفَدَ دَوَ ∴ كَ عُفِمِ

نِمِجِ ∴ مُحَمَّدَا ∴ كَدَاغِ ∴ مَدَاقُرْسَ بِكُنْ ∴ دَدَمْسَ

إِدَّوُ ∴ كَفَدَ دَوَ ∴ كِجَتَارُ شِ فِيتَا مُغَدَا ∴ عَمُرْ يَدَاوُ قَبْ

'A me ya fāru? Kad ka je.' [12] Ya che yaa je, ta che, 'Mu je.'
Su-ka-tafi. Da su-ka-je, sai ta goda masa [13] rufēwa
na māna, ya shiga. Shi kūa mai-gida ba shi gida;
[14] yā tafi dāji. Ta che, 'Kā gani yā tafi dāji, ama kar
ka yi mōtsi idan yā zō.' Ya zamna chiki,
har marēche ya yi. Mai-gidan ya zō. Shi-na-fadi
'[15] Ina-ji(n) wārin mutun.' Maatarsa ta che, 'Akwai wani mutun
nan, ba ni ba?' Hakanan idan ya che shi-na-jin wārin mutun,
sai ta che, 'Akwai wani mutun nan, ba ni ba? Idan
ka-na-sō ka chinye ni ne, tō, bābu kōwa,
sai ni.' Shi kūa kāto ne, magananfa kamar
hadari, gīwa gōma shi ke chi. Idan gari ya
wāye, shi kare kumalō da guda daia, kāna

'Oh, what is the matter? You had better not come.' (But) he said he would come; and she said, 'Let us be off.' They set out. When they arrived (at the house) then she showed him a place for storing meat, (and) he got inside. Now he, the master of the house, was not at home; he has gone to the bush. She (his wife) said, 'You have seen he has gone to the bush; but you must not stir if he has come.' He sat inside till evening came. The master of the house came. He keeps saying, 'I smell the smell of a man.' His wife said, 'Is there another person here? It is not I.' Thus, if he said he smelled the smell of a man, then she would say, 'Is there another person here. Is it not I? If you want to eat me up, well and good, for there is no one else but I.' Now he was a huge man, his words like a tornado; ten elephants he would eat. When dawn came, he made his morning meal of one; then

عما بيا قادر ∴ تكر كجي ∴ ميبث يأجن ∴ تنبا ميس

شكتبم ∴ د لسكجي قسر تقد امسن ∴ زجكوا ∴ =

تنام ∴ ميشغ ∴ شيكو ∴ قيفدن ∴ مداشغد / ∴

يافقدا ∴ تثكد غنم ∴ ميدا تقدا ∴ آمد كم

كمو ط ∴ إكرن ∴ ميدا فرا ∴ ميدم من ∴ تكم ∴

تم صنر مث ∴ ميم مينفدن ∴ ميدو ∴ شنا فحي ∴

إلما ثوا نفش ∴ مشرس ∴ تث أكوبو قفشم ∴

فر با فيب ∴ تكفر إكرن ∴ ميابث ∴ لشغا جن ∴ وا نفش

اسن قث ∴ أكويو نفشن ∴ فر با فيب ∴ إكرن ∴

كنا لسو ∴ كتنيمن ∴ ثو ∴ ماب كورا ∴

سبينم ∴ شيكو ∴ كا قوبي ∴ ففنس ∴ كمر

تدر ∴ غيوا ∴ غوتم ∴ شبكي ∴ إدر غمر ميد

وايمن ∴ شكبر كملو ∴ دغدادتن ∴ كان ∴ =

shi tafi dāji, idan [16] daa ya gani mutume nan, daa ya kashe shi. Yau shi-na chikin runbu yā bōye. Maatar mai-gidan ta gaia masa ta che, ' Kar ka yi mōtsi har shi yi kwāna, idan kā gani wuri da dufu, bai yi kwāna ba, idan kā gani wuri yā yi kashe, yā yi kwāna ke nan, ka fita ka gudu.' Ana-nan sai ya gani wuri yā yi haske kamar rāna. Sai ya fita. Shi-na-gudu, shi-na--gudu har gari ya wāye, shi-na-gudu, har rāna ta fitō shi-na-gudu, bai tsāya ba. Sai mutume nan ya falka daga kwāna, sai ya che, ' Ina-jin wārin mutun, ina--jin wārin mutun.' Ya tāshi, ya bi wurin da mutume nan ya bi. Shi-na-gudu. Shi kuma, wa(n)chan, shi-na-gudu

---

he went to the bush, and if he should see a person there he would kill him. Now he (A Man-among-Men) was in the store-house, hidden. The man's wife told him, saying, ' You must not move till he is asleep. If you have seen the place dark, he is not asleep; if you have seen the place light, that is a sign he is asleep; come out and fly.' Shortly after he saw the place has become light like day, so he came out. He was running, he was running, until dawn, he was running, till the sun rose he was running, he did not stand. Then that man woke up from sleep and he said, ' I smell the smell of a man, I smell the smell of a man.' He rose up, he followed where the man had gone. He was running. He also, the other one, was running

لِشَفِ دَامِ ؞ إِدَنْ دَأْ ؞ بَقَنِ مُتُمْتَنْ ؞ دَ أَيِدَ كَبْشِيشْ

يَوْ شَنَا تِكَنْ رُفْبُوأْ ؞ يَابُجُ وِپِي ؞ مَدَاقَنْ مَيْغِدَنْ

تَفِيَا مَسَنْ مَتَبْ كَمْ كَتِّ مُوطِمِ ؞ حَمْ شِيَّكُ وَافَمَنْ ؞

إِكَزْكَ اغَنِم ؞ وُرِي ؞ دَمْ دَفْ ؞ بَمِنْ كُوَافَ دَبَ ؞ إِدَنْ زَكَ

غَنِم ؞ وُرِي يَاتِّي ؞ حَسْكِنْ يَا تِّي كُوَافَمْ ؞ بِكَنْ

بَجِتَ ؞ كَغُدَ ؞ أَفَا قَنْ ؞ لَسْ يَقَنِ وُرِي ؞ يَاتِّي ؞

حَسْكِنْ ؞ كَحَمْ رَافَمْ ؞ لَسْ يَجِتَ شِنَا غُدَ ؞ شِنَا

غُدَ ؞ حَمْ غُمْرِي يَوَاپِي ؞ شِنَا غُدَ ؞ حَمْ رَافَسُو ؞

تَبُتُوا ؞ شِنَا غُدَ ؞ بِمْ طَيَابَ ؞ لَسْ مُتَبَنْتَنْ ؞ يَقَلْكَ

دَغُكُوَافَمْ ؞ لَسْ مِيَتْ إِفَا جِمْ ؞ وَارْ فُغْتَنْ ؞ إِفَا

جِمْ ؞ وَارْ فُغْتَنْ ؞ يَمْتَا الشْ ؞ يَبِ وُرْفَدَ مُتَبَّسَنْ

يَبِ ؞ شِنَا غُدَ ؞ شِيكُحَمْ ؞ وُقَنْ شِنَا غُدَ ؞

har ya tarda masu-[17]sasabe, su-ka-che me ya fāru. Ya che, 'Wani mutun ya kōrō ni.' Su-ka-che, 'Tsāye nan har shi tafō.' Zūa anjima, sai iskansa ya zō, shi-na-daukansu, shi-na-kaiyaswa. Sai ya che, 'Tō iskansa ke nan, tukuna shi dakaisa bai zō ba, idan ku-na-iyāwa ku gaia mani, idan ba ku iyāwa ku gaia mani.' Su-ka-che, 'Yi gaba.' Sai ya shēka da gudu, ya je ya iske wadansu, su-na-[18]fūda. Su-ka-che, 'Me ya kōrō ka?' Ya che, 'Wani mutun ya kōrō ni.' Su-ka-che, 'Wani irin mutun ya kōrō kamanka.' Ya che, 'Wani ne wai shi Namiji-Mijin-Maza.' Su-ka-che, 'Ba Mijin-Maza ba, Mijin-Māta, tsāya har shi tafō.' Ya tsaya. Shi-na-nan, iskansa ya zō, shi-na-tunkude

---

till he met some people who were clearing the ground for a farm, (and) they asked what had happened. And he said, 'Some one chased (is chasing) me.' They said, 'Stand here till he comes.' A short time passed, and the wind caused by him came; it lifted them (and) cast them down. And he said, 'Yes, that is it, the wind he makes (running); he himself has not yet come. If you are able (to withstand him) tell me. If you are not able, say so.' And they said, 'Pass on.' So he ran off, and came and met some people hoeing. They said, 'What chased (is chasing) you?' He replied, 'Some one pursued (is pursuing) me.' They said, 'What kind of a man chased (is chasing) (one) such as you.' He said, 'Some one who says he is A-Man-among-Men. They said, 'Not a man-among-men, a man-among-women. Stand till he comes.' He stood. Here he was when the wind of him came, it was pushing about

جَمْ مِتْرِدَ ∴ قَدانْ لَسَمِي ∴ لِسكُثْ ∴ مِجَادُرُ ∴

مِبْ وَفِفْتُنْ ∴ يَكُوزُرُنْ لَسكُثْ ∴ طِيَا قَمْ ∴ جَمْ

ثُسَتَبُوا ∴ دُوَا ∴ أَفْجَمَ ∴ تَسِنْ إِلْسَكَفْسَنْ مِيخُوَا ∴

ثِنَادُ وَكَنْفْسَنْ ثِنَاكَدَ مِيسُوَا ∴ آسَنْ يَبُثْ ثُو

∴ إِلْسَكَنْلَنْ ∴ بِكَنْمْ ∴ تُكُمْ ∴ ثِمْ دَكَنْيَسْ ∴ قِنْجُوَا

إِدُّنْ ∴ كَنْدَا عِيَدَوَا ∴ كُغِيَامِرْ ∴ إِدَّنْ ∴ مَدَا كَعِيَاوَا

كُغِيَامِرْ ∴ لَسكُثْ ∴ يَغُبْ ∴ تَسَنْ يَيشَكْ ∴ دَغُدْ

مِجِي مِيَ إِلْسَكَنْ ∴ وَدَفْسَنْ ∴ لَسَنَا فُودَا ∴ لَسكُثْ

مِيَكُدُ وُرَكْ ∴ مِبُثْ وَنْفُتُنْ ∴ يَكُوزُرُنْ ∴ سَ

لَسكُثْ ∴ وَفِدِ وَنْفُتُنْ ∴ مِيكُوزُرُوَا كَمْنَكْ ∴ مِبُثْ

وَفِنْبُنْ ∴ وَمِيشَمْ ∴ نِمِجْ ∴ مِجِنْفُدَا ∴ لَسكُثْ

بَا مِجِنْفُدَابُ ∴ مِجْمْ مَادَا نْتَا ∴ طِيَاجَمْ ∴ ثِتَبُو

يَطِيَ ∴ ثِنَا قَمْ ∴ إِلْسَكَفْسَنْ ∴ يَجُوَا ∴ ثِنَا نْتَكُمْرُ

māsu-nōma. Sai ya che, 'Kun gani iskansa ke nan,
19 takuna shi dakaisa bai tafō ba, idan ku-na-iyāwa,
ku gaia mani, idan ba ku iyāwa, ku gaia mani.' Sai su-ka-che,
'Yi gaba'; sai ya shēka da gudu. Shi-na-gudu ya iske māsu-
-shibka. Su-ka-che, 'Me ka kewa gudu?' Ya che, 'Wani ya kōrō ni.'
Su-ka-che, 'Wane irin mutun ne ya kōrō kamanka?' Ya che,
'Sunansa Namiji-Mijin-Maza.' Su-ka-che, 'Zamna nan
shi zō.' Yaa zamna. Aka-jima kadan sai iskansa ya zō.
Shi-na-daukansu, shi-na-kāyaswa. Sai su-ka-che, 'Wane irin
iska ne haka?' Shi, mutume nan da aka-kōrō shi,
ya che, 'Iskansa ke nan.' Sai su-ka-che, 'Yi gaba.' Su-ka-yāda
abin shibka, su-ka-shiga dāji, su-ka-bōye,

---

the men who were hoeing. So he said, 'You have seen, that is the wind he makes; he has not yet come himself. If you are a match for him tell me; if not say so.' And they said, 'Pass on'; and off he ran. He was running. He came across some people sowing; they said, 'What are you running for?' He said, 'Some one chased (is chasing) me.' And they said, 'What kind of a man is it who chased (is chasing) the like of you?' He said, 'His name is A-Man-among-Men.' They said, 'Sit here till he comes.' He sat down. In a short time the wind he made came (and) it lifted them and cast them down. And they said, 'What kind of wind is that?' He, the man who was being pursued, said, 'It is his wind.' And they said, 'Pass on.' They threw away the sowing implements, (and) went into the bush (and) hid,

مداسفو مو : لس ميث كنغنم :: اسكنسن بجنن

تكندا اشي :: دم كنيسن : ميسقواب :: ادون كندا عيدا وارا ::

كفيا ممن : ادون : مدا كعيدا وارا :: كفيا ممن : لس سكب :: ب

يقب : سع بيثنك :: دم غمد : بشندا غد :: بير اسكبي : مداس

شبك :: اسكب :: بمكجوا اغد :: بيب ونيكو رون ::

لسكب :: وبد ارو : مستن فسو : بكورو كمنك :: بيب

موقنسن نعج : معنفد ا :: لسكب :: دمندا قمن

شدورا : بد ممن : اكجم كدون : لس اسكنسن : مدورا

لقندا دو كنسن : شندا كدا بسوا :: مس سكب :: وبدارون

اسكدا بن : تك :: شيفنجقن : داك كوو وش =

ميب اسكنسن بجنن لس سكت :: يقب :: سلكيا د

امنشبك :: سكيشع :: داج :: لسكبو بين :: =

shi kūa wanchan shi-na-gudu. Ya je, ya tarda wani gawurtachen mutun, shi kadai gutsun kūka shi-na-zamne.
Ya [20] kasō giwāye, shi-na-banda, shi kūa, gīwa
ishirin shi ke chi, da sāfe shi karia kumalō da bīar.
sūnansa, Dungun-Dāji. Sai ya tanbaye shi, ya che,
'Ina zaa ka da gudu?' Ya che, 'Namiji-Mijin-Maza ya kōrō ni.'
Sai Dungun-Dāji ya che, 'Tafō, zamna har shi zō.'
Ya zamna. Aka-jima iskan Namiji-Mijin-Maza ya zō,
ya dauke shi, zaa shi da shi, sai Dungun-Dāji ya būga
tsāwa ya che, 'Kōmō.' Ya che, 'Ba ni dakaina ke tafia ba,
iskan mutume nan ke dauka na.' Sai Dungun-Dāji ya yi fushi.
Ya tashi, ya kāmō [21] hannunsa, ya sainya karkashin

---

but that one was running on. He came (and) met a certain huge man; he was sitting alone at the foot of a baobab tree. He had killed elephants and was roasting them, as for him, twenty elephants he could eat; in the morning he broke his fast with five. His name was 'The Giant of the Forest.' Then he questioned him and said, 'Where are you going in all this haste?' And he said, 'A-Man-among-Men chased (is chasing) me.' And the Giant of the Forest said, 'Come here, sit down till he comes.' He sat down. They waited a little while. Then a wind made by A-Man-among-Men came, and lifted him, (and) was about to carry him off, when the Giant of the Forest shouted to him to come back. And he said, 'It is not I myself who am going off, the wind caused by the man is taking me away.' At that the Giant of the Forest got in a rage, he got up and caught his hand, and placed it under

شِبِكُو ۔ وَرْفَشَرْ ۔ شِنَا غُدُ ۔ فِجِي مِتَرْ دَ ۔ وَرْفِغَا وُزْ تَبْشَرْ

مُثْرِ ۔ شِبِكَ سُ ۔ غُوطَرْ ۔ كُوكِ ۔ شِنَا دَ مُبِنْ

يَا كَسُوا ۔ فِيوَا اِكِ ۔ شِنَا بِفْدَ ۔ شِبِكُو ۔ غِيوَا

عِشِرِ ۔ شِبِيشِ ۔ دَ تَسَا فِكِ ۔ شِكَرَ ۔ كُمَلُو ۔ دَبِيَرْ

سُو فَلْفَشَ دُ مُغُنْ دَرَ اِجِ ۔ تَسُنْ يَتَنْ بِيشِ ۔ يِبَ

اِتَلَا دَ أَكِ ۔ دَ غُدُ ۔ يِبَ نَهِج مِنْفَدَا ۔ يَكُو وُزْ نُكُ

سُنْ دَ مُغُنْ دَرَ اِجِ ۔ يِبَ تَفْوَا دَ فَنَا ۔ حَرْ شِدُوَا

يِدْ مَرَ أَكِحَ ۔ اِسْكَرْ نَهِج مِنْفَدَا ۔ يِدُوَا

يَدَ وُكَكَشِ دَ أَشِرْ دَ يَشِ ۔ تَسُنْ دُ مُغُنْ دَرَ اِجِ ۔ يِبَغِ

طَدَ وَا ۔ يِبَ كُو فُوَا ۔ يِبَ بَدَلِيدَ كَبْنِتْ كَتَفِيَا بِ

اِسْكَرْ مُثْبَتَرْ ۔ يَدَ وُكَدَوَشِ تَسُنْ دَ مُغُنْ دَرَ اِجِ يِسُنْ فُشِ

يَتَلاشِ ۔ يَكَ مُوَا ۔ فَنْفُفَسُ ۔ يِبِشِيَا كَنْ كَيْشِنْ

chinyasa. Shi-na-zamne har Namiji-Mijin-Maza ya zō, ya che, 'Kai wa ke zamne, masu-rai, kō masu--mutūa?' Sai Dungun-Dāji ya che, 'Karanbani garē--ka.' Sai Namiji-Mijin-Maza ya che, 'Idan ka-na-sō ka sāmu lāfia, ba ni ajiana.' Sai Dungun-Dāji ya che, 'Tafō ka dauki.' Sai ya yi fushi, ya zaabura, ya kāma shi. Su-na-kōkūa. Da su-ka-nada ma majuna hardia, su-ka-tuma, su-ka-yi bisa. Har wa yau su-na-chan, su-na-kōkūa. Idan sun gaji, su za--mna, su fūta, idan sun tāshi kōkūa, shi ne ka kan ji chida chikin samau, su ne su ke kō--kūa. Shi kūa, wanchan, ya sāmu kansa, ya je gida, shi-na-bāda lābāri. Sai maatarsa

---

his thigh. He was sitting until A-Man-among-Men came up and said, 'You sitting there, are you of the living, or of the dead?' And the Giant of the Forest said, 'You are interfering.' And A-Man-among-Men said, 'If you want to find health give up to me what you are keeping there.' And the Giant of the Forest said, 'Come and take (him).' And at that he flew into a rage and sprang and seized him. They were struggling together. When they had twisted their legs round one another they leaped up into the heavens. Till this day they are wrestling there; when they are tired out they sit down and rest; and if they rise up to struggle that is the thunder you are wont to hear in the sky; it is they struggling. He also, that other one, found himself (escaped), and went home, and told the tale. And his wife

شُيُسَ شُنَا دَ فَقَّنْ ⁖ فَرْنَجِ مِجِنَمْدَا ⁖ يِغُرَا ⁖

يِشِكَوْ ⁖ وَارَكَ دَ فَبْنِي ⁖ مَسُورِيْ ⁖ كُوَ مَسُو

مُشُوَ ⁖ سَنْ دُ مُغُرْ دَاجِ ⁖ يِشِ كَرْ قَبَانْمِ ⁖ غَمِ

لَكَ ⁖ سَنْ نَمِجِ ⁖ بِجِنَمْدَا ⁖ يِجِ إِدَّرْ ⁖ نَمَنْدَا سُو ⁖

كَسَانْ ⁖ لَابِقُو ⁖ بَادُوْ ⁖ أَجِيَا قُو ⁖ سَنْ دُ مُغُرْ دَاجِ

يِشِ ⁖ قَبُوَا ⁖ كَدَّ وُكِ ⁖ سَنْ يِمُوْ فِشِنْ ⁖ يِزَا يِرَ ⁖

يَكَا مَدَا شِنْ ⁖ سُنَا كُوكُوَ ⁖ دُ سُمَكَنْدَا مِجُوْمَا

قَرْ دِيَا ⁖ سُكُشُمَ ⁖ سُكَنِّ مِلَنْ ⁖ قَرْ وَبَّوْا ⁖

سُنَا قَرْ ⁖ سُنَا كُوكُوَ ⁖ إِدَّرْ ⁖ سُنَاغِجِ ⁖ سُنَجِ

مَرَ ⁖ سُبُقُوتَ ⁖ إِدَّرْ ⁖ سُنَنْتَا شِنْ كُوكُوَّ ⁖ شِيبِنِي

كُكَنْجِ ⁖ شِدَ شِكَمْ ⁖ سَمَدَا ⁖ سُو قِبِّي ⁖ سُبَكَكُو

كُوَ ⁖ شِيكُوَ ⁖ وَاقَمْ ⁖ مِسَانْ ⁖ كَمَسَنْ ⁖

يَجِمَ نَمْدَا ⁖ شِنَا بِدَا لَابِدَا ⁖ سَنْ هَا قَمْ مَنْ

ta che, 'Dōmin hakanan ni ke gaia maka, kulum kōmi
ka ke yi, [22] dinga ragāwa. Idan [23] karfī, idan sarauta,
idan kurdi, idan tsīa, ka ke takama, duka dai,
wani ya fi ka, ka che, karīa ne, gā shi, [24] kā gani
da idānunka.' [25] Kungurus kan kūsu.

---

said, 'That is why I was always telling you whatever you do, make little of it. Whether it be you excel in strength, or in power, or riches, or poverty, and are puffed up with pride, it is all the same; some one is better than you. You said, it was a lie. Behold, your own eyes have seen.' Off with the rat's head.

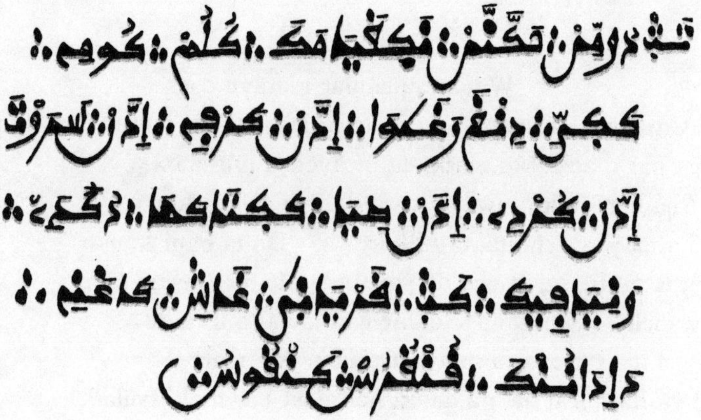

No. 13.

Wanan tātsūnīar marāyu che.

[1] Gātanan, gātanan. Ta je, ta kōmō. Wani mutun [2] ya mutu
ya bar dīansa bīū maza, da uwāyensu bīū mātā.
Ana-nan chikin uwāye māta daia ta sāmu chīwō.
Ta-na-jinya chiuta, ta ki karēwa. Da ta gani kamar
[3] taa mutu, sai ta che da yar uwa tata, ai [4] kīshīa tata,
wanche, 'Kin gani [5] chiutar nan tawa ta ki karē-
-wa, na san zaa ni mutūa ne, idan Ala taala
[6] yā karbi rai na, ga danki nan, [7] nā bar maki taulafi,
dōmin Ala da anabi.' Ta che, 'Tō, nā ji.' Ana-nan sai
ranan ta mutu, yārō kūa ba shi da wāyō. Aka-yi kō-
-mi da kōmi aka-gama. Aka-yi kwānaki bāyan
mutūanta, ana-nan danta da dan wachan su-na-

This story is about orphans. A story, a story. Let it go. Let it come. A certain man died and left two sons, and their mothers, two women. Then among the mothers one fell sick. She was taking medicine for her illness, (but) it refused to mend. When she saw she was apparently going to die; then she said to her sister, that one (her late husband's) second wife, 'You have seen this illness of mine will not go away. I know I am going to die, when Allah, the exalted one, has taken my life from me, behold there is a son (lit. your son) I have left to you and put in your charge, for the sake of Allah and the prophets.' She said, 'It is well, I have heard.' And it came to pass the day came when she died, and the boy had not reached an age when he had full knowledge. Then the funeral rites were completed. Some time passed after her death. Now her son and the son of the other (woman) possessed

وَقَّرْ قَتَا طُوفِيَّرْ ؞ مَرَابُوثْ

نَمَا قَنَّنْ ؞ نَغَدَ قَنَّنْ تَجِي تَكُومُوا ؞ وَنِقَنْ ؞ يَمُتَ

يَجَبْ ؞ دِيَقَنْ ؞ بِيُو مَدَا ؞ دَعُوَابِرْسَ ؞ بِيُو مَاقَدَ ؞

أَقَّا قَنْ ؞ تِكِنْ ؞ عُوَابِنْ مَدَاتَا ؞ دَتَّ ؞ قَلْدَامْ ؞ قِيُو ؞

تَقَاجِمْنَ ؞ قِنُوقَلِي ؞ تَكَدَبْرُ مَوَا ؞ دَقَنْغِمْ ؞ كَمَرَ

تَأُمُثْ ؞ اَسِنْ قَبْتَ ؞ دَبِّرْ عُوَاقَتَ ؞ أَيْ كِيبِيَتِيَا قَتَ ؞

وَقْبَن ؞ يَكَنْغِمْ ؞ نِقُوقَتَرْ قَنْ ؞ قَدَاوُ ؞ قَدَكِ ؞ كَدَبُ

بَوَا ؞ قَدَ اسَوُ ؞ دَأُونْ ؞ مُتُوَابِقَّ ؞ إِلَّارَنْ ؞ أَلَّ ؞ تَقَدَالَي

يَدَكُرْبِ ؞ وَقِيقَدَا ؞ غَدَ نِكَنْ ؞ قَدَ بِرْ مَكِ ؞ قَوُلَبِ

دُوقِّنْ ؞ أَلَّ ؞ دَأَقَّبِ ؞ قَبْتُو ؞ قَدَاجِ ؞ أَقَدَ قَنْ ؞ اَسِنْ

وَقَنْ ؞ تَمُتَ ؞ بِيَارُوكُوَّ ؞ بَدَاتِدَ وَرَابِيُوَا ؞ أَعِرْ كُو

مِ ؞ دَحُومِ ؞ أَكَعَمَ ؞ أَكِنْ كُوَا قَكِمِ ؞ بَدَابِّنْ

مُتُوقْتَ ؞ أَقَدَ قَنْ ؞ عَقَتَ ؞ دَدَقُوقَنْ ؞ يُسَدَ

da kāji, su-na-kīwō, nasa guda, na marāya guda.
Ranan ta dauki sanda, ta buge na marāya da gangan,
ta kashe, ba shi gida. Da ya zō, ya gani kāza
tasa matachīa, bai che kōmi ba, sai ya che,
'Wayō Ala mai-girma yau kāzata tā mutu.'
Sai ya dauki, ya fīge, ya babake, ya gerta da keau,
ya dōra tukunia bisa wuta, ya dafa da keau,
ya dauki, ya kai kāsua. Kōwa ya zō, ya che
shi na sō shi saia, sai shi che, shi, ba shi
sairwa, sai dōki. Ana-nan dan sarki, wanda
shi ke sō, ya zō, shi kūa yārō ne kankane.
Shi-na bisa algarma, sai ya che, nāman kāza nan
shi ke sō sai asai masa. Marāya kūa ya che,

---

fowls, (and) were rearing them, he (had) one, (and) the orphan one. One day she lifted a stick, and hit the orphan's (fowl) on purpose, (and) killed it (when) he was not at home. When he returned he saw his hen dead; he did not say anything except 'Alas! Allah, the powerful one, to-day my hen has died.' Then he picked it up, (and) plucked it, (and) put it on the fire, and prepared it well, (and) placed a pot on the fire, (and) cooked it thoroughly. He took it up, (and) went (with it) to the market. Whoever came and said he wanted to buy it, he would answer he would not sell it, except for a horse. Then the chief's son came, the one the chief loved; he too was quite a little boy. He was mounted on a powerful horse; and he said the flesh of this hen was what he wanted and it must be sold to him. But the orphan said,

دكاجم ؞ سنا كيو و ؞ نا اس غدا ؞ قمو يا غدا ؞

وقم ؞ تمدر وك ؞ اسندا ؞ تبغي ؞ قما وم ؞ د غنكم

تكشي ؞ بدا شغدا ؞ د يغ وا ؞ يقنم كدا دا

تمس ؞ متشيا ؞ ينب كو ميب ؞ اسن يب ؞

وميو ؞ أل ؞ ميغم مو ؞ يو كدا ذا ات ؞ قدا مث ؞

بسن يدرك ؞ ييغي ن يسبكي ؞ يغم تو ؞ د تو

يدرو ؞ تكنيا ؞ يسو قم ؞ ميدق ؞ د قو ؞ —

يدرك ؞ يكن ؞ كدا سوا ؞ كوا يغوا ؞ يب

شدا سوا ؞ شاسيا ؞ اسن شب ؞ شيبا ش ؞

اسيروا ؞ اسن د وك ؞ اقدا قم ؞ د قسم كم ؞ رقد

شكمسوا ؞ يعوا ؞ شيكو ؞ يدا وبو ؞ فنقبر

شدا بسن ؞ ألقزم ؞ اسن يب ؞ ندا مر كدا د قمز

شكسوا ؞ اسرأ اسيقسن ؞ مرليا كو ؞ يب

idan ba dōki aka-ba shi ba, shi kūa bābu mai-chin nāmansa. Yau sai aka-ba shi dōki, aka-baiwa dan sarki nāma, shi kūa ya kāwō dōkinsa gida.

Sai uwa tasa ta che, ' Dauki dōkinka ka sainya achikin dākinga, ka līke da kasa, kāmin kwāna bakwoi, idan ka būde, sai ka gani yaa yi kiba, kamar zai pashe dākinsa. Zatonta idan ya yi hakanan sai shi mutu.' Shi kūa yārō shi-nazatō gaskīa ne. Sai ya sainya dōki chikin dāki, ya līke kōfa. Aka-kwāna kamar gōma, ya būde kōfa, sai ya gani dōkinsa ya yi kiba. Sai kīshiar uwa tasa ya yi bakin chiki dōmin da dōki

---

if he did not give him the horse, as for him, no one would eat his meat. So he was given the horse, (and) the chief's son the meat, and the former took his horse home. But his mother said, ' Take your horse (and) put it in this house, and close up the door with earth ; in about seven days, if you open it, you will see it has become fat enough to burst its house.' Her idea was if he did so it (the horse) would be dead. Now the boy thought this was true, so he put the horse in the house, and plastered up the door. When about ten days had elapsed, he opened the door, and he saw his horse had become fat. But his step-mother got black of heart because the horse

إِدَنْ مَدَّ زُكِ ∴ أَكَبَاشِبَ ∴ شِيكُوَّ ∴ بَدَبِ ∴ فِيشِنْ

فَدَمَنَسَنْ ∴ مِيوُسَنْ أَكَبَاشِدُ زُكِ ∴ أَكَبِيوَ ∴ دَفْلَسْرِكِ

قَدَمْ ∴ شِيكُوَّ ∴ يَكَدَاوُ ∴ دُوكِنْسَنْ غِدَنْ ∴ =

تَسْ غُوَا أَمْسَنْ ∴ قَبْشْ دُ زُكِ ∴ دُوكِنْكَ ∴ كَلَسْفِيَ

أَمْكِنْدَا كِنْغَ ∴ كَلِيفِنْ دَكَمْسَنْ ∴ كَدَامِنْ ∴ كُوَانْ

بَكُمْنْ إِدَّنْ كَبُوجِنْ ∴ تَسْ كَقَنِمْ ∴ مَيْأُنّْ ∴ كِبَ

كَمْرْ ∴ دَبِيقَبْشِنْ ∴ دَاكِنْسَنْ ظَمْتُوقَ ∴ إِغَّنْ ∴

يَدَنّْ ∴ قَكَمْنْ ∴ تَسْ شِمْفُ ∴ شِيكُوَ ∴ يَدَوُرْ ∴ شِنْدَ

ظَنْتُو غَسْكِيَا قُنَّ ∴ تَسْ يَلَسْفِنْ ∴ دُرُوكِ ∴ ثِكِمْ دَاكِ

بِلِيفُنْ كُوقَ ∴ أَكَكُوَا أَمُنْ ∴ كُمْ غُوتَمْ ∴ يُبُوجِنْ

كُوقَ ∴ تَسْ بِغَنِمْ ∴ دُوكِنْمَسْ ∴ يَدَانْ كِبَ ∴ آسَنْ

كِيشِيَّرْ ∴ غُوَاقَسَنْ ∴ فَنّْ بَكِنْشِكِ ∴ دُوفِمَّرْ ∴ دَدُوكِ

bai mutu ba. Yau ana-nan ranan ta che, 'Yau bābu karan da-fūa.' Shi saiar da dōkinsa, shi sayō kara. Sai ya che, 'Haba uwāna, ana wada ake sai da dōki, asai kara?' Ta che, 'Dōmin ba uwa(r) ka ni ke ba, dōmin hakanan ka ke gardama da ni?' Ya che, 'Ba gardama ni ke yi ba, naa tafi in bīdō kara.' Ta che, 'Bari idan ba ka sai da dōkinka ka bari.' Sai maraya ya che, 'Bābu laifi.' Ya je, ya sai da dōki, ya karbō kara. Ya kāwō mata. Ta kōne kara duka, ba ta rege kō kadan ba, sai yan guntāye guda uku su-ka-saura. Ya tsinche, ya dunka yar jaka, ya dūra su achiki. Sai wata rāna ya tāshi, ya je wani gari yāwō,

---

did not die. Well, things went on, and one day she said, 'To-day there are no grain-stalks to cook with.' He must sell his horse and buy stalks of grain. But he said, 'Oh my mother, why must the horse be sold to buy stalks of grain?' She said, 'Because I am not your mother, because of that do you argue with me?' He said, 'I am not disputing, I shall go and seek the grain stalks.' She said, 'Stop! If you do not sell the horse leave things as they are.' And the orphan said, 'It cannot be helped.' He went and sold the horse and received the grain stalks, (and) brought them to her. She burned all the stalks; she did not leave any at all, except three very small pieces which were left. He picked them up, sewed a little bag and tied them inside. Another day he rose up and went to another village for a walk,

ܒܥܩܒܗ܂܂ܝܘܐܡܐܡܢ܂ܪܩܢܪ܂܂ܬܒܝܘܓܐܒ܂܂ܟܪܦ̈
ܒܘܐ܂܂ܐܫܠܝܢܪܢܪܘܟܣܢܣܬ܂ܝܫܠܝܘ܂܂ܟܪܐ܂܂ܐܣܪܝܣܝ̈
ܩܒ܂܂ܥܘܐܡܝ܂܂ܥܘܐܡܘܕܐܟܣܝܢܕܪܘܟ܂܂ܐܣܝ
ܟܪܐ܂܂ܬܒܕܪܝܬܢ܂ܒܡܐܥܘܟ܂܂܂ܢܟܒ܂܂ܕܪܩܡ
ܩܟܢܪ܂܂ܥܓܟܢܪܡ܂܂ܕܪܥ܂܂ܝܒܒܡܐܥܪܡ܂܂
ܢܟܣܝ܂܂ܢܠܡܩܝ܂܂ܐܫܝܘܐܘ܂ܟܪܐ܂ܬܒܩܡ܂܂ܐܪܢ
܂ܒܡܐܟܣܝܝܡ܂ܪܘܟܢܟ܂܂ܟܒܝܪ܂܂ܐܣܪܡܪܐܡ

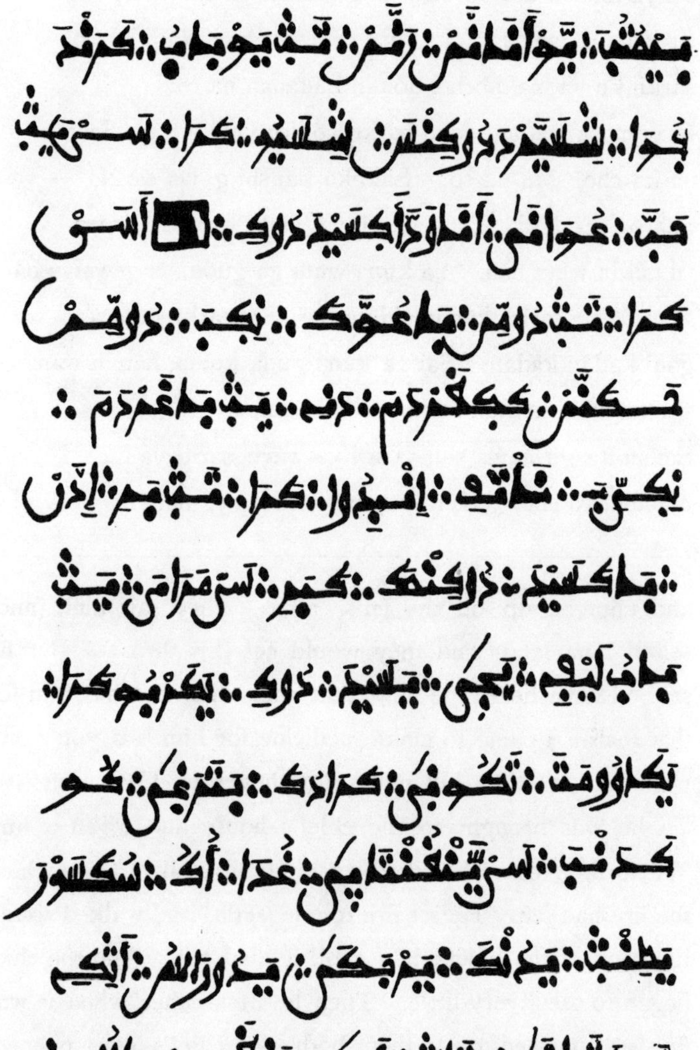

sai ya hau [8] matsāfa. Su-ka-gane shi, su-ka-kāma shi, su-ka-che, zaa su yanka shi. Sai ya che, 'Nā ji lābāri sarkinku ya makabche, dōmin hakanan na zō in yi masa māgani, idan ba ku sō, ku yanka ni.' Sai su-ka-che, 'Mu-na-so.' Sai aka-kai shi gidan sarki, aka-ba shi dāki. Dare ya yi, ya dauki karansa, saura-n bākin wuta nan. Ya kuna wuta ga guda, ya gewaiya bā-yan dākin sarki, kāmin shi mutu. Sai sarki ya fāra gani kadan kadan. Sai ya kuna guda kuma, kāmin wanan shi kāre, sai idānun sarki ya būde duka.
Sai su-ka-girmama shi. Gari ya wāye, sarki ya tāra mutāne, ya che, [9] 'Kun ka gani yārō ya yi mani māgani.

---

and climbed up on the fetish altar. They saw him, (and) seized him, (and) said they would cut (his throat). But he said, 'I have heard the news that your chief is blind, and for that reason I came to make medicine for him. If you don't want (me to) then kill me.' But they said, 'We wish (it).' So he was brought to the chief's house and given a hut. When night came he lifted up his grain stalks; these which the fire had left. He set fire to one (stalk) and walked round the back of the chief's house till it died out. And the chief began to see a very little. Then he lit another, when it was finished (burned out), then both the chief's eyes opened. Thereupon they gave him honour. At dawn the chief assembled the people (and) said, 'You have seen the boy has made medicine for me.

سن يعو مطاقي ∴ سككبش ∴ سككلماش ∴

سككب ∴ دأس ∴ ينكاش ∴ سن يب ∴ فاج للبار ∴

لسركنك ∴ يا مكبب ∴ دوقمر ∴ ككثر ∴ مدرا ∴ =

إفيمس ∴ ماغنيم ∴ إدفبا كسوا ∴ كينكار ∴ لسن

سكب ∴ مفاسوا ∴ لسن أككيش ∴ غم فلسركم ∴

ك

أكباش ∴ داك ∴ دربيمق ∴ يمرنكر فلس ∴ لسنور

نباكر ∴ وتمر ∴ بكرودا ∴ غغدا ∴ يغموتن ∴ با

يفداكم ∴ لسركم ∴ كامر ∴ يشمت ∴ لسن لسركم ∴ يقار

غنيم ∴ كدتكدن ∴ لسن يكرغدا اكم ∴ كامر ∴ وقس

يشكبوكس ∴ لسن إ افم لسركم ∴ يبوجرد ك ∴ =

لسن لسكغر مماش ∴ غمر ميواجي ∴ لسركم ∴ يتلر

متدافين ∴ يب كنكغنيم ∴ يدار ∴ ميا يمر ∴ هاغنيم

Idānuna ya warke, ama naa ba shi rabin gari,
shi chi sarauta.' Sai ya che, 'Ni falke ne, ba ni chin sarauta.'
Su-ka-che, 'Idan ba ka chin sarauta, ka dībi abinda
ka ke sō, ka tafi.' Sai ya dēbi bāyi, da shānu,
da kōmi masu-chau, ya tafō da su, ya shigō
gari da su. Mutāne su-na-māmāki. Sai
kīshīar uwa tasa ta che, 'Tafō mu je hainya
rāfi, nā gani wani kūsū, yā shiga rāme,
ka gina mani, in yi mia.' Sai ya che, 'Haba uwana
wane irin nāma, ga zābi, ga kāji, ga rāguna?'
Sai ta che, 'Ansani ka-na da dūkīa, ni dai nā-
-man kūsu ni ke so.' Sai ya che, 'Bābu laifi
mu tafi ka gwoda mani.' Ashe tā gani rāmen kumurchi ne

My eyes are healed, and I shall give him half of the town to rule over.' But he (the boy) answered, 'I am only a trader, passing, and I do not rule.' They said, 'If you will not rule, take whatever you wish and go.' So he took slaves, and cattle, and everything beautiful, and went off with them, and entered (his) town with them. The people were astonished. But his step-mother said, 'Come, let us go to the road by the stream, I have seen a rat enter a hole; you dig it for me to make soup.' And he said, 'Come now, my mother, what kind of meat (is a rat's)? Behold guinea-fowls, and hens, and rams.' And she said, 'We all know you have wealth; as for me though, rat's meat is what I want.' So he said, 'There is no harm in that. Let us go, you show me.' Now really she has seen it was a snake's hole (but she told him this)

إِدَ اُفُوقُمِي ۞ يَدَاوُرْبُكُي ۞ آمَّا قُدْ بَدَ اِشْ ۞ رِيمُفُرِي ۞

يِشَّ لَسَرُوتَّ ۞ لَسِي يَبُّ ۞ فِي بَلُبْكُنْ ۞ بَدَارِ شِنْ لَسَرُوتَّ

۞ سُكُبُّ ۞ إِدَّنْ ۞ بَدَ اَعِيْشُ لَسَرُوتَّ ۞ كَحِ مِيبِ ۞ آبِنْدَ ۞

كُبْكُسُو ۞ كُتَّقِي ۞ لَسِنْ يَحِي مُجِي ۞ بَدَ يِيبِ ۞ دَ شَّدَ اَنُو

دَ كُحُومِ ۞ مُكُسِّ ۞ شُوْ ۞ يَتَّبُوَّ اُدَ سُوَا ۞ يَيشَ قُحُو ۞

قَمِرِي ۞ دَ سُوَا ۞ مُتَدَ بُكُنْ ۞ سَنْدَ اَمَدَ مَدَكِ ۞ لَسِي

كَيشَيَّرْ عُوَ اَتَّسْ ۞ قُتُّ تَّبُوَا ۞ مُجَمُّ ۞ مُنْسُ ۞

رَاوِم ۞ قَدَ غِيمِ ۞ وَ نَكُوسُ ۞ يَدَ اِشْقَ ۞ رَابِسِي

عَقَّدَ اَمِنْ ۞ اِمُّ مِيَّ ۞ لَسِنْ يَبُّ ۞ قَيَّ عُوَ اَمَّسْ ۞

وَبَارِ فُنْدَ اَمْ ۞ غَدَ دَابِي ۞ غَدَ كَدَ اَجِي ۞ غَدَوَ اَ غَسْ

۞ لَسِنْ تَبُّ ۞ آلْحَسَنِي ۞ كَنْدَ اَ دُرْ كِيَا ۞ فِيدَ نِي ۞ قَدَ

مُنْكُوسُ ۞ نَبْكُسُوَا ۞ لَسِنْ يَبُّ ۞ بَدَ اَبْ لَبِّجِمِ ۞

مُتَّبِجِي ۞ كُكُدَ اَمِنْ ۞ آبْشَ ۞ قَدَ غِيمِ ۞ وَابِ سُكُمُرْ شِيبِيُّنْ

dōmin ta kai shi shi halaka. Sai baban bāwansa ya tāshi. Ta che, 'Zamna, nā gane ka, mai bāyi, kai dakainka zaa mu da kai, idan ba ka zūa, ka bari.' Sai ya che bāyinsa su zamna, shi shii tafi. Su-ka-zamna, su-ka-tafi tāre da kīshīar uwa tasa. Ta je, ta gwoda masa rāmen; zaa shi gina, sai ta che, 'Ajie hauya, tūra hanunka.' Sai ya tūra hanu. Sai ya jāwo kwandage. Ya che, 'Ga shi.' Ta che, 'Ba shi ba, kūsu na che akwai shi nan.' Sai ya tūra hannu kuma, sai ya zārō kwanda-ge na zīnāria. Sai ta yi fushi, ta kōma gida, ta kirāwo danta. Ya zō, sai ta che shi tūra hannu, shi kāmō mata kūsu. Da tūra hanunsa, kumurchi ya chīje hannunsa, sai aka-dauke shi

---

in order that she might bring him trouble. Now a big slave of his rose up (to accompany him). She said, 'Sit down, I have seen you are the owner of slaves, but it is you alone we (I) will go with. If you will not come, then stay.' So he told his slaves to sit down and he would go (alone). They sat down. They set off, (he) and his step-mother. She went and showed him the hole. When he was about to dig, then she said, 'Put down your hoe (and) push in your hand.' So he put in (his) hand and drew out a bracelet. He said, 'There it is.' She said, 'That is not it. A rat, I said, was there.' So he put in his hand again and drew out a golden bangle. But she got angry and went back home. She called her own son; he came, whereupon she said he must put in his hand and catch a rat for her. On putting in his hand a snake bit his hand, and they carried him

دوقمن تكيش .. شعلو لسن ببم .. بداو فنلن ..

ينكاش تبد مفنى .. قد غبسك .. هيبا يم .. =

كيد كنك .. د أفد كن .. إدن بد اهد ق .. كبر ..

لسن يبد بد ايفلن .. لسغ فمن .. يشم شفتهم .. لسكد فمن

لسكتهم .. قارمد بهيشير .. عواتفلن تجو تغد ا

مسن .. وامو .. داشن .. غمنى .. لسن قبد .. أجبن دويد

ثور قفنك .. لسن يثور .. قفوا .. لسن بجاور كند عمى

يبد غداش .. قبد بد اشيب .. كوس .. قبد .. اكو بيشن

قمن .. لسن بثور قفوا .. كم .. لسن بداور .. كند ..

بجون مد بمدا ريا .. لسن قنى .. فيشم .. تكوتم بمدا

تكماو .. د مقد بدوا .. لسن قبد يثور .. قفوا .. =

شكا فوقد .. كوس .. دقور .. قفلن ..

كمقم .. يقجم .. قفنس .. لسن اكداو بكش

zūa gida. Bai kai gida ba, sai ya mutu. Ita kūa kwā-
-nanta uku, sai ta mutu. Marāya ya gāde gida.
Mafāri ke nan akan-che, 'Aki marāya da rīgan
būzu, agane shi da ta [10] karfē.' Shi ke nan.
[11] Kungurus kan kūsu.

---

home. He died before they reached home. She also died in three days. The orphan inherited the house (property). This is the origin of the saying, 'The orphan with the cloak of skin is hated, but when it is a metal one he is looked (favourably) on.' That is all. Off with the rat's head.

اكّوا ∴ تَكُوَّ ∴ إِتَّكْ ∴ تَسْرِيمُتْ ∴ غْدَاب ∴ يَنِكْنْ ∴ غْدَا ∴ دُوَّ

قْنْتَ ∴ أُكْ ∴ تَسْرِ تَمُتْ ∴ مَرَايَدْ ∴ يَغْلْ جَرْ مْغْدَا ∴

مَقْلِرِ ∴ بِجِّنْ ∴ أَكْنْشْ ∴ أَكْمَرَا تْرِ ∴ دْرِ يَغْنْ

بُوذْرَا ∴ أَغْنِبْشْ دْ تْكْنْرُوكْ ∴ شِيكْنّْ ∴

فُنَغْمْ سْ ∴ كْنْفُوسْ ∴

No. 14.

Wanan tātsunīar makīsanchi che.

[1] Gātanan, gātanan, ta je, ta kōmō. Wani mutun shi-na chikin birni, sai [2] ya tāshi, ya kōma dāji dōmin kar anemi [3] maatansa, har wata rāna sar-kin [4] garin ya ji lābāri, sai ya che, 'Wanda ya je, ya nemi maatarsa, idan ya zō, [5] naa ba shi dōki, da rīga, da kurdi, zanba dari.' Sai wani mutun ya che shi [6] yaa tafi, ya kwāna da maatarsa, gaban idānunsa. Sai ya je ya bidi yāyan kūka. Ya fūde, ya ger-ta chikinsu da chau, ya nemi kurdi kankanāna, ya zuba chiki. Ya je, ya kai, ya ba shi keauta. Sai ya pasa, ya gani kankanānan kurdi ke chiki, ya pasa wani kuma. Hakanan ya pasa wani kuma hakanan.

This is a story about a jealous man. A story, a story. Let it go. Let it come. There was a certain man who used to live in a town, but afterwards he rose up and went to the bush, lest people might go after his wives, until one day the chief of the t own heard about him) and he said, 'He who goes and seduces his wives, if he comes (to me) I will give him a horse, and a cloak, and one hundred thousand cowries.' Then a certain man said he would be the one to go and lie with his wife before his eyes. Then he went off and sought some baobab seeds. He opened them, (and) cleaned out the inside well; he sought for some very small pieces of money and poured them inside. He went, reached (the place where the man was) (and) gave him a present of them. When he broke (one) open he saw the small money inside. He broke another also, (and) in the same way broke open another.

وَقَّرْقَا طُونِيرْ ⁖ مَكِبَشِيبْ

عَمَا اتَمَّرْ ⁖ عَمَا اقَمَّرْ ⁖ تَجِمْ تَكُومُوا ⁖ وَنِقُمْتَرْ م

شِنَا تَكِمْ ⁖ مَرْ نِي ⁖ لَسِ وَقَدَاشِنْ يَكُوم ⁖ دا ج

دُوقّرْ ⁖ كَمْ اَيْمِ ⁖ مَا اتَمَلُسُ حَمْ وَقَمْ اَمُوْ ⁖ لَسَمْ

كَنْ ⁖ عَمْ قَيْجِ ⁖ لَابَادِرْ ⁖ لَسِ يَبْ ⁖ وَقْمِ يَجِي ⁖ =

يَنِمْ ⁖ مَا اتَمْ لَسِنْ اِمْ قَيجُوا ⁖ قَلْمَاشِنْ دُوكِ ⁖ دَ

وَيَقُوْ ⁖ دَ كُمْ دِي ⁖ دَقَبْ دَرِي ⁖ لَسِ وَنِمُقْتَرْ يَبْ

شِمْ يَا اتَقِي ⁖ يَكُوا اوْ دَ مَا اتَمْ لَسِنْ ⁖ عَمْ بَمْ اِعْ اقْتَلَسْ

لَسِمْ تَجِيْ ⁖ يَمِي يَا مَيْرْ ⁖ كُوكْ ⁖ يَقُودِنْ ⁖ يَعْمْ

تَ ⁖ تَكِمْ سُوْ دَ قُوْ ⁖ يَنِمِ ⁖ كُمْ دِي ⁖ فَنْقَدَانْ

⁖ يَدِبْ ⁖ تَكِمْ ⁖ يَجِي تَكُوْ ⁖ يَمَاشِ ⁖ كُوقُمْ ⁖ =

لَسِ يَقَسِنْ يَعْنِمْ ⁖ قَقْفَا اقَمْرْ ⁖ كُمْ دِي ⁖ يَتَكِمْ

يَقَسْ ⁖ وَنِكُمْ ⁖ تَكَمَّرْ ⁖ يَقَسِنْ وَنِكُمْ ⁖ تَكَمَّرْ

Sai ya che, 'Abōki-na ba ka gwoda mani wurin da kūka nan ta ke?' Ya che, 'Wurin kūka nan shi-na da nīsa.' Ya che, 'Kai ni.' Ya che, 'Ba shi hauuwa sai da tsāni, bābu wanda ya san wurin da ta ke sai ni.' Sai ya dinga lālāshi, shi kūa kwar-tō, sai ya che, 'Mu tafi in kai ka, ama ba dōmin kai ba, ba ni kai kōwa.' Sai su-ka-tafi tāre da maatar-sa. Da su-ka-isa wurin kūka, sai kwartō ya daukō tsāni, ya dangana, ya che mai-maata shi hau. Sai ya hau. Da ya hau ya kāre, sai ya dauke tsāni, ya kai wani wuri, ya aje, ya kōmō, ya kāma maatar, ya kayas. Shi-na nasa abu, mai-maata shi-na gani, ba shi iya sabkōwa, sai ya che, 'Naa zuba maku miau, naa zuba maku miau.' Har su-ka-gama abinda su ke yi. Kwartō

And he said, 'My friend, will you not show me where this baobab tree is?' He replied, 'The place where this baobab tree is is far away.' (And) he said, 'Take me (to it).' And he said, 'It cannot be climbed except by a ladder, (and) no one knows where it is save me.' And he continued to entreat him; and at last the seducer said, 'Let us go, I will take you there, but if it was not for you, I would not show any one the place.' So they set out along with his wife. When they came to the baobab tree then the seducer lifted the ladder and placed it (against the tree), (and) told the woman's husband to climb up. So up he climbed. When he had finished climbing, then he lifted away the ladder, (and) carried it somewhere else (and) set it down, (and) came back. He seized the wife and threw her down. He did what he intended, the woman's husband looking on (and) not able to descend; but he said, 'I shall spit on you, I shall spit on you,' until they had finished what they were doing. The seducer

تسن يب آبو كينا : بد كنكم امين : ورفد كو عنن

تكن : يب ورنكو كنن : شنا د فيعن : يب كيم

يب بد اشعو وا : تسن د طان : مداب ورفد يسن : ورفد

تنكن تسين : تسن يد فنغ : لالا اشم : يشيكو كم

شوا : تسن يب متيم : انكيك : آمابادو مين :

كنب : بد انكيكو وا : تسن تسكتيم : تد ود مدانم

تسن د تسكاسن ورنكوك : تسن كم قو : ميد ركو

طان يد فنغنا : يب مبيدا من : شحو : تسن يحو

د يحو : يكد رمن : تسن يد ركن : طان يكن ورفو وري

يا بن : يكو مو : يكد تم : مدانم : يكد ايسن :

يسنا ما سران : مبيدا من : شنا غنم : بد اشعن

تسنكو وا : تسن يب مند بدامك : ميو : مدانم يد

مك : ميو : تم تسكنم : آمند تسبكن : كم نو

ya yi [7] tafiasa. Ya je, ya gaia wa sarki kamar da su-ka-yi.
Sarki ya ba shi lāda tasa, ya kāra masa keauta.
Ya che, 'Māganinsa ke nan.' Shi kūa maatarsa
ta yi kōkari, ta daukō tsāni, ta kāwo masa,
ya sabka. Da zuansa gida, sai ya [8] tatara kāyansa,
ya kōmō chikin gari. Ya che, 'Kīshī-na
ya jāwō mani haka, idan ina-nan, mutāne su halaka ni.'
Shi ke nan. [9] Kungurus kan kūsu.

---

went his way. He came, (and) told the chief what they had done. The chief gave him his reward, and added to his gifts. He said, 'That 's the medicine he required.' As for the (jealous) man, his wife with difficulty lifted the ladder, (and) brought it to him, (and) he descended. On his return home he collected all his goods, (and) returned (to live) in the town. He said, 'My jealousy dragged me into this ; if I remain here, people will destroy me.' That is the story. Off with the rat's head.

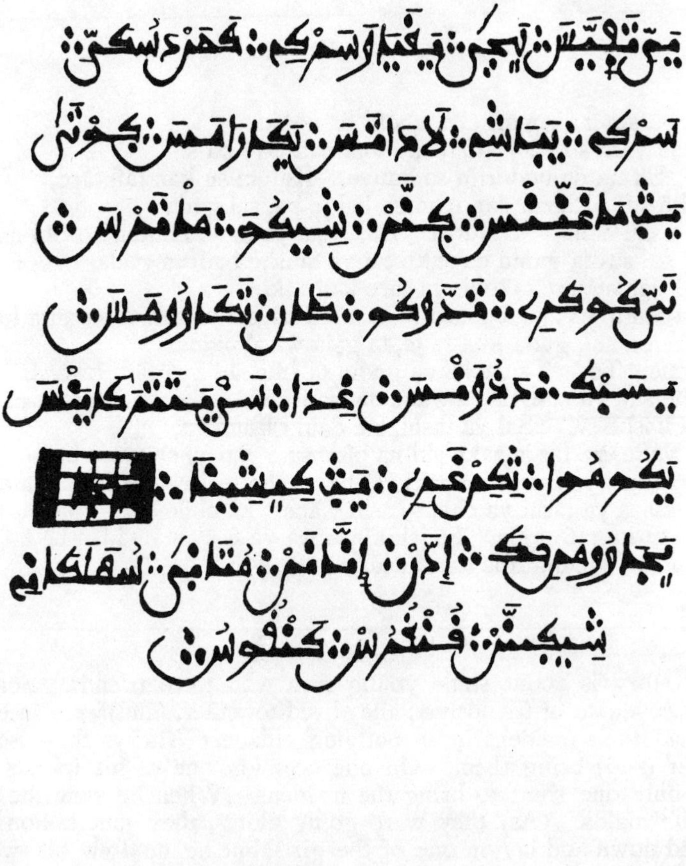

No. 15.

Wanan tātsunīar samāri che, abōki da abōki.
Wadansu yāra su-ka-yi abūta; su-na nan tāre ba su rabūa. Su-na da buduri(n)su kauye. Kulum su kan tafi tāre, su daukō su. Ranan dan uwansa bai je ba, sai guda daia [1] ya tafi daukō [2] budurin. Da ya je, ya daukō buduri. Shi-na--zakua, sai su-ka-gamu da zāki, sai ya taushe budrua guda, sai shi kūa, ya zāre takōbi, ya sāre kan zāki.
Zāki ya mutu, ya tāda budrua ba ta mutu ba, sai ya che ta kwanta karkashin zāki tāre da shi, guda kūa ta je, ta gaia wa abōkinsa.
Sai ta che, 'Tō.' Ta shēka da gudu, ta iske shi [3] yā fāra kwāna.
Ta tāshe shi, ya che, 'Ana wāne da wānche?' Ta che, 'Su-na-chan, zāki ya kashe su.' Sai ya tāshi, bai dauki kōmi ba, ya tafi, ya je, ya tarda zāki, shi-na bisansu. Bai yi shāwara ba, sai ya zābura, ya hau bissa zāki. Shi-na-che mai-rai ne, ashe matache ne.
Sai abōkinsa ya tāshi ya che, 'Tāshi wāne, [4] kā chika dā.' Sai su-ka-tāda budrua, su-ka-tafō gida. Tō, chikinsu wa ya fi wani? Idan ba ka sani ba, shi ke nan. [5] Kungurus kan kūsu.

This story is about some young men who were friends. Some boys made a covenant of friendship; they lived together, (and) were inseparable. They had their maidens in an outlying village. Always they used to go together (and) bring them. On one occasion, one of his friends did not go, so only one went to bring the maidens. When he went, he brought back the maids. (As) they were going along, they met a lion; and it knocked down and lay on one of the girls, but he, he drew his sword and cut at the lion's head. The lion died, and he found the maiden was not dead. And he told her to lie down beneath the lion along with him, and one of them was to go and tell his friend. So she consented, (and) ran off (and) found he has begun to sleep. She roused him, (and) he said, 'Where are So-and-so and So-and-so?' And she said, 'They are out there, a lion has killed them.' And he rose up, he did not take anything with him he went along and came and reached (where) the lion was; it was above them. He did not hesitate, but sprang and climbed on the lion. He thought it was alive. Truly it was dead. Then his friend rose up and said, 'Rise, So-and-so, you have proved yourself (a free-born) man.' So they lifted up the maiden (and) went home. Now among them who was better than another? If you do not know, there it is. Off with the rat's head.

وقتن قتا طوقيم :: لسقاوي ث :: ابوكيم :: دابوكيم ::

ودّ مسر بدوا :: لسكي ابو تتو :: لسنا قمر :: قاربو :: مداس

ربوا :: لسنا د بدرسن كحوبين :: كلم :: لسكنهجي قابرن

لسد وكوسن وقمن ء ملعوقسن بيجعب :: اسن غدا

دتن :: يتهي دركوبدرن دبجي بد وكوبدري :: لشنا

مكوا :: اسن لسكعم دداك :: اسن بتوشن :: بدروا غدا ::

اسع شيكو :: بيد ارين تكوبي :: بلساون كنداك ::

داك يفث :: يتاد بدروا :: هتحت :: اسن بيت تكنت :: كركش

داك :: تادرعرشم :: غدالكو :: تجي تغياو :: ابو كشن

اسن قث ثو :: تنشك د غد :: قا اسكشن يا قار :: كوافي

تتنا شمش :: بيث اماوا مي شدروامث :: قث لسنا ثمن =

داك :: يداكشمسن اسن بتاشن بيدرك :: كوبيب ::

بيتف :: بجي قتر داك :: لشنا بلسمس :: بنتي شدا وراب ::

اسن بدابر :: بجوبسن داك :: شدات :: ميم ميمن :: ابشي متحنش

اسر ابو كمسن بتلش :: بيث متانتر وامو :: كدانك دا :: اسر لسكناد

بدروا :: لسكتغو غدا :: قوتكسن :: وبجور :: ادو :: بكلسيت

شبعثن :: قنغمسن :: كرفوس

No. 16.

Wanan tātsunīar gwanāye che. [1] Gātanan, gātanan. Wani sarki [2] ya haifu dīansa uku maza. Ranan fāda-nchi ya tāru, ya che shi shi-na-sō shi gani gwani chikinsu. Akwai wata gāwurtata kūka fagashin sarki. Ya che shi-na-sō su hau dawāki, su zō, su gwoda gwaninta, wurin kūka nan. Sai su-ka-hau algarmu, su-ka-tafi da nīsa. Babansu ya yi sukūa, ya zō, ya nashi kūka nan da māshi. Māshi ya zarche, [3] ya bi ta kafar māshi nan da dōkinsa, ya wuche. Ma-bi baban ya tafō. Da ya kusa da kūka, sai ya kinkimi dōkinsa, sai ya tsalache kūka. Da autansa ya yi sukūa ya zō, sai ya chire

---

This story is about a (test of) skill. A story, a story. A certain chief begat children, three males. One day his councillors assembled. He said he himself wished to see the most skilled among them. There was a huge baobab tree (near) the entrance to the chief's house. He said he wanted them to mount (their) horses, (and) come (and) show their skill, where this baobab tree was. So they mounted their chargers, (and) went far away. The eldest galloped (and) came, (and) thrust that baobab with (his) spear. The spear went right through and he followed, passing through the hole made by the spear, with his horse. And he passed on. The next to follow the eldest came on. When he was near to the baobab tree he lifted his horse (on the bit) and jumped the baobab. When the youngest galloped, he came, (and) pulled

وقمرتا صوفيير .: قمنا يبش .: قما تتمر غما قمر .:

وفسركم .: يتعيف ديمنسر اكي .: مغ ا .: وقمر .: قدام

نشم .: قيا قتدو .: يبش يشم يشندا سوا .: يشكنم غنم

قفشن .: كوك .: قتوزر قندار .: اكومر .: قكنسن

سنغ وا .: اكي .: سعو دوا .: شنداسو .: يبش يشنا .: سركم .:

سعو .: لسن سكر .: كوكنر .: ونكتنث .: غمنت .: سعد .:

الفرمو ا .: سكنتبع دفيلس .: تبجنسن يبش

سكوا .: يغدا ميقشن كوكنر .: م د قدا يشن .: قدا يشن

يغدرث .: يب تكبقز قدا يشقنر .: م د دوركنسن .: يبوبه

قسيم بنبر .: يقتبوا .: د يكلس د كوك .: تسن

بيكنيكم .: دوركنسن تسن يطلب كوك .: =

دا وقتنسن يبر سكوا .: يغد وا .: اتسن يشبر

kūka duka da sauyanta, ya je, ya yi ma ubansu jinjina. Sai [4] gūda ta gama wuri. Yanzu tanbaya ka na ke yi, chikinsu wa ya fi. Idan ba ka sani ba, shi ke nan. [5] Kungurus kan kūsu.

---

up the whole baobab, roots and all, and came on waving it aloft at his father, and the place rang with applause. Now I ask you who excelled among them. If you do not know, that is all. Off with the rat's head.

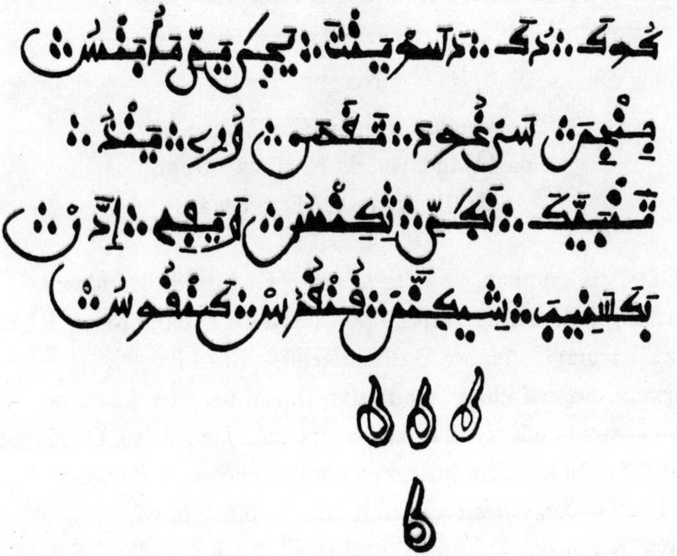

تُحُوكَ ⁘ دُرْكَ ⁘ تَدَرْسُويَنْتَ ⁘ يِجِمْ يَمِّ مَاتُبُنْسَ ⁘

يِنْجِمْ سَنْ غُوَمْ ⁘ تَقْعُصُ وُرِ ⁘ يَنْفُدُ ⁘

تَنْبِيِّكَ ⁘ نُكَيِّ ⁘ ثِكِنْفُسُ اَرِيحِه ⁘ إِدِّنْ ⁘

بَكِسِنِيبَ ⁘ يِشِيكَتَنْ ⁘ فُنْقُرْسَ ⁘ كَتَفُوسَ ⁘

No. 17.

Wanan tātsunīar Gishiri che,
da [1] Daudawa, da Nari, da [2] Gabū,
da Tankūa, da [3] Daudawar
batsō.

[4] Gātanan, gātanan, ta je, ta kōmō. Gishiri, da Daudawa, da Nari, da Gabū, da Tankūa, da Daudawar batsō, su-ka-ji lābāri wani sarmāyi, sūnansa Daskandarīni. Shi kūa sarmāyi ne mai-chau (keau), dan Iblisai ne. Su-ka-tāshi su-ka-zama buduri masuchau, su-ka-tafi. Da [5] zaa su, Daudawar batsō [6] ta bi su. Su-ka-kore ta su-ka-che ta-na da wāri. Sai ta [7] make, har su-ka-tafi, ta dinga binsu bāya bāya, har su-ka-kai gurin wani rāfi. Su-ka-tarda tsōfūa, ta-na-wanka. Ta che, su chūda mata bā-yanta, sai wanan shi che, 'Ala shi tsare ni in dauki hanu na

---

This story is about Salt, and Daudawa (sauce) and Nari (spice), and Onion-leaves, and Pepper and Daudawar-batso (a sauce). A story, a story! Let it go, let it come. Salt, and Daudawa, and Ground-nut, and Onion-leaves, and Pepper, and Daudawar-batso heard a report of a certain youth, by name Daskandarini. Now he was a beautiful youth, the son of the evil spirit. They (all) rose up, (and) turned into beautiful maidens, (and) they set off. As they (Salt, Onion-leaves, &c.) were going along, Daudawar-batso followed them. They drove her off, telling her she stank. But she crouched down until they had gone on. She kept following them behind, until they reached a certain stream. (There) they came across an old woman; she was bathing. She said they must rub down her back for her, but this one said, 'May Allah save me that I should lift my hand

وقَرْ قَنَا طُوفِيَّيرْ :: غِشْرِيبْ

دَدَوْدَوَا :: دَفَلِ :: دَغَبُو

دَقَنْكُوا :: دَدَوْدَوَرْ

بَطُوا

غَلَقَنَّ :: غَاقَنْ تَجُو تَكُو هُوا :: غِشْرِ :: دَدَوْدَوَا ::

دَفَلِ :: دَغَبُو :: دَقَنْكُوا :: دَدَوْدَوَرْ بَطُوا :: سُكَجِ لَابَدُورَ ::

وَفِسَمْ مَيَّمْ :: سُوفَفْسَ دَسْكَنْكَ رِمِيفِ :: شِيكُو ::

سَمْ مَيِيبْ مَيْنُوْ :: دَفَمْ فِلَيسِيبَنْ سُكَتَاشْ =

سُكَدَمْ :: بَجْرِ :: مَاسْتُوْ :: سُكَتَفِ :: دَدَ أَسْ :: دَوْدَوَر

بَطُوا :: قَبِيسْ :: سُكَكُورُكَتَ :: سُكَبْ :: قَنَا دَوَارِ

سَنْ تَفَوْل :: حَرْ سُكَتَفِ :: قَحِ فَمْغْ :: بِفَسْ بَدَاسَ

بَدَاسَ :: حَرْ سُكَكَ :: غَجِ فُوفَرَاقِ :: سُكَتَرْ دَ ::

طُوفُوَا :: قَنَا وَنْكَ :: قَبْ سُيُو دَافَتْ :: بَدَ

يَفْنَا :: سَنْ وَقَرْ شِبْ :: أَلْشَطَمْ مَرْ إِفْدَوَرِ قَنُومْ

in taba bāyan tsōfūa.' Sai tsōfūa ta [8] kyale.
Su-ka-wuche, aka-jima, Daudawar batsō ta zō, ta ishe ta,
ta-na-wanka. Ta gaishe ta, ta amsa, ta che, 'Yārinya,
ina zaa ki?' Ta che, 'Zaa mu wurin wani sarmāyi ne.' Ta che, 'Chūda mani
bāyana.' Sai ta che, 'Tō.' Ta tsāya, ta chūda ta da chau.
Tsōfūa ta che, 'Ala shi yi maki albarka.' Ta che, 'Sarmāyi nan
da ku ke zūa wurinsa, kun san sūnansa?' Ta che,
'Aa ba mu san sūnansa ba.' Sai tsōfūa ta che, 'Dāna ne, sūnansa Daskandarīni, ama kar ki gaya
masu.' Ita kūa ta kyale, ta-na-binsu, bāya bāya,
har su-ka-kai wurin yārō. Zaa su shiga. Sai aka-che,
'Ku kōma, ku shigō daia daia.' Su-ka-che. 'Tō.'
Su-ka-kōma. Sai Gishiri ta zō, zaa ta shiga,

---

to touch an old woman's back.' And the old woman did not say anything more. They passed on, and soon Daudawar-batso came, (and) met her washing. She greeted her, (and) she answered (and) said, 'Maiden, where are you going?' She replied, 'I am going to where a certain youth is.' (And) she (the old woman) said, 'Rub my back for me.' 'She said, 'All right.' She stopped, (and) rubbed her back well for her. The old woman said, 'May Allah bless you.' And she said, 'This youth to whom you are (all) going to, have you known his name?' She said, 'No, we do not know his name.' Then the old woman said, 'He is my son, his name is Daskandarini, but you must not tell them.' Then she ceased. She was following them far behind till they got to the place where the boy was. They were about to enter, but he said, 'Go back, (and) enter one at a time.' They said, 'It is well,' and returned. And then Salt came forward, (and) was about to enter,

إِقَتَب ؞ مَدَ يَفطُوبُوَا ؞ لَسَن ظُوبُوَا ؞ تَبَكِّيوُ ؞

سَكُوبُ ؞ آكِيجَم ؞ دَرْدَّ وَزَمَظُو ؞ قَتَغَرَا ؞ قَمَ ثِبَتَ

قَدَوَرَنكِي ؞ قَتَغَيبْشَتَب ؞ قَتَأمَس ؞ قَتَبْ يَدَرِمُهِي ؞ ـ

إِقَادَ أَكِ ؞ قَتَبْدَأَم ؞ وَرِمُوَفِهَنزَ مِيبِينِي ؞ قَتَبْ ثُوكَرَامَس

بَدَ يَبَا قَنِي ؞ لَسَنقَتَب قَتُو ؞ نِقَظَتَي ؞ قَتِثُو دَاقَ ؞ كَهَمُو ؞

طُوبُوَا ؞ قَتَبَ آرَشِيقَكِ اَلجَبْرَك ؞ قَتَب آمَس مَيِّيمَن

هَعَجَبِدَ أَرَ ؞ أُرُوقَسَ ؞ كُفَنَسَ ؞ لَسُوقَفَسَ ؞ قَتِثَ

عَدَعَ ؞ بَهْ سَقَلُو قَقَلَسَب ؞ لَسَن ظُوبُوَا قَتِثَ ؞ دَا

قَدَ بُو ؞ سُوقَفَسَ ؞ دَسَكَنَدَ رِيمُ ؞ آمَدَكَرْكِفَا

مَسَن ؞ إِنكُو ؞ تَبكِّلُ ؞ قَتَابِنَسَن ؞ بَدَ مُوقَدَ تَسَ

تَمِسَكَتَ ؞ أُرِفِيَدرَا ؞ دَأَسَن ؞ شَعَو ؞ لَسَن أَكَثِ ؞

كُكُومَ ؞ كُثِقُوَا ؞ دَتَ دَقَ ؞ سَكَبَ قَتُو ؞

سَكُومَ ؞ لَسَن غِثَم ؞ قَغَرَا ؞ دَأقَفِحَو

aka-che, 'Wānene nan?' Ta che, 'Ni che.' 'Ke che wa?' 'Ni che Gishiri, mai mia da zāki.' Su-ka-che, 'Wānene sū-
-nā na?' Ta che, 'Ban san sūnanka ba dan yārō, ban san sūnanka ba.' Aka-che, 'Kōma da bāya yārinya, kōma da bāya.' Ta kōma. Sai Dau-
-dawa ta zō. Zaa ta shiga aka-che, 'Wacheche?' Ta che, 'Ni che.' 'Ke che wa? Wāne sūnanki?' 'Sūnana Daudawa, mai-mia da dādi.' Sai ya che, 'Wane sūnana?' Ta che, 'Ban san sūnanka ba dan yārō, ban san sūnanka ba.' Ya che, 'Kōma da bāya yārinya, kōma da bāya.' Ta kōma, ta zamna. Sai Nari ta tāsō, ta zō. Zaa ta shiga sai aka-che, 'Wānene nan yā-
-rinya? Wānene nan?' Ta che, 'Ni che ke gaisua dan yārō,

---

when she was addressed with, 'Who is there?' She said, 'It is I.' 'Who are you?' 'It is I, Salt, who make the soup tasty.' They (he) said, 'What is my name?' She said, 'I do not know your name, little boy, I do not know your name.' Then he said, 'Go back, little girl, go back.' She turned back. So Daudawa came forward. When she was about to enter, she was asked, 'Who are you?' She said, 'It is I.' 'Who are you? What is your name?' 'My name is Daudawa, who makes the soup sweet.' And he said, 'What is my name?' She said, 'I do not know your name, little boy, I do not know your name.' He said, 'Turn back, little girl, turn back.' She turned back, (and) sat down. Then Nari (spice) rose up and came forward, (and) she was about to enter when she was asked, 'Who is this little girl? Who is this?' She said, 'It is I who greet you, little boy,

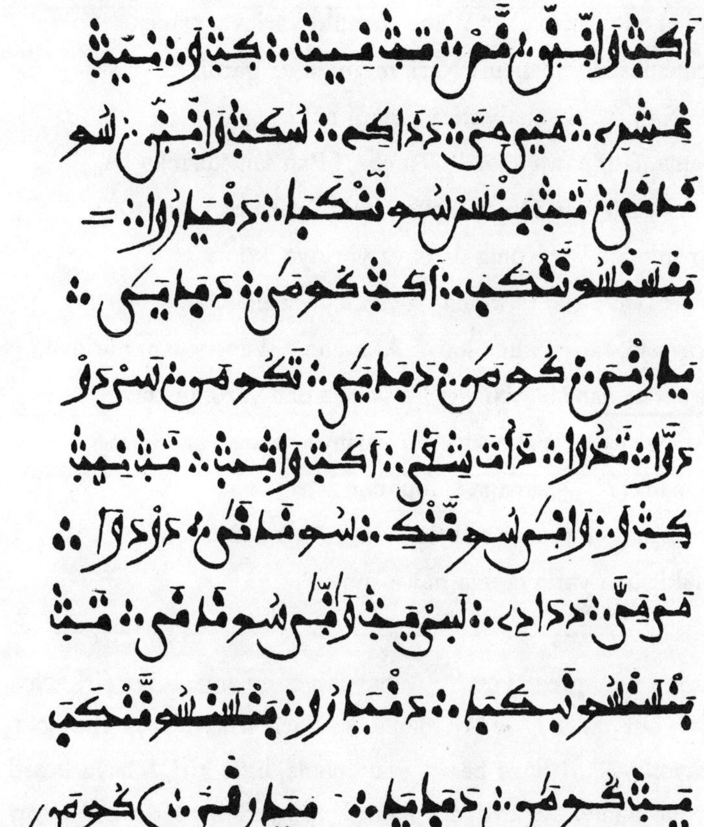

ni che ke gaisua.' 'Wāne sūnanki yārinya, wāne
sūnanki?' 'Sūnana Nari, mai-mia da gardi.'
'[9] Nā ji nāki sūna yārinya, nā ji nāki
sūna, fadi nāwa sūna.' Ta che, 'Ban san sūnanka ba
dan yārō, ban san sūnanka ba dan yaro ban san su-
-nanka ba.' 'Kōma da bāya yārinya, kōma
da bāya.' Sai ta kōma, ta zamna. Sai Gabū
ya tasō, sai ya kuna kai. Aka-che, 'Wānene nan yārinya,
wānene nan?' 'Ni che ke gaisua dan yārō, ni che
ke gaisua.' Wāne sūnanki yārinya, wāne
sūnanki?' 'Sūnana Gabū, dan yārō,
sūnana Gabū, mai-mia da kamshi.' Ya che, 'Naji
nāki sūna yārinya, ina nāwa sūna?'

---

it is I who greet you.' 'What is your name, little girl, what is your name?' 'My name is Nari, who makes the soup savoury.' 'I have heard your name, little girl, I have heard your name. Speak my name.' She said, 'I do not know your name, little boy, I do not know your name.' 'Turn back, little girl, turn back.' So she turned back, (and) sat down. Then Onion-leaves rose and came up, and she stuck her head (into the room) and was asked, 'Who is this little girl, who is this?' 'It is I who salute you, little boy, it is I who salute you.' 'What is your name, little girl, what is your name?' 'My name is Onion-leaves, who makes the soup smell nicely.' He said, 'I have heard your name, little girl. What is my name?'

نيب بكغفيسوا ∴ والنم سوننك ∴ يدرمن ∴ وانم

سوققنك ∴ سونامن قسير ∴ ممرمن ∴ دغمردي ∴

قسطاج ∴ قناك سوقني ∴ يدرقن ∴ قناج قناك

سوقني ∴ قجي ناو ∴ سوقمن ∴ قتب بنسنسو ننكب

دقيا روا ∴ بنسنسو ننكبا دقيدروا ∴ بنسنسو

ننكب ∴ كومو دبايي ∴ يدرقن ∴ كومو

دبايي ∴ سع تكوم ∴ قذمر ∴ سع غبوا ∴

يتداسوا ∴ سن تكمر كون أكب وانبن نمر ∴ يدرن

وانبن قمر ∴ نيب بكغفيسوا ∴ دقيدرا ∴ قيب

بكغفيسوا ∴ وانم سوقنك ∴ يدرمن ∴ وانم

سوننك ∴ سونامن ∴ قبوا ∴ دقيارو ∴

سونانا غبوا ∴ منمر دكمشي ∴ يثناج

ناك سوقلي ∴ يدرقن ∴ إناناو ∴ سوقلي ∴

Ta che, 'Ban san sūnanka ba dan yārō, ban san sūnanka ba.' 'Kōma da bāya dan yārō, kōma da bāya.' Sai ta kōma. Sai Tankua ya zō, ya che, 'Gāfaran [10] kudai dan yā-rō, gāfara kudai.' Aka-che, 'Wānene nan?' Ya che, 'Ni che, Tankua dan yārō, ni che tankua, mai-mia da yāji.' 'Nā ji nāki sūna yārinya, nā ji nāki sūna, fadi nāwa sūna yārinya, fadi nāwa sūna.' 'Ban san sūnanka ba dan yārō, ban san sū-nanka ba.' Aka-che, 'Kōma da bāya yārinya, kō-ma da bāya.' Sauran Daudawar batsō, sai aka-che, 'Ke ba ki zūa?' Ta che, 'Mu tafi gida, mutānen kirki sun tafi, ankōrō(n)su, bale ni mai-wāri.' Aka-che,

---

She said, 'I do not know your name, little boy, I do not know your name.' 'Turn back, little boy (girl), turn back.' So she turned back. Now Pepper came along; she said, 'Your pardon, little boy, your pardon.' She was asked who was there. She said, 'It is I, Pepper, little boy, it is I, Pepper, who make the soup hot.' 'I have heard your name, little girl, I have heard your name. Tell (me) my name, little girl, tell (me) my name.' 'I do not know your name, little boy, I do not know your name.' He said, 'Turn back, little maid, turn back.' There was only left Daudawar-batso, and they said, 'Are not you coming?' She said, 'Can I enter the house where such good people as you have gone, (and) been driven away? Would not they the sooner (drive) me out who stink?' They said,

تَبْ بَنْلَسَنْسُو تَنَّكَبَ مَ ؞ دِ قَيَارُو ؞ بَنْسَنْسُو تَنْكَبَ

كُوتَمُو ؞ دِ بَمَا مَيَا ؞ دِ نَيَارُوا ؞ كُوتَمُو ؞ دِ بَمَا مَيَّن ؞ تَسَنْ

تَكُوتَمَ ؞ تَسَنْ تَنْكُوَا ؞ مَيَّدُو نِيَبْ عَمَّا بَاقَكَدَ ؞ دِ نَيَ

رُوَا ؞ عَمَّا قَمَّ كُدَ ؞ أَكَبْ ؞ وَاقَّنَّ قَمَّن ؞ مَيَبْ نِيَبْ ؞

تَنْكُوَا ؞ دِ قَيَارُوَا ؞ مِنِيَبْ تَنْكُوَا ؞ مَبِيمِنَّ ؞ دِ يَامَ

قَامَ ؞ قَمَاكِ ؞ سُوقَمُ ؞ مَيَارُقَمَّ ؞ قَامَ قَمَاكِ ؞

سُوقَمُ ؞ قَدِ مَاوَ ؞ سُوقَمُ ؞ مَيَارُقَمُ ؞ قَدِ مَاوَ

سُوقَمُ ؞ بَنْلَسَنْسُو تَنْكَبَا ؞ دِ نَيَارُوَا ؞ بَنْلَنْسُو

تَنْكَبَ ؞ أَكَبْ ؞ كُوتَمُو ؞ دِ بَمَاسَّ ؞ مَيَارُقَمَ ؞ كُو

تَمُو ؞ دِ بَمَاسَّ ؞ لَسُوقُدُودِ قَاوَ ؞ مَطُوَا ؞ تَسَنْ أَكَبْ

بَكُو بَمَاكِ خُوَرَ ؞ تَبْ مُتَقِ عِدَا ؞ مَتَابَقَن ؞ كَكُرِكِ

؞ سَنْتَقِ ؞ أَنْكُورُ لَسُ ؞ مَبَلُوقِمَ مَيْوَارِ ؞ أَكَبْ

'Tāshi, ki tafi.' Sai ta tāshi, ta je. Aka che, 'Wānene nan yārinya wānene nan?' Sai ta che, 'Ni che ke gaisua dan yārō, ni ke gaisua.' 'Kāka sūnanki yārinya, kāka sūnanki?' 'Sūnana Batsō, dan yārō, sūnana Batsō, mai-mia da wāri.' Aka-ka che, 'Nā ji nāki sūna yārinya, nā ji nāki sūna, sauran nāwa sūna.' Ta che, 'Daskandarīni da-n yārō, Daskandarīni.' Sai aka che, 'Shigō.' Aka-shinfida mata [11] kilīshi, aka-ba ta tufāfi, aka-ba ta tākalmin zīnāria, dada sai wadan da ke [12] kōran ta wanan shi che. '[13] Naa dinga yi maki shāra.' Wanan shi che, 'Naa dinga yi maka daka.'

'Rise up (and) go.' So she got up (and) went. He asked her, 'Who is there, little girl, who is there?' And she said, 'It is I who am greeting you, little boy, it is I who am greeting you.' 'What is your name, little girl, what is your name?' 'My name is Batso, little boy, my name is Batso, which makes the soup smell.' He said, 'I have heard your name, little girl, I have heard your name. There remains my name to be told.' She said, 'Daskandarini, little boy, Daskandarini.' And he said, 'Enter.' A rug was spread for her, clothes were given to her, and slippers of gold; and then (of) these who had driven her away one said, 'I will always sweep for you'; another, 'I will pound for you.'

تَمَالِشْ ∴ كِتِجِم ∴ اَسِنْ تَمْتَالِشْ ∴ قَجِي ∴ أَكِبْ وَابْنَمْ فَمْ

ثِيَادِ وَمْ ∴ وَابْنَمْ فَمْ ∴ اَسِنْ قَبْ ∴ فِيبْشْ كَخِيسُوا

دَنْيَادَارْ ∴ نِيكَ خَيْسُوا ∴ كَدَاكْ ∴ اَسُوقَنْكِ يَادَوْمْ

كَدَاكْ ∴ اَسُوقَنْكِ ∴ اَسُوقَمْ ∴ مَطْلُوا ∴ دَنْيَادَارْ

اَسُوقَمْ قَابْطُوا ∴ قَيْمَوْ ∴ دَرَارِي ∴ آكِبْ قَدَاجِ

تَدَاكْ ∴ اَسُوقَمْ ∴ ثِيَادَوْمْ ∴ قَدَاجِ قَدَاكْ ∴ اَسُوقَمْ

[illegible]

[illegible]

[illegible]

[illegible] [redacted]

[illegible]

[illegible]

Wanan shi che, 'Naa dinga yi maki dauka rua.' Wanan shi che, 'Naa daka maki mia.' Wanan shi che, 'Naa tūka maki tūō.' Su duka su-ka-zama [14] kuyanginta. Dōmin hakanan, idan ka gani mutum talaka ne, kar ka rēna shi; ba ka sani ba wata rāna shi fi ka. Shi ke nan. [15] Kungurus kan kūsu.

Another said, 'I will see about drawing water for you'; and another, 'I will pound (the ingredients) of the soup'; and another, 'I will stir the food.' They all became her handmaids. And the moral of all this is, if you see a man is poor do not despise him; you do not know but that some day he may be better than you. That is all. Off with the rat's head.

وَقَّمْ شِبْ ∴ مَادٰى مْغَ يِچِكْ ∴ دَمْ وُكْرُ آرَا ∴ وَقَمْ شِبْ ∴

مَذَمْ كَدَامَكِ ∴ مِيَّ ∴ وَقَّمْ شِبْ ∴ مَدَأْتُو كَدَامَكِ ∴ =

تُوْرُو ∴ شُودُكَ ∴ اُكَذَمْ ∴ كُيِغْشَّ ∴ دُوَرِّمْ

مَكَّنْتَّ ∴ اِدَّرْ ∴ تَكَا غَشِّمْ ∴ فُتُمْ ∴ تَالَكِنّمْ ∴ تَكَرْ

تَكْمَغَاشِنْ بَكَسِيْبِ ∴ زَقَمْ اقَلِّ ∴ شِقِيكِ ∴ =

شِيكَّمْ فَنْغُرْشِ ∴ تَكَرْ فُوشِ ∴

No. 18.

Wanan tātsunīar [1] Mūsa che.

[2] Gātanan, gātanan, ta je, ta kōmō. Wani sarki [3] ya haifi dīansa guda biu, da mache da namiji. Su-ka-girma. Aka ba ta miji, ita mache, ta che ba ta sō, sai wanta ta ke sō. Idan aka-che, ta je, ta kirāwō Mūsa, sai ta je, ta che, '[4] Wāne wai ka zō.' Hakanan kulum, ranan sai wanta ya che, '[5] Naa yi māganinsa.' Akwai wata kōrama garinsu, yāra na wanka chiki, idan rāna ta yi; akwai wani itāche tsakan kōrama garin nasu, buduri na danri bante ne. Sai Mūsa ya [6] kyale, saada su-ka-zō, sun shiga achikin rua, su-na-wanka, su-ka-aje bantunansu gefē, sai ya zō ya kwā-
-che duka, ya je, ya hau itāchen tsakan [7] ruan

This story is about (a boy called) Musa. A story, a story. Let it go. Let it come. A certain chief begat children, two in number, a girl and a boy. They grew up. A husband was found for her, the daughter, (but) she said she did not want him; only her big brother she loved. If she was told to go and call Musa, then she went, (and) said, 'What's-your-name, they say you are to come.' And it was always so, (till) one day her brother said, 'I shall cure her of that.' (Lit. I shall make its medicine.) There was a small stream at their village, the children used to bathe in it when the sun was up; there was a tree in the middle of the stream at their village where the girls used to fasten their little loin-cloths. And Musa waited in the meantime. When they had come (and) entered the water (and) bathed they laid aside their loin-cloths at the water's edge. Then he (Musa), came and took them all away, and went and climbed the tree in the middle of the water

وَ

فَرَقَ طُوفِيَرْ ؞ مُوسَبْ ؞

عَلَمَتَنْ غَدَ اَقْتَنْ ؞ قَجِي تَكُومُوا ؞ رَفِسَرْكِمَ ؞ يَجَيِي

دِيَفْلَسَ ؞ غُدَ اِمِيُوا ؞ دَمَبْ ؞ دَنِمَجِ ؞ سُكِفْرِمَ ؞ ا

اَكَبَا قَمِجِ ؞ اِقَ مَتْ ؞ مَتْ بَدَ اَقْتَسُوا ؞ لَسَرْوَمْنَتْ ؞ =

تَكُسُوا ؞ اِدَّنْ ؞ اَكَبْ قَجُو ؞ تَكِمَ اُوَرْ ؞ مُوسَنْ ؞ لَسِي

قَجُو تَمَبْ ؞ رَاَمَنْ ؞ وَنْكَخُوَا ؞ حَكَنْتَنْ ؞ كُلُمْ ؞ وَقَّمْ

لَسَرْوَقْتَ ؞ يَمَبْ مَقْ يَمَا غَتِفْسَنْ ؞ اَكُوَمِيْ ؞ وَتَكُوَرَمْ

غِمْ فَسَنْ ؞ يَدَوَا ؞ قَدَوَنْكَنْ ؞ تَكِمَ ؞ اِدَّوْ ؞ وَرَاَمْ قَمِّ

اَكُوَمِيْ ؞ رَنِدَ اَقَافْ ؞ طَكَنْ ؞ كُوَرَمْ ؞ غِمْ نَنْدَاسَ

بُدُو ؞ قَدَا دَمِرْ ؞ بَنْتَبُو ؞ سَرْمُوسَ ؞ يَكِّلُبُو ؞

سَقَدْ سَكَخُوَا ؞ لَسَنْشِغْ ؞ اَتِكِمْ ؞ رُوَا ؞ سُنَدَ اَوَنْكَنْ

سُكَاجِيْ ؞ بَنْتَنْتَسْ ؞ غِّبُونْ سَرْمِيدُوَا ؞ يَكُوَا

بِشَرْ ؞ دِكَ ؞ يَجِيْ قَجَوْ اِمَامِيْ ؞ طَكَنْ رُوَّنْ

tsatsakin ruan, kōwa ya fitō bai gani bantensa ba,
sai shi dinga kūka. Sai Mūsa kūa shi-na bisa, shi-na-
-gani, har su duka su-ka-fitō, ya che, 'Ku duka gā
bantunanku wurina, kōwa ya kirāyi sūnana
naa ba shi bantensa, idan ba hakanan ba; ba ni ba ku.'
Sai wata ta zō, ta che, 'Kai; Mūsa, kai Mūsa, Mūsa
[8] gaia, Mūsa dan sarākai, dōmin Ala Mūsa ba ni
bantena.' Sai shi ba ta. Hakanan hakanan har su duka
su-ka-karbi bantunansu. Sauran kanua tasa.
Sai aka-che, 'Tafi ki karbi bantenki.' Ruan kūa
iyākan idānun sau shi ke. Sai ta shiga [9] ruan,
ta che, 'Kai Mūsa, Mūsan gaia Mūsa dan sarā-
-kai dōmin Ala Mūsa ba ni bantena.' Sai Mūsa ya che,

(middle of the water), each one who came out did not see his (her) cloth, whereupon he (she) began to cry. And Musa was up above and watching till they all came out. He said, 'All of you, see, your cloths are with me. Whoever calls out my name, I will give him (her) his (her) cloth; otherwise I will not give you.' Then one girl came forward. She said, 'You, Musa, you, Musa, Musa the spiteful one, Musa the son of chiefs, for Allah's sake, Musa, give me my loin-cloth.' And he gave her (it). And so on, and so on, until they all received from him their cloths, and there was only left his little sister. And she was told, 'Go and get your cloth.' Now the water was up to the ankles. Then she entered the water (and) said, 'You, Musa, Musa, the spiteful one, Musa the son of chiefs, for Allah's sake, Musa, give me my loin-cloth.' But Musa said,

كَطِكِمْ ؞ زُوَّنْ كُوَرَا ؞ بِيِڢِثُوا ؞ بِيْغَمَ ؞ بُنْبُنْسَبِ ؞

تَسَنْ لِشِ ڢَعَمْ ؞ كُوكَوْ ؞ تَسَنْ مُوسَ كُوَّ ؞ لِشَدَ مِلَمْ ؞ لِشَدَ

ڢَنِمْ ؞ قَمْ سُودَكَ ؞ سَكَ ڢِثُوا ؞ يِبْ كُودَكَ ؞ غَدَ

بُنْبُنْكَ ؞ وُرِينَدَ ؞ كُوَنْ ؞ يِكَرَاتِ ؞ سُوڢَلَڢُ ؞ =

ڢَ بَاشِ ؞ بُنْبُنْسَنْ ؞ اِدَّنْ ؞ بَاكَكِنْدَ ؞ بَادَرْ ؞ بَاكَ

؞ تَسَنْ ؞ وُقَدَوْا ؞ تَبْ كِيمُوسَنْ كِيمُوسَنْ ؞ مُوسَنْ

غَمِيَا ؞ مُوسَنْ ؞ دَڢَلَكِنْ ؞ دُوقَمْ ؞ اَدَّنْ ؞ مُوسَنْ ؞ بَادَ

بُنْبُنْدَ ؞ تَسَنْ شِبَاتَ ؞ ڢَكَنْ ؞ ڢَكَنْ ؞ ڢَرْسُودَكَ

سَكَكَرْبِ ؞ بُنْبُنْسَنْ ؞ سُورَ ڢَڢُوا ؞ ڢَسَنْ ؞ =

سَعَ اَكَبْ ؞ تَبِمِ ؞ كِكَرْبِ ؞ بُنْبُنْكَ ؞ زُوڢَ كُوَا

اِيَّا كَنْ ؞ اِدَا ڢُنْسُوا ؞ ڢُشْكَ ؞ تَسَنْ تِشَعْ ؞ زُوَّنْ ؞

تَبْ كِيمُوسَنْ كِيمُوسَنْ ؞ مُوسَنْ غَمِيَا ؞ مُوسَنْ ؞ دَڢَلَا

كَمْ ؞ دُوقَمْ ؞ اَدَّا ڢُوسَنْ ؞ بَاڢُنْبُنْدَ ؞ تَسَنْ مُوسَنْ ؞ يِبْ

'Ba ni ba ki sai kin kāra fadi, saanan in ba ki.' Ashe
tā manche ne da ta tuna sai ta che, 'Kai wāne, kai wāne
wānen gaia, wāne dan sarākai, dōmin Ala wāne
ba ni bantena.' Sai ya che, 'Nā ki ba ki, nā ki ba ki,
sai kin che, Kai Mūsa, kai Mūsa, Mūsan gaia, Mū-
-sa dan sarākai, dōmin Ala Mūsa ba ni bantena.'
Sai nan da nan rua ya kāma mata kwobri. Sai ta che,
'Kai wāne, kai wāne, wāne(n) gaia, wāne dan sar-
-akai, dōmin Ala wāne ba ni bantena.' Sai rua
ya kāma ta ga katara. Sai Mūsa ya che, 'Na ki ba ki
sai kin che, Kai Mūsa, Mūsan gaia, Mūsa
dan sarākai, dōmin Ala Mūsa, ba ni bantena.'

'I do not give it to you till you have said it again, then I will give it to you.' Now she has forgotten (for a minute that she would not say his name); when she remembered, then she said, 'You, What's-your-name, you, What's-your-name, What's-your-name the spiteful one, What's-your-name the son of chiefs, for the sake of Allah, What's-your-name, give me my cloth.' But he said, 'I have refused to give you, I have refused to give you, till you say, You, Musa, you, Musa, Musa the spiteful one, Musa the son of chiefs, for the sake of Allah, Musa, give me my cloth.' Now by this time the water was up to her shins. Then she said, 'You, What's-your-name, you, What's-your-name, What's-your-name the spiteful one, What's-your-name the son of chiefs, for Allah's sake, What's-your-name, give me my loin-cloth.' But now the water had reached her thighs. But Musa said, 'I have refused to give you unless you have said, You, Musa, Musa the spiteful one, Musa the son of chiefs, for the sake of Allah, Musa, give me my cloth.'

أفشى ∴ إبداكِ ∴ سعتمْ ∴ قدِ ∴ وكنكاد ∴ سِنْ ∴ بداكِ بدار

وانبل وانبى

[redacted] كِنْ [redacted] كيتبْ تسنْ ∴ مشترة ∴ دبنبى تناهنبن

وانبر واكبر وانبر

[redacted] أآل ومنو دُ ∴ اكمْ سسمَ دِ [redacted] قيلنقن

بداتبنبتنى ∴ سنْ بيشْ قداكِ بداكِ ∴ قداكِ باكِ

سنْ كنبنْ ∴ كيفوسنْ ∴ كيفوسنْ ∴ موسنْ غياتْ ∴ مو

سنْ دِ فسنمَ اكمْ ∴ دُ ومْ أآلِ موسنْ بدارِ بنبنا ∴ =

سنْ قرْ دِ قمْ ∴ ورابكا اما مت ∴ كبرِ ∴ سنْ تنى

وانبس وانبى وانبس وانبل

كيموسنْ كيموسنْ موسنْ غيدا موسنْ دِ فسنمْ

وانبى

اكمْ دُ ومْسْ أآلِ موسنْ بدارِ بنبنْ سنْ وآرا ∴

يكامات ∴ كمكنرة ∴ سنْ موسنْ بيشْ ∴ قداكِ بداكِ

سنْ كنبنْ ∴ كيموسنْ ∴ موسنْ غيا ∴ موسنْ ∴ =

دِ فسنمَ اكمْ ∴ دُ ومنْ أآلِ موسنْ بدارِ بنبنبنى =

Ta che, 'Kai wāne, kai wāne, wānen gaia, wāne dan sarā-
-kai, dōmin Ala wāne ba ni bantena.' Sai Mūsa
ya che, 'Nā ki ba ki, nā ki ba ki sai kin che, Kai Mū-
-sa, kai Mūsa, Mūsan gaia, Mūsa dan sarākai
dōmin Ala Mūsa ba ni bantena.' Sai rua ya kāma ta
ga kirji. Sai ta che, 'Kai wāne, kai wāne, wānen gaia,
wāne dan sarākai, dōmin Ala wāne ba ni bantena.'
Sai Mūsa ya che, 'Nā ki ba ki, sai kin kirāyi sū-
-nana.' Sai rua ya kāma ta ga wia. Aka-che, 'Ke fadi
sūnansa, idan ba ki fadi ba rua [11] yaa chi ki.'
Rua kua shi-na kōkari, shi kāma ta ga haba,
sai ta che, 'Kai Mūsa, kai Mūsa, Mūsan gaia

She said, 'You, What's-your-name, you, What's-your-name, What's-your-name, the spiteful one, What's-your-name the son of chiefs, for the sake of Allah, What's your name, give me my loin-cloth.' But Musa said, 'I have refused to give you, I have refused to give you, unless you say, You, Musa, you, Musa, Musa the spiteful one, Musa the son of chiefs, for the sake of Allah, Musa, give me my cloth.' And the water reached to her breasts, but she said, 'You, What's-your-name, you, What's-your-name, What's-your-name, the spiteful, What's-your-name the son of chiefs, for Allah's sake, What's-your-name, give me my cloth.' But Musa said, 'I have refused to give you till you have called out my name.' And the water was up to her neck. And they said, 'Speak his name; if you do not speak the water will swallow you up.' Now the water was trying hard to reach her chin. Then she said, 'You, Musa, you, Musa, Musa the spiteful one,

قب كيبوابى كيبوابى وابقر غيا وابى د قسرا

كم دوم آر وابى بدار بنشق تسر موسن

يب قدك بدك قدك بدك تسر كنب كيمو

تسن كيموسن موسن غ يد موسد قسرا كم

دوم آ موسن بدو بم تبشق تسر و وا يكامات

غكرج تسر قب كيبوابى كيبوابى وابقر غيا

وابى د قسراكم دوم آ وابى بدو بم تبشق

تسر موسن يب قدك بدك تسر كنكرابى تسو

قدقى تسر و يكامات قموتن آكب بكجى

سو قلسن اكر بكجى ميب وا يا قيك

وكو شقد كوكرم شكامات قمب

تسع قب كيموسن كيموسن موسن غيا

Mūsa dan sarākai dōmin Ala Mūsa ba ni bantena.'
Sai ya che, 'Kāra fadi.' Ta fadi. Ya che, 'Kāra.' Ta kāra har uku.
Ya che, 'Kii kāra fadi ni mijinki?' Ta che, 'Aa.'
'Ki-na sō mijin da aka-ba ki?' Ta che, 'I.' Mafāri
ke nan, wa ba shi auren kanua. Shi ke nan.
[12] Kungurus kan kūsu.

Musa the son of chiefs, for the sake of Allah, Musa, give me my cloth.' But he said, 'Repeat it.' She said it (again). He said, 'Again.' She repeated it, until three times. He said, 'Are you going to say again that I am your husband?' She said, 'No.' 'Do you want the husband whom you have been given?' She said, 'Yes.' This was the beginning (of the custom) that a brother should not marry his sister. That is all. Off with the rat's head.

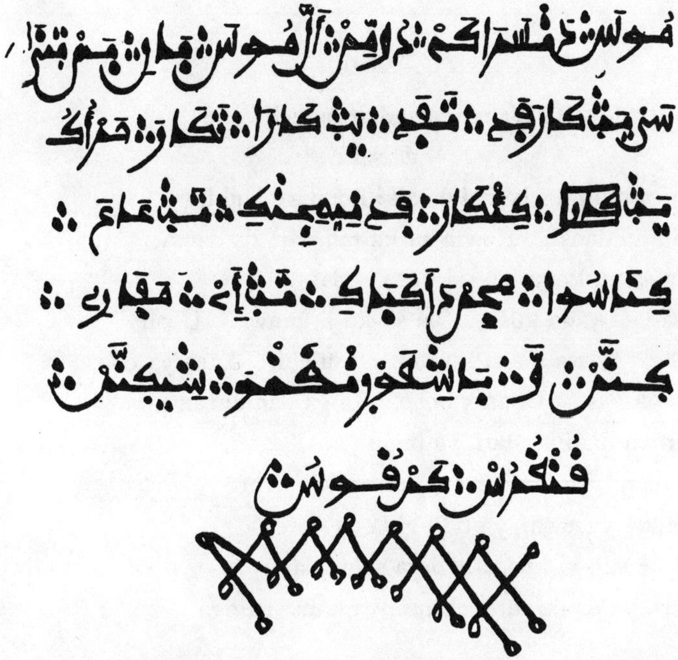

No. 19.

Wanan tātsunīar mahalbi che
da sarki.

Wani mutun ne, ba shi da aiki kōmi sai halbi,
da shi da dansa. Ranan su-ka-tafi dāji, da dansa,
ba su sāmu kōmi ba, sai kūsu. Sai
dansa [1] ya yāda kūsu. Sai su-ka-ji yunwa. Uban
ya che, '[2] Gasa muna kūsunmu, mú chi.' Yārō ya che,
'Ai [3] nā yas.' Uban ya che, 'Ka ga dan durun uwa.'
Uban ya dauki gātari, ya buge yārō,
ya sūma. Ya [4] tafia(r)sa, ya bar shi. Yārō
ya falka, ya tāshi, ya tafō gida da dare.
Ya iske sun yi kwāna, sai ya shiga dā-
-kinsa, ya dauki tarkachensa, ya kāma hainya,

This tale is about a hunter (lit. a shooter) and a chief. There was once a certain man who had no other work but hunting, both he and his son. One day (he) they went to the bush with his son. They did not find anything but a rat, and his son threw the rat away. But they became hungry (and) the father said, 'Roast our rat for me, (and) let us eat.' The boy said, 'Oh, but I have thrown it away.' The father said, '. . .' (cursing him), (and) the father lifted (his) axe and struck the boy; he fainted. He (the father) went his way, (and) left him. The boy came round, he rose up, and went home by night. He found them asleep, so he entered the room and lifted his belongings. He took the road,

وَنَّمْ قَدْ طُو فِيِيرْ :. مَحَلِبِهِ ث

دِسَمْ كِم :.

وَنِمُشْثَمْبُنْ بَدَاشِدْ أَيْكِ :. كُوهِم :. سَمْ قَلْبِ :.

دِلِشْم :. دددفَلَسْ رَفَّمْ سُكْتَقِمْ :. دَرَاجِ :. دددفَلَسْ

بَهْسْ لَسَامْ :. كُوهِمْبَ :. لَسْمْ كُوسْ لَسَسْ

دِفْلَسْ مَبَادِ :. كُوسْ سَمْ سُكِمْ :. يِمْنُو :. أُبَمْ

يَثْ غَسَمْ مُمْ :. كُوسُغُمْ :. فَثْ :. يَدَارُويَثْ

أَ :. فَدَامِيسْ :. أُبَمْ يَثْ :. كَدَاغَدْ نُمْدُرُو نُمْقُوَّ :.

أُبَمْ يَدْوِكِ :. غَدَاقَمْ :. يِمْبُغْ :. يَدَاوُ :.

يِسْوَمَمْ :. يِتَّبِيِّسْ :. يِسِمْبُرِشْ :. يَدَارُوثْ :.

يَقَلْكَ :. يِتَّدَاشْ :. مِتَّبُو :. غَدَا :. دَدَبْرَسْ

يَدَاسْكَسْ :. لَسَمْ :. كُحَوَامْ :. لَسْ :. يِشِغْ :. دَ ٩

كَنْلَسْ يَدَّوِكِ :. نَمْ كَبْشْلَسْ يَكَمْ مَ تَمَّ

shi-na-zūa wani gari. Da ya kai gari da dare, sai
ya shiga chikin gari. Kōwa ya yi kwāna.
Shi-na-tafia chikin gari har ya kai gidan sarki.
Ya shiga har chikin gida, funtu, bābu rīga,
bābu wandō. Sai ya tāda sarki. Sarki
ya che, 'Daga ina?' Ya che, 'Daga gari kaza.' Sai sarki
ya che, 'Lāfia?' Yārō ya che, 'Da ni da ubana mu-ka-je
dāji yāwō halbi, ba mu sāmu kōmi, sai
kūsu guda daia, ya ba ni rikō, na manche shi
wani wuri. Da mu-ka-ji yunwa sai ya che, Kāwō kūsu,
mu gasa, mu chi. Sai na che, Nā yashe shi ban sani ba.
Sai ya yi fushi, ya dauki gātari, ya buge ni,
na sūma. Da mareche ya yi, sai na falka na tāshi,

(and) was going to a certain town. When he reached the town it was night; he entered into the town. Every one was asleep. He proceeded into the middle of the town until he reached the chief's house. He entered until he was right in the house, (he was) naked, without clothes, without trousers, and he met the chief. The chief said, 'From where?' (And) he replied, 'From such and such a village.' And the chief said, 'Is it well with you?' The boy said, 'Both I and my father went to the bush to walk and shoot. We did not find anything but one single rat, he gave (it) me to keep, I forgot it somewhere. When we became hungry, then he said, Bring the rat that we may roast it and eat. And I said, I have dropped it, I do not know where. Thereupon he became angry. He lifted his axe (and) struck me. I fainted. When evening came then I recovered (and) rose up,

شنداور ∴ ونغمر ∴ ديكن غمر ∴ دكرور آسي ∴

يشغ ∴ تكن غمر ∴ كووا ∴ تايكواشس ∴

شنا تبي ∴ تكن غمر ∴ تمر بكن ∴ غد مسركم ∴

يشغ ∴ تمر تكن غدا ∴ فنتو ∴ بداب ∴ ريحي

يداب ∴ وفدور ∴ لسن ويتاد ∴ لسركم ∴ سركم ∴

يث ∴ دغ اقلي ∴ يث دغغر ∴ كدا ∴ سن سركم ∴

يث ∴ لافي ∴ يداور ∴ يث دفي دابداقل ∴ مكجي

داج ∴ يداور ∴ قلب ∴ بحسام ∴ كوم ∴ نسي

كوسن غداد تن ميبارو ∴ فو ∴ تمتبشن

ونور ∴ دمكج ∴ فنو ∴ لسن يث ∴ كداور كوس

مغس ∴ مث ∴ سن مث ∴ قد يد ابشن ∴ مسيب

سني يمي ∴ فشم ∴ بيمي وكي ∴ غدا قبري ∴ يبغنيم

نسومري ∴ دمم مث ∴ يمر سن ∴ مبلك ∴ قتا يش

na zō nan.' Sarki kūa ya je yāki, aka-kāma dansa aka yanke shi. Sarki ba shi da dā, namiji. Sai sarki ya che, 'Yanzu ba ka rufa mani asīri?' Yārō ya che, 'Rufin asīri kaman kāka? Sarki ya che, 'Ba ni da dā namiji, in gari ya wāye, in che kai dāna ne, da aka-kāma wurin yāki, ka gudānō, ka zō.' Yārō ya che, 'Wanan ai ba shi da wia.' Sarki ya shiga dāki, ya daukō bindiga, ya buga chikin dare. Sai [5] uwar gidansa ta fitō, ta che, 'Alfanda zāki bāda rāzana, bindigar me ka ke bugu da da darenga?' Sarki ya che, 'Wāne [6] yā zō.' Sai uwar gida ta rangada [7] gūda. Sai gari ya tāshi tsaye, ana-che, 'Menene ya fāru, gidan sarki ana-buga bindiga da dadarenga?' Aka-che dan sarki ya zō wanda aka-kāma

---

(and) came here.' Now the chief had gone to war, and his son had been captured and killed. The chief had no male child. And the chief said, 'Now will you not keep a secret for me?' The boy said, 'What kind of a secret?' The chief said, 'I have no male child, when dawn comes I shall say you are my son, who was caught at the war, and that you ran away and came back.' The boy said, 'That is surely not difficult.' (Then) the chief entered his room (and) took up his gun (and) fired it (it was) in the middle of the night. And 'the mother of the house' came out (and) said, 'King, lion who causes fear, what is the gun you are firing in the night?' The chief said, 'So-and-so has returned.' Thereupon the mother of the house raised the sound of joy, and the town rose up, (and) they were asking, 'What had happened at the chief's house, (seeing that) they are firing a gun at this time of night?' (And) they said that the chief's son had come, he who had been caught

مَغُ وَقَّنْ سَرْكِمْ ∴ كُوَّ ∴ يِ جَنْ يَدَاكِ ∴ أَكْكَامْ ∴ دْ قْسَرْ
أَكِينْكُوشْ ∴ لَسَرْكِمْ ∴ بْدَاشْدَا ∴ نْمِجْ ∴ لَسْ لَسَرْكِمْ ∴
يَبْ ∴ يِقْغُ ∴ يَدَاكْرْ قَامِنْ ∴ أَسِيمِي ∴ يَدْرُو ءَايْبْ رُقِمْ
أَسِيمِي ∴ كَمَّنْ كَدَاكْ ∴ أَسَرْكِمْ ∴ يَجّْ يَدَّوْ ∴ دْ عَدَّا ∴ نَمِجْ
إِنْقْرِي ∴ يَعْدَا وَامِّيشْ ∴ إِنْشْ كَرْ ∴ دَاقْلْأَقْرْ ∴ دْأَكْكَامْ ∴
وُرْقْبَاكْ ∴ كَغْدَا أَقُو ∴ كَدْوْ ∴ يِدْرُو ∴ يَبْ وَقَّرْ
أَ ∴ بْدَاشْدْ رُوبَا ∴ سَرْكِمْ ∴ يَقْلْغْ دَاكْ ∴ يَجّْ وُكْوَا ∴ بْنَدِغْ
يَبْغْ ∴ تْكْرْجْ دْرَنْ ∴ لَسْ عُورْ ∴ غْدْ قْسَنْ ∴ قْبْجْتُو ∴ قَتْ
أَلْقَنْدْ ∴ ذَاكْ ∴ بْدَادَ رَادَقَنْ ∴ يِقْدِ غَمْ يَبَنْ ∴ كَبَ بْغْ
دْ ∴ ءَدّْرْ يَمْغْ ∴ لَسَرْكِمْ ∴ يَبْ وَأَبَنْ ∴ يَلْغْرْو ∴ لَسْ عُوَّرْ عَدَا ∴
تَمْ قْغَدَ ∴ غُودَ ∴ لَسْ غَمِي ∴ يَتَّاشْ طَيَّنْ ∴ أَقَابْ ∴
مَبْنَنْ ∴ يَبْقَاوْ ∴ غْدْ قْسَرْكِمْ ∴ أَقْنَا بْغْ ∴ يَقْدِ غْمْ ∴ ددد
دْ ∴ ءَدّْرْ يَمْغْ ∴ أَكْبْ ∴ دْقَمْرْكِمْ ∴ يَغْدْو ∴ وَقْدْ أَكْكَامْ

wurin yāki.' Aka che, 'Mādala, mādala.' Gari ya wāye,
yārō ya yi wanka, sarki ya gama masa
kāya, ya fitō. Fādanchi, wadansu su-na-chewa,
'Ba dansa ba ne.' Wadansu su-na-chewa, 'Dansa ne.' Ranan
sai sarākai su-ka-gama kai, sú-ka-che, 'Ku bari
mu gani, izan dansa ne.' Su-ka-gama ma dīansu
kāya, su-ka-damra masu sirida bisa angarmu,
su-ka-hau, su-ka-che masu, 'Ku bi gidan sarki,
ku kirāyi dansa, ku che ku tafi kilīsa.' (sk)
Su-ka-che, 'In kun je, kun yi sukua, in kun zāme,
ku sabka, ku sāre dawākin, ku kōmō gida.'
Kōwa ya ba dansa kansakali, ya rātaya,
su ka je gidan sarki, su ka kira yārō. Ashe

---

at the war.' And they said, 'Indeed! indeed!' When it was dawn the boy bathed (and) the chief gave him (gifts) goods (and) he came forth. (Among) the councillors some said, 'It is not his son.' Others said, 'It is his son.' Now one day the head-men joined their heads together, (and) said, 'Wait, and we shall see if it is (really) his son.' Then they added goods (presents) to those their children already had, (and) they put the saddles on the war-horses for them. (And) they (the children) mounted, (and the fathers) said to them, 'Go to the chief's house and call his son, and say you are going to take horse exercise.' And they said, 'When you have gone and galloped and pulled up, you must dismount, (and) kill your horses, (and) come home.' (And) each one gave his son a sword (and) he slung it on his shoulder, (and) they came to the chief's house and called the boy. Now truly

وُرْفِيَاكِ ∴ أَكْتُبْ مَادَّلَهْ ∴ مَادَّلَهْ ∴ غَمِرْ مِيَوَ ابِى

يَادُوِرْ ∴ يَمِيّ ∴ وَنْكَرْ ∴ سَرْكِمْ ∴ بَغْمَرْ ∴ مَسَّنْ

كَدَايَا ∴ يَبِتُو ∴ قَادَمْنِشْ ∴ وَدَمُسَنْ ∴ لُسَنَابْتُوَا

بَادَمْسَبَنْبَنْ ∴ وَدَمْسَنْ ∴ لُسَنَابْتُوَا ∴ دَمْسَبْنَنْ ∴ وَمَّرْ

سَنْسَرَاكُنْ ∴ سُكَغَمَ كَنْ ∴ سُكَبْ ∴ كُبَجِمْ

مُغَنِمْ ∴ إِدَرْ ∴ دَمْسَبَنْ ∴ سُكَغَمَنْ ∴ مَدِيَمْسَ

كَدَايَا ∴ سُكَدَ مَرْ ∴ مَسَنْ ∴ لِسِرِدَا ∴ بِسَنْ ∴ أَنْكُمْ مُو

لُسَكَجَوْ ∴ سُكَبْمَسَنْ كُبِمِ غَدَمْسَرْكِ ∴ ∴

كُكِمَارَ ∴ دَمْسَنْ ∴ كُبْكَنْبِمْ ∴ كِلِيبَسَنْ ∴ سَكْ

سُكَبْ ∴ إِرْكُنْجَمْشِ كُمْتّ ∴ لُسَكُوَا ∴ إِرْكُمْ دَامِى

كُسَبَكْ ∴ كُسَدِبَرَنْ دَوَاكِمْنْ كُكُو مُوغِدَا

كُوَوَا ∴ يَبِعَمْسَنْ كَنْسَفِلِمْ ∴ مِيرَاتَيَا ∴

لُسَكِمَنْ غَدَمْسَرْكِمْ ∴ سُكَكِمَ ∴ يَادُوِ ∴ آنْبَسَ

makwarmachi yā ji, ya je, ya gaya ma sarki. Sarki ya yi shiri ya aje ya che, 'Funtu ya yi rawa, bale mai-rīga.' Sarki ya kirāyi yārō, ya fada masa, ya che, 'In kun je, kōmi ka gani sun yi, kai ma ka yi.' Yau yāra su-ka-zō, su-ka-kirāyi dan sarki, su-ka-tafi. Da su-ka-je, su-ka-yi sukua, sai su-ka-sabka, su-ka-sāre dawāki. Yau ɗan sarki, shi ma ya yi suka, ya zāme, ya sabka, ya sāre dōkinsa. Su-ka-kōmō gida. Sai sarakai su-ka-che, 'Karia ne, gōbē ku kōma, gari ya wāye su-ka-zō, su-ka-kira shi.' Sarki ya sa dōgarai, su-ka-damra masa sirdi bisa baban dōki, su-ka-tafi. Da su-ka-je

---

some tale-bearer has overheard, (and) he went and told the chief. The chief made similar preparation (horse, &c.) and put the things aside, (and) said, 'If the naked man can dance, much more can the man with the cloak.' The chief called the boy, (and) told him, (and) said, 'When you have gone, everything you see they have done, do you also do.' So the boys came, (and) called the son of the chief, (and) they set off. As they went they galloped; then they dismounted (and) killed their horses. So the son of the chief he too galloped, pulled up, dismounted, (and) killed his horse. They went home. And the head-men said, 'It is a lie, to-morrow you go back.' When it was dawn they came (and) called him. The chief caused (his) body-guard to fasten the saddle on a great horse for him. They went off; as they went

ܡܟܡ ܡܫܢ :. ܝܡܐܓܚ :. ܝܓܚ :. ܝܓܢܝܐ ܩܣܪܟܡ :.

ܣܪܟܡ :. ܝܫܢ ܫܪ :. ܝܡܐܓܚ ܝܢܬ :. ܦܢܬܘܐ ܝܣ

ܙܘܐ :. ܡܒܚ ܡܝܪ ܡܓܚ ܣܪܟܡ :. ܝܟܡ ܐܪܢ :. ܝܡܐܪܘ

ܝܩܕܐ ܡܣܢ ܝܬܐ ܐܪܟܢܓܚ ܟܘܡܡ :. ܟܚܢܡ

ܣܢܢ ܟܢܡܢ :. ܟܢ :. ܝܚܝܕܐ ܘܐ :. ܣܟܕܘ :. ܣܟܟܪܐܢ

ܕܩܣܪܟܡ :. ܣܟܬܡ :. ܕܣܟܓܚ ܣܟܢ :. ܣܟܘܐ :.

ܣܢ :. ܣܟܣܒܟ :. ܣܟܣܕܐ ܪܢ ܕܘܐ ܟܡ :. ܝܣܘ :.

ܕܩܣܪܟܡ :. ܫܝܡܢ :. ܝܣܢ ܣܟܡ :. ܝܕܐ ܡܢ :. ܝܣ

ܝܣܒܟ :. ܝܣܕܐ ܪܢ :. ܕܘܟܢܣܢ ܣܟܟܘ ܡܘܓܕܐ

ܣܢ :. ܣܪܐ ܟܢ ܣܟܬ :. ܟܪ ܝܕܐ ܒܡܢ :. ܓܡܘ ܒܢ

ܟܟܘܡ :. ܓܡ :. ܝܚܘ ܝܡܢ :. ܣܟܕܘ :. ܣܟܟܪܐܫ

ܣܪܟܡ :. ܝܡܢ :. ܕܘܓܡܝ :. ܣܟܡ ܡܪܐ ܡܣܢ :. ܒ

ܝܣܪܕ :. ܝܣܢ ܝܒܡܢ :. ܕܘܟ :. ܣܟܬܡ :. ܕܣܟܓܚ

su-ka-yi sukūa. Sai su-ka-sasabka, [8] su-ka-sasāre dawākinsu. Dan sarki, shi kuma da ya yi suk(u)a, sai ya sāre dōkinsa, su-ka-kōmō gida. Sai sarākai su-ka-bai dīansu bāyi, buduri māsu-chau, su-ka-che, 'Ku tafi da su chikin dāji, ku sasāre su.' Makwormachi ya je, ya kwormata ma sarki, sai sarki ya ba dansa [9] kuyangi bīū, ya che, 'Ku tafi, kōmi ka gani sun yi, kai ma ka yi.' Su-ka-tafi dāji, yan sarākai su-ka-sasāre kuyanginsu, dan sarki shi kuma ya sasāre nāsa, su-ka-kōmō gida. Sai su-ka-che dansa ne. Ana-nan,

---

they galloped. Then they dismounted, (and) killed their horses. The chief's son also, when he had galloped, then he killed his horse, (and) they returned home. Then the sub-chiefs gave their sons slaves, beautiful maidens, (and) said, 'Take them to the midst of the bush (and) slaughter them.' The tale-bearer (again) went and informed the chief, and the chief gave his son two female slaves, he said, 'Go, whatever you see they have done, do you do too.' They went to the bush. The sons of the head-men killed their female slaves (and) the chief's son also killed his, (and) they returned home. And they said, 'It is his son.' And so time went on,

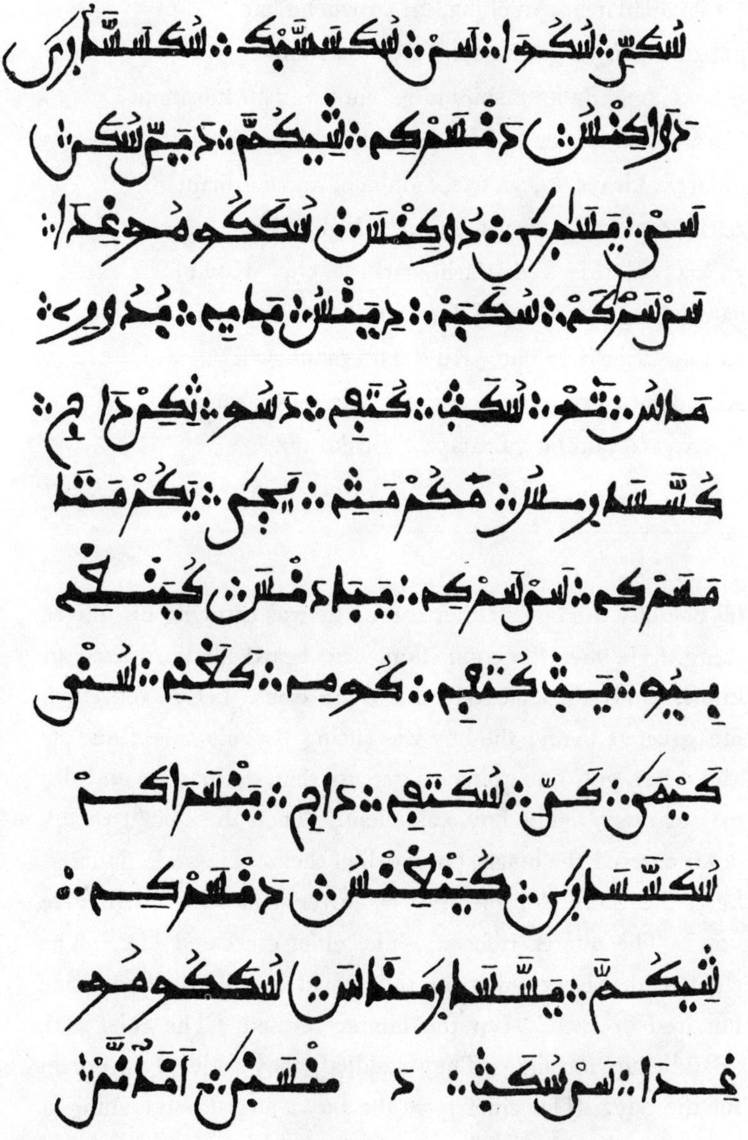

sai ranan uban yārō ya zō, shi-na-rātaye da kwori.
Ya iske fādanchi, ya chika, sai ya wuche har
gaban sarki, ya gaishe su. Yārō na zamne.
Sai ya che, 'Ba ka tāshi, mu je, mu yi ginan kūsanmu?'
Yārō shi na kurum. Sai sarki ya tāshi, ya shiga
gida, ya kirāye su, ya che, 'Mahalbi ka rufa mani
asīri, kōmi ka ke sō naa ba ka.' Mahalbi
ya kia. Sarki ya yi lālāshi, sarki ya che, 'Kōmi
na dunianga [10] naa baka dari dari.' Sai mahalbi
ya kia. Sarki ya che, 'Ku damra mani sirdi.'
Aka-damra sirdi, aka-damra ma yārō sirdi, sarki
ya ba yārō takōbi, ya rātaya. Su-ka-tafi

---

till one day the boy's father came; he was carrying his quiver slung. He met the councillors; he heard all he wished to know, (and) then passed on till (he came) before the chief. He greeted them; the boy was sitting (by his side); and he said, 'Are you not going to get up that we may go and dig for our rats?' The boy was silent. Then the chief rose up, (and) entered the house, (and) called them. He said, 'Hunter, keep the secret for me, and whatever you wish I will give you.' The hunter refused. The chief entreated him. The chief said, 'Everything in the world I will give you, one hundred of each.' But the hunter refused. The chief said, 'Saddle up for me.' They saddled, they saddled (a horse) for the boy. The chief gave the boy a sword, (and) slung it across his shoulder. They went off

تسرو قمر .: ابص ميداوو .: يمذو .: لشناواتسين دكري

يااسكن .: قاد منشم .: بيدثك .: تسريجوث .: حسر

غسبر لسركم .: يخيبشسش يداوو نماذمفي

تسويبث .: بداكتنااشن مجكمو .: غنمن كوسنم

يداوو .: شناكرم .: تسرتسركم .: يتداشن يشح

غدا .: يمكراميسش يبث معلبم .: كرقامر

اسيري .: كومم .: تكجكسوا .: قمباك .: معلبم

يكنن .: سركم .: يسلااشم .: تمركم يبث .: كومم

نذرنينغ .: قاباك .: عررزي .: تسر معلبم .:

يفن .: لسركم .: يبث كدمرامن .: لسرذ .: اكدمر

لسرذ .: اكدمرا .: ميداوو .: لسرذ .: لسركم .:

يبأيداووا .: تكوبم .: يمراتيا .: لسكتنفم .:

dāji. Sarki ya tsaya, ya che ma yārō, '[11] Au ka sāre ni, ka dauki kāyanga, ka ba ubanka, ku kōma gari, ku chi duniarku, au ka sāre ubanka, ni da kai mu kōma, mu zamna.' Yārō ya yi barkatai.

Tō in kai ne Batūre, chikinsu,
wa zaa ka sārewa chikinsu ?
In ba ka san wanda zaa
ka sāre ba,
shi ke nan.
[12] Kungurus kan kū-
-su.

---

to the bush. The chief halted (and) said to the boy, 'Either you kill me, (and) take these goods (horse, &c.), (and) give to your father, (and) return to the town, (and) enter into your (kingship) world, or you kill your father, (and) you and I will go back and live (as before).' The boy was distracted, (not knowing what to do). Now if it were you, O white man, among them whom would you kill ? If you do not know whom you would kill, there it is. Off with the rat's head.

دَاجِ: لَسْنكِم: مِيطَن: مِيثَمِيَاوُو: أَوْكَسَدَارَمِيم

كَدَوْكِ: كَدِيفْخ: كَبَا: أُمَنْكَ: كُكُو مَ:

غَمِرِ: كُنِذُوفِيمْكَ: أَوْكَسَدَارَمِن أُمْنكَ:

فِمِ دَكَن: مَكُوَمَ: مُخَّ مَرْنْ يَادُرُ: يِمِ بَمِنْكَنْش

تُو: إِرْكِيَنْ جَتْوُرِ تِكَنْش

وَلِهْ ذَا أكَسَدَارْمُوَلِهْ تِكَنْس

إِرْبَكَسَفُو فَدَ دَ أُ

كَسَدَارَبَ

شِيكَفَم

فَنْغَمْسِ

كَرْفُو

سْ

No. 20.

Wanan tātsūnīar
dumā che da yārinya

Wani mutum ne, sūnansa Alabarma, atājiri.
Shi-na da kurdi dayawa, bai sāmu haifua ba.
Sai chikin sādakunsa, wata ana-che mata Watapansa,
ita che [1] ta haifi dīa guda daia, mache, shi kūa
Alabarma ba shi sō abinda ke taba yārinya
nan. Ita kua yārinya sūnanta, Furaira.
Yau ranaṉ uwa tata ta gōya ta, su-ka-tafi dāji
dōmin ta yi tōrōtso. Sai Furaira ta ga
dan dūme guda daia, shi ke nan gare ta, bābu
wani kuma. Sai ta che, 'Alabarma, tsumke mani dan dumē

This is a story about a pumpkin and a maiden. There was a certain man by name Alabarma, a rich man. He had much money, (but) he had not any children. But among his concubines was one called Watapansa, (and) she had given birth to one daughter; and he, Alabarma, did not wish anything to touch this little girl. Now the girl's name was Furaira. And one day her mother took her on her back and they went off to the bush in order that she might ease herself. And Furaira saw one young pumpkin, that was all she (the mother pumpkin) had; there was not another. And she, (the little girl) said, 'Alabarma (Watapansa?) pluck the baby pumpkin for me

وَأَمْر تَتَا طُوفِيَّمْ
دُمَا : فِيهِمَا رُفِّسَّ

وَنِفْتُنْبِنُ مُ سُوفُنْسَنْ أَلَّ : مَرِمْ :. أَمْتَا جِرِ
شَنَا دُكُرْدِ :. دَمِيُّو : مِيْسَامُ :. فَكِيِّقُوا ب
سَنْ تَكُرْسَا دُكُولَسْ رَتْ ! أَمْثَا بَثْمَتَ :. وَرَتْبَقْنَسْ
إِمْشِ :. تَحِيدِ :. دِ مِيَا غْدَا ادمَّرْ :. مَجُ :. شِيكُوَّ
أَلَّ مَرِمْ :. مَا شِسْمُو :. أَمِنْدَ بِكَتَبْ :. مِيَارُنْسَ
نَمْ تَا إِتَكُوَّ مِيَارُّنْ سُومُنْتَ فُرْمِيْرَا
مِيُورُمْنْ :. عُوَّانَتَ :. تَعُومِيَاتْ :. سَكَتِقِمْ دَاج
دُومِمْنْ قَمْ :. شُورُوطُو :. سَوْ فُرِيمْ :. فَتْخ
دُفْدَ مِمِ :. غُدَا دَرَّ :. شِيكُفْنُ غَمْ مُتَّ :. مَجَابْ
وَمِكُمْ :. سَرْتَبْا أَلَّ مَرْمَ :. طَهْبُكُمُنْ دُفْدَ مِمْ

in yi wāsa.' Sai Alabarma ta che, 'Haba Furaira
kāka dan dūme guda daia shi ke nan,
ga uwa(r)sa, ni ke tsumkēwa, in ba ki.' Sai Furaira
ta rika kūka, sai uwa tata Alabarma
ta che, 'Idan ki yi kūka ne, sai ki yi, ama
ba ni tsumke dan dumē guda dai in ba ki.'
Su-ka-zō gida, yārinya ta-na-kūka.
Ubanta ya tanbaya, uwa ta gaya masa
mafāri. Sai uban yārinya ya che, 'Kōma,
ki tsumke, ki ba ta.' Yau, ta kōma,
ta tsumke, ta ba ta. Ana-nan, sai ranan
dan dumē ya rika bin yārinya, shi-na-
-fadi, 'Nāma in chi Furaira, nāma in chi.'

---

to play (with).' But Alabarma (Watapansa?) said, 'Come now, Furaira, how is this? One solitary baby pumpkin is there. See, there is its mother, (which) I will pluck and give you.' But Furaira began to cry and her mother Alabarma (Watapansa?) said, 'If you are going to cry you must just cry, but I am not going to pluck the solitary baby pumpkin to give you.' They returned home, (and) the little girl continued weeping. Her father asked (the cause). Her mother told him from the beginning. And the little girl's father said, 'Go back, (and) pluck (it), and give to her.' So she returned, (and) plucked it, (and) gave her. Then that day the baby pumpkin commenced to follow the maiden. It kept saying, 'Meat I must eat, Furaira, meat I must eat.'

إِنْتِي ؞ وَالسَّنْ سَرْ أَلَّ بَرْمَ ؞ تَشْ جَبَرْ قَرَيْمَرَا ؞

كَدَكَ ؞ دَقْدُ مَبَنْ غُدَادَمَّرْ شَيْبَكُقَّرْ ؞

غُقُوسَّنْ نَبَكَطَمْبَكُوَا ؞ إِقْبَاكِ ؞ سَنْ قُرَيْمْ

تَمْرَكْ ؞ كُوكَكَنْ سَنْ عُوَ أَتَّقْ أَلَّبَرْمَمْ ؞

تَشْ ؞ إِدَّرْ كِيَّكُوكَابَنْ لَسَنْ كِيَّ ؞ أَمَّا

بَدَانِطَمْبَكَ ؞ دَقْدُ مَبَنْ غُدَادَمَّرْ ؞ إِقْبَاكِ

سُكُدُو ؞ غَدَا ؞ يَادُ وَقَّنْ تَمْدَا كُوكَسْ

أُبَقْتَ ؞ يَتَنْبَيَا ؞ غُوَاتَخَيْدَا قَّسَنْ

مَقَارِي ؞ سَنْ أُبَرْيَادُوتَّرْ ؞ يَشْ كُومَسْ

كِطَمْبَكَنْ ؞ كَبَاتَ ؞ يَبُوتَكُومَ ؞ مَ

تَطَمْبَكَنْ تَبَاتَ ؞ أَقَّا أَقْمَرْ سَنْ رَقْتْ

دَقْدُ مَبَنْ يَبَرَكْ ؞ يِقَنَيْدُ وَقَنَ ؞ شِتَا

قَجِ ؞ قَدَامَ ؞ إِقْتِي ؞ قُرَيْمَ ؞ قَدَامَيَّا ؞ أَقْتِ

Sai aka-zō, aka-shaida masa, aka-che, 'Gā Furaira dan dumē na-bin ta, shi-na-che, wai nāma shi chi.' Alabarma ya che, 'Aje chikin akuyōyi.' Aka-kai shi chikin akuyōyi, ya chinye. Aka-kai shi ga wadansu, ya chinye, hakanan har ya chinye garken awāki dari uku da hamsin. Sai dumē ya kōmō, shi-na-fadi, 'Nāma in chi Fūraira, nāma in chi.' Aka-zō, aka-fada ma ubanta, sai ya che, 'Akai-shi garken tumāki.' Aka-kai shi, ya chainye garke dare bakwoi na tumāki, ya kōmō, shi-na-bin yārinya, shi-na-fadi, 'Nāma in chi Furaira, nāma in chi.' Sai aka-che, '[2] Yā chainye garken

---

And they came and bore witness to him saying, 'Look at Furaira, the baby pumpkin is following her (and) saying he must eat meat.' Alabarma said, 'Put it among the goats.' It (the pumpkin) was put among the goats. It ate them up. It was taken to some others. It ate them up. And so on till it had devoured three hundred and fifty flocks of goats. But the pumpkin returned and said, 'Meat I must eat, Furaira, meat I must eat.' They came and told her father and he said, 'Let it be taken to the sheep-fold.' It was taken, and ate up a flock of seven hundred sheep. It came back, (and) kept following the maiden, (and) saying, 'Meat I must eat, Furaira, meat I must eat.' And they said, 'It has eaten the flock of

سَرْ أَكْذُو ∴ أَكْشِيمْ امْسَنْ أَكْثْ ∴ غْ ابْقُرْمِيمْ ∴

دْقْذْ مِنْ قَدْمِغْتْ ∴ شَنَا بْقُوبْنَامْ ∴ شِيغْ

آلْهَمْرَمْ ثِيغْ أَجِنْ ثْكِمْ ∴ أَكِيُّومِيمْ ∴ أَكْكِيْنِشْ

ثْكِمْ أَكِيُومِيمْ ∴ يِقْشْنِينْ أَكْكْبْنِشْ ∴ غْمُودْقْسْ

يِشْقِينْ تَكْنَنْ ∴ حَمْ يِشْنِينْ غَمْ بْكِنْ ∴ أُوَاكِمْ

دُرِي أَكْ ∴ دْقْخْسِمْ ∴ سَنْ دْمِكْ ∴ يَكُومُوا

شَنَا قْدِي ∴ قْمَامْ ∴ إِنْشْ بْقُرْمِيمْ ∴ قْمَامْ ∴ إِمْقْ

أَكْذُو ∴ أَكْبْدَامْ ∴ أُبْمِغْتْ ∴ سَنْ يَبْ ∴ أَكْبْنِشْ

غَمْ بْكِنْ ∴ قْمَلْكِمْ ∴ أَكْكِيْنِشْ يِثْنِينْ

غَمْ بْكِنْ ∴ دْرِي بْكَنْ ∴ قْتْمَلْكِمْ ∴ يَكُومُوا

شَنَا بْحِيَا رْقَمْ ∴ شَنَا قْدِي ∴ قْمَامْ ∴ إِمْقِشْ بْقُرْمِيمْ

قْمَامْ إِمْقِي ∴ سَرْ أَكْثْ ∴ يَامْقْشْنِينْ ∴ غْمْرِيكْسْ

tumāki, [3] yā kōmō, shi-na-bin-ta.' Ubanta ya che, 'Akai shi garken shānu.' Aka-kai shi garken shānu, ya chainye garken shānu duka. Ya kōmō, shi-na-bin yārinya, shi-na-fadi, 'Nāma in chi Furaira, nāma in chi.' Sai aka-zō, aka-gaya ma ubanta, sai shi kuma ya che, 'Akai-shi garken rākuma.' Aka-kai shi garken rākuma, sai ya chainye, ya kōmō, shi-na-bin yārinya, shi-na-fadi, 'Nāma in chi Furaira, nāma in chi.' Sai ya che, 'Akai-shi gidan bāyi?' Akai-shi gida-n bāyi, ya chainye-su, ya kōmō, shi-na-bin yārinya, shi-na-fadi, 'Nāma in chi Furaira, nāma in chi.'

---

sheep, (and) has come back and is following her (the maiden).' Her father said, 'Let it be taken to the cattle kraal.' It was taken to the cattle kraal. It ate up the whole kraal of cattle. It returned, (and) was following the maiden (and) saying, 'Meat I must eat, Furaira, meat I must eat.' And they came and told her father, and he again said, 'Let it be taken to the camel kraal.' It was taken to the camel kraal; but it ate them up, (and) returned. It was following the maiden (and) saying, 'Meat I must eat, Furaira, meat I must eat.' And they said, 'Let it be taken to the slaves' quarters.' It was taken to the slaves' quarters, it ate them up; it returned, (and) was following the maiden, (and) saying, 'Meat I must eat, Furaira, meat I must eat.'

ثُمَالِكُمْ ؞ يَالْكُو مُو ؞ شِنَا مِنْتَ ؞ أُمَنْتَ يِبْ

أَكِبِشْ نَمْ بِكِنْ ؞ شَا قُوا ؞ أَكَكِيشْ نَمْ بِكِنْ

شَا قُوا ؞ يِتِشِپِنْ ؞ نَمْ بِكِنْ ؞ شَا نْوا ؞ دِك

يَكُو مُوا ؞ شِنَا مِنْ ؞ يِدِ رِفْنَ ؞ شِنَا قِبِ نَمَ حَمِ

إِفْتِ ؞ فُرْمِيرَ ؞ نَمَ إِمْشِ ؞ سَمْ أَكُذُورِ ؞

آكِفِيَامَ ؞ أُمِنْتَ ؞ سَمْ شِيكُمَ ؞ يِبْ ؞ أَكِيشِ

نَمْ بِكِنْ رَافُمَ ؞ أَكَكِيشِ نَمْ بِكِنْ رَافُمَ

سَمْ مِتِشِپِنْ يَكُو مُوا ؞ شِنَا مِنِيَا رِفْنَ ؞

شِنَا قِبِ ؞ نَمَامَ ؞ إِمْشِ فُرْمِيرَ ؞ نَمَامَ إِمْشِ ؞

سَمْ مِيبْ أَكِيشِ نَمْ قِبَايِمِ ؞ أَكَكِيشِ نَمْ بَ

نْبَايِمِ ؞ يِتِشِپِسْ يَكُو مُوا ؞ شِنَا بِنِيَا رِفْنَ

شِنَا قِبِ ؞ نَمَامَ إِمْشِ ؞ فُرْمِيرَ ؞ نَمَامَ إِمْشِ ؞

Ubanta ya che, ‘Ku kai shi ruga.’ Aka-kai shi ruga,
ya chainye mutānen ruga, ya kōmō, shi-na-fadi,
‘Nāma in chi Furaira, nāma in chi.’ Hakanan
har ya chainye mutāne duka, shānu, akuyōyi
tumāki, rākuma, dawāki, duka ya chainye,
hata kāji, zābi, agwagwa, tantabara,
duka, sauran mai-gida kadai. Sai ya bi yārinya,
sai ta gudu, ta bi ubanta, sai ubanta ya che,
‘Bābu kōmi kuma sai ni kadai, idan ni
‘zaa ka chi, dauke ni, ka chi.’ Sai dan dumē ya dauke shi,
ya hadē. Sai ya bi yārinya, ta gudu, ta je
wurin rāgo lahia ubanta. Sai ya je, zaa shi kāma (ya)

Her father said, ‘Take it to the cattle grazing ground.’ They took it to the grazing ground (and) it devoured all the people on the ground, (and) came back, (and) said, ‘Meat I must eat, Furaira, meat I must eat.’ And so on, until it ate up all the people, cattle, goats, sheep, camels, horses, all it devoured, even the fowls, guinea-fowls, ducks, pigeons, everything (and) there remained only the master of the household. And it (the pumpkin) followed the maiden, and she ran, (and) went after her father, and her father said, ‘There is nothing left but I myself. If it is I you would eat, take me, (and) eat me.’ And the baby pumpkin took him up and swallowed him; then it followed the maid. She fled, and came to the paschal ram of her father's. And it came on, (and) was about to seize

أبنت يب ∴ ككيش زغم ∴ أككيش زغم

بشين متا بمن زغن يكومو ∴ شنا قد

قلم ∴ إفش فجرير ∴ نقام إفش ∴ قكنش

قم ميشين متابمن ذك ∴ شاقوا ∴ أكيو ميم

نقاكيم ∴ وافحم ∴ دراكم ∴ ذك ∴ ميا قنبيس

كتن كاجم ∴ قربم ∴ أغواغ ∴ قنتبرا ∴ =

ذك ∴ سورقميغدا ∴ كدي ∴ سن ميم ∴ ميا وقس

سن نغذ ∴ قب أبنت ∴ اسن ∴ أبنت يبث

باب كومم ∴ كم ∴ اسبنم ككدي ∴ إدّ وقم

قاكش ∴ دوبجم ∴ ككش ∴ اسن دمد مس ∴ يكتنس

و

يحجكن اسن ميم ∴ ميا وقم ∴ قنكد تجس ∴

وزقم اغشو ∴ نيحر أبنت ∴ سن يحكن ذ اشكا مبا

yārinya, sai rāgon lahia ya zābura,
ya buga dan dumē da kafō. Sai ya pashe,
sai tumāki, da akuyōyi, da shānu, duka
su-ka-rika fitōwa. Shi ke nan. [5] Kunguru-
-s kan kūsu.

---

the maiden, but the paschal ram sprang forward, (and) struck the young pumpkin with his horn. And thereupon it split open, and sheep, and goats, and cattle, all kept coming forth. That is all. Off with the rat's head.

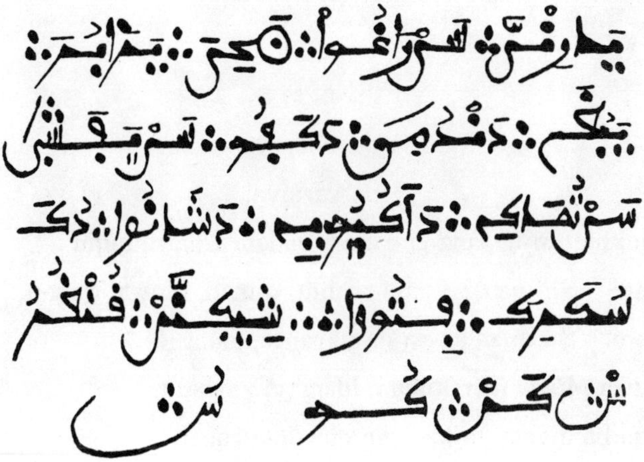

No. 21.

Wanan tātsunīar gāwō che
da yārinya.

Wani mutun ne, ana-che masa mālam Umaru mijin
[1] Lādi. Shi-na da [2] mātansa bīū, wanan, Mōwa, wanan,
Baura. Su duka su-na da yāyansu, mātā.
Wanan Mōwa nan, kulum, idan [3] tā yi shāra,
sai ta ba dīanta, ta kai gun gāwō, ta zubar.
Gāwō kūa shi-na da wani abu kamar chībi,
idan yārinyar nan ta kai shāra, sai ta taba,
ta che, 'Gāwō da chībi.' Kulum hakanan
ta ke yi. Ranan ta je, ta zuba shāra, sai ta taba.

This story is about a 'gawo'-tree and a maiden. There was a certain man, by name, Doctor Umaru, the husband of Ladi. He possessed two wives, one (called) Mowa, one (called) Baura. They both had children, girls. The one called Mowa, always, if she has swept, then she used to give (the sweepings) to her daughter, (and) she took them to where the gawo-tree was and threw (them) away. Now the gawo-tree had some growth on it that looked like a person's navel, and if this maiden took the sweepings (there) she used to touch (it) and say, 'The gawo-tree with the navel.' And it was always so she used to do. One day she went, (and) threw out the sweepings, (and) then touched (the mark).

ونّ قاطو فييرْ ∴ غداورْ

ديدو قنْ ∴

وفرْ منتبنْ ∴ آمّا قْهسّنْ مالّمْ ∴ عمْرْ ∴ بجمْ

اللّاح ∴ شنّادها قنّلسْ بيوْ ∴ وقّمْ مُووْنْ ∴ وقّمْ

بوْرْ ∴ سُودكْ ∴ سْنّاد يبّا ينّسْ ∴ ماقْسْ ∴

وقْمْ ∴ مُووقّمْ ∴ كُلّمْ ∴ إدّرْ ∴ قدايسّ ∴ شّدا راهْ ∴

سْ قنْباد يبنشْ ∴ تكسْ ∴ غنْغداورْ ∴ تدبرْ ∴

غداورْ ∴ كُوّ ∴ يشنّاد وبلّابْ ∴ تكسْ ∴ ثيببْ ∴

إدّرْ ∴ ميدار نبيرقّمْ ∴ تكسْ ∴ يشّد واهْ ∴ سمْ متّبْ ∴

تبْ ∴ غداوْ ∴ دثيبْ ∴ كُلّمْ ∴ تكنْ ∴ كْ

تكسْ ∴ زقْمْ تجمْ ∴ تّمخْبْ ∴ ثلّاد راهْ ∴ سْ متّباهْ ∴

Sai gāwō ya chire, ya bi ta, shi-na-fadi,
'Da sāfē, gāwō da chībi, da yama gāwō
da chībi.' Sai yārinya ta shēka, gāwō
ya bī ta. Ta je, ta iske māsu-shibka,
su-ka-che, 'Ke yārinya me ya fāru?' Ta che, 'Wani abu ne
ke bii na.' Su-ka-che, 'Zamna nan har shi zō.
Mu dauki abin shibka, mu bubugē shi, mu kashe.'
Aka-jima kadan sai gāwō ya zō, shi-na-
-fadi, 'Da sāfē gāwō da chībi, da yama gāwō
da chībi.' Sai māsu-shibka su-ka-che,
'Yārinya kāra gāba.' Sai yārinya
ta shēka, ta je, ta iske māsu-noma,
sai su-ka-che, 'Ke yārinya me ya fāru?'

But the gawo-tree pulled himself out (of the ground) (and) followed her, (and) was saying, 'Of a morning it's, The gawo-tree with the navel; of an evening it's, The gawo-tree with the navel.' Then the maiden ran away, (and) the gawo-tree followed her. She came (and) met some people sowing, (and) they said, 'You, maiden, what is the matter?' She said, 'Something is following me.' (And) they said, 'Sit down here till it comes. We will take the sowing implements, (and) beat him (and) kill (him).' They waited a little and then the gawo-tree came along. He was saying, 'In the morning it's, The gawo-tree with the navel; in the evening it's, The gawo-tree with the navel.' Thereupon the sowers said, 'Maiden, go further on.' And the maiden ran on. She came and met some people hoeing, and they said, 'Maiden, what is the matter?'

تسن : غداور : ييشمبر : ميبيتة : شندا قبه :

دصافبن : غداور : دشيبب : دتيحم غداور :

دشيبب : تسن يداوفن : تقبشك : غداور :

تيبيتة : تبجن : تماسبكن : مداستيشيك :

تسكب : بجيداوفن : ميقداور : تتب : ومامبني

بجبنتو : تسكب : دمقامن دحم شدو :

مدوك : امبشبك : مبجشن مكشبي

اكبجم : بكدن تسن غداور : ميدو شنا

قبه : دصافبن غداور دشيبب دتيحم غلوو

دشيبب : تسن مداستيشبك : تسكب :

ميدوفن : كداوا : غجبن : تسن يداوفن

تقبشك : تبجن تماسبكن : مداسفومن

تسن تسكب : بجيداوفن : ميقداو :

Sai ta che, 'Wani abu ke bii na.' Su-ka-che, 'Tsaya nan
shi zō, kō hauyōmu ba mu dauki, mu [4] bubuge shi,
mu kashe?' Aka-jima, sai gāwō ya tafō,
shi-na-fadi, 'Da sāfē gāwō da chībi, da yama
gāwō da chībi, yau kī ga gāwō da chībi.'
Sai su-ka-che, 'Yārinya kāra gāba.' Sai ta kāra
gāba, ta je, ta iske māsu-fūda, su-na-
-fūda, sai su-ka-che, 'Ke yārinya me ya fārū?'
Ta che, 'Wani abu ke bii na.' Sai su-ka-che, 'Zamna
nan har shi zō.' Aka-jima, sai gāwō
ya tafō, shi-na-fadi, 'Da sāfē gāwō da
chībi, da yama gāwō da chībi, yau kī ga

And she said, 'Something is following me.' (And) they said, 'Stand here, let him come. Can we not then lift our hoes, (and) hit him, (and) kill (him)?' They waited a little while, then the gawo-tree came towards them; he was saying, 'In the morning it 's, The gawo-tree with the navel; in the evening it 's, The gawo-tree with the navel; to-day you see the gawo-tree with the navel.' And they said, 'Maiden, pass on.' So she passed on, and went and met some people ploughing. They were ploughing, and they said, 'You, maiden, what is the matter?' She replied, 'Something is following me.' And they said, 'Sit down here till he comes.' In a little while, then the gawo-tree came up; he was saying, 'In the morning it 's, The gawo-tree with the navel; in the evening it 's, The gawo-tree with the navel. To-day you see

طيبا امْ ∴ سكب نبيتشن بك ∴ باب زنا ∴ تشب تس
مبيڧش ∴ كرو موجب ∴ موبوتوكو ∴ رو شذ
مكشبن أكجم ∴ لسن غداورو ∴ يتبڧوا ∴ =
شناڧب ∴ دصاڢي غداورد ڧيب ∴ عميم
غداورد ڧيب ∴ بجوكيغ ∴ غداورد ڧيب
تسن تكداو ∴ كداراغب ∴ ياورمن ∴ سكب تسن
غجب ∴ تبجكن تنا اسكن ∴ مداسجودا ∴ لسنا
ڢودا ∴ لسن ∴ سكب ∴ بكيارڧن ∴ جيڧبدار ∴
تشب ∴ وڧاب ∴ بكيتشن لسن سكب ∴ دمڧن
ڧمش حن شذو ∴ أكجم ∴ لسن غداورو ∴
يتبڧو ∴ شناڧبد ∴ دصاڢي غداورد ∴
شتيب ∴ دميم غداورو دڧيب ميوكيغ ∴

gāwō da chībi.' Sai su-ka-che, 'Yārinya kāra gāba.'
Sai yārinya ta shēka. Sai ta je ta iske kadangare,
shi-na-sāka, shi-na-fadi, 'Kiryan, ba kiryan ba,
zarta dāma, zarta hagu.' Sai ya che. 'Ke yārinya
ina zaa ki, ki na gudu?' Ta che, 'Wani abu ke kōra na.'
Ya che, 'Tsāya nan har shi zō.' Yārinya ta labe gun
kadangare, shi-na-fadi, 'Kiryan, ba kiryan ba,
zarta dāma, zarta hagu.' Har gāwō ya zō, shi-na-fadi,
'Da sāfē gāwō da chībi, da yama gāwō da chībi,
yau kī ga gāwō da chībi.' Sai yārinya ta che,
'Ga shi chan zakūa.' Sai kadangare ya che,
'Bari shi zō, ama in yā zō, ina-raba ki da shi,
ki-na-amre na?' Ta che, 'I.' Yau, sai gāwō ya zō.

---

the gawo-tree with the navel.' Thereupon they said, 'Maiden, pass on.' So the maiden ran on. Then she came (and) met a lizard; he was weaving and was saying, 'Kiryan, not kiryan, throw to the right, throw to the left (of the shuttle).' And he said, 'You, maiden, where are you going (that) you are running (so)?' She said, 'Something is pursuing me.' He said, 'Wait here till it comes.' The maiden nestled close up to the lizard, (who) was saying, 'Kiryan not kiryan, a cast to the right, a cast to the left,' until the gawo-tree came up. He was saying, 'In the morning it 's, The gawo-tree with the navel, in the evening it 's, The gawo-tree with the navel; to-day you see the gawo-tree with the navel.' And the maiden said, 'See, there he is coming.' And the lizard said, 'Let him come, but if he has come, (and) I save (lit. separate) you from him, are you going to marry me?' She said, 'Yes.' Now the gawo-tree came up.

غماور ∴ دم شيب ∴ سم ∴ سكش ∴ يداومر ∴ كداوغب
سم يداومر ∴ تبشك ∴ سم تجبم تداسكم ∴ كدنغبر
شنداسدك ∴∴ شنداقد ∴ كم يمن مداكم يمب
دم تمدام ∴ دم قمحغ ∴ سم يمش ∴ بكيدارمر ∴ =
إقدادك ∴ كندغد ∴ قش ومداب ∴ بككوواقم
يمش طيمن ∴ قم شدو ∴ يدرفمن ∴ قلبمن ∴ غمن
كد نغبمر ∴ شنداقد ∴ كم يمن ∴ مداكم بمن ب
دم قدام ∴ دم قمحغ قم غداور ∴ يمدو ∴ شنداقد
دصادفمن ∴ غداور دم شيب ∴ دميم غداور دم شيب
يمكيغ غداور دم شيب ∴ سم يداومر ∴ قش
غدا شنمر ∴ دكوا ∴ سم كد نغبر ∴ يمش
بم شدو ∴ أمد ∴ إريدادو ∴ إن فمر مداك ∴ دم شيم
كندا أمر مغدا ∴ قش إد ∴ يموسم ∴ غداور ∴ يمدو ∴

Ya che, 'Ina ajīana?' Kadangare ya che, 'Wani ajīa ka ba ni?' Gāwō ya che, 'Yārinya nan, da ke bāyanka.' Kadangare ya che, 'Wanan yā-rinya ta fi harfinka.' Sai gāwō ya che, 'Kadangare karanbani garēka.' Sai kadangare ya che, 'Ai namiji tonka ne, sai antaba, akan-san mai-yāji.' Sai gāwō ya yi fushi, ya kāma kadangare, ya hade, sai ya fitō ga idānun gāwō. Sai ya kuma kāma shi, ya hade, sai ya fitō ga kunuwansa. Sai ya kuma kāma shi, ya hade, sai ya fitō ga kirjinsa. Sai ya kuma kāma shi, ya hade, kadangare ya fitō

He said, 'Where is the thing I gave you to keep for me?' The lizard said, 'What did you give me?' The gawo-tree replied, 'The maiden who is behind you.' The lizard said, 'This (maid) is stronger than you.' And the gawo-tree said, 'Lizard, you are forward.' But the lizard replied, 'Ah! A man is like the little red peppers, not till you have touched (tasted) them do you know how hot they are.' Then the gawo-tree got angry. He seized hold of the lizard. He swallowed him, but he came out of the gawo-tree's eyes. Then he caught him again (and) swallowed him, but he came out at his ears. Then he caught him again and swallowed him, but he came out of his breast. Then he caught him again and swallowed him, but the lizard came out

يبا إنا .. أجيا نا .. كدا مغجرس .. ميا ..

ونا جيا .. كبا ن غدا ور .. جيا .. يدا رفمرمش

كبا يبنك .. كدا مغجر شيا .. وفمريا

ومس .. تدا ف .. كرونك .. سن غدا ور ..

يبا كدا مغجر .. كم مجار .. غجر نك .. لسن

كدا مغجر .. يبا .. أامج .. شنكا بس

سن .. أمتب .. أكنسن مني ماج .. سن

غدا ور نيمن فشه .. ميكا م .. كدا مغجر

يحجكن .. سن .. ببقتوا .. غدا أفنغا ور ..

سن يكحم .. كا امدا لش .. يحجن سن ببقتو أ

غكنغنومنلن .. سن يكحم .. كا امدالش .. يحجن

سن يقتوأ .. غيكم بنلن .. سن يكحم كدا امدالش

يحجمون .. سن كدا مغجر .. بقتو .. تم

ga chībīarsa. Sai gāwō ya fādi, ya mutu.
Sai kadangare ya che, 'Tāshi in rake ki gida.'
Sai ta tāshi. Su-ka-je gidansu, ya tsaya bākin
kōfar gida, ita kūa ta shiga gida, ta yi
zamanta. Aka-tanbaye-ta, 'Ina ki tafi?' Ta [5] kyale. Sai
ubanta ya fitō, ya iske mutun [6] tsugunē
kōfar gida. Sai ya che, 'Lāfia.' Ya che, 'Ni da
yārinya nan mu-ka-zō, kāji kāji wada
mu-ka-yi da ita.' Sai ubanta ya che, 'Ai ba ta fadi ba.'
Sai ya shiga gida, ya gaia ma mātā. Sai
aka-che, 'Kāka ki zō, ba ki fada ba?' Sai
ta che, 'Ala shi kyāshe ni, in amri kadangare.'
Sai ubanta ya kōma waje daia, ya kirāyi Baura,

---

at his navel. And the gawo-tree fell down and died. And the lizard said, 'Rise up, and I shall accompany you home.' So she rose up. They went to their (her) home. He (the lizard) stood at the entrance to the door of the house, but she entered into the house and went about her affairs. They asked her, 'Where did you go to?' She did not make any answer. Then her father came out, (and) met a man sitting at the door of the house. And he said, 'Greetings. Are you well?' He replied, 'I and the maiden have come, and so on, and so, and so, and so (relating all that happened), we did with her.' And her father said, 'Oh, she did not talk about (it).' And he entered the house, (and) told the women. Then they said, 'How is it you came and did not say anything about it?' And she said, 'May Allah save me from marrying a lizard.' Then her father went aside, (and) called Baura,

غشيبير سن ءسن غما اور ؞ يقاح ؞ يمث ؞ ب

ءسن كد نغجر ؞ يمث تداشن اور بكك ؞ غدا

ءسن تتاشن سكجم ؞ غد قسن يطم واقم

كو قم غدا ؞ اتكو ؞ قفشغ ؞ غدا ؞ تمى

دمنت اكتنبيت ؞ اما كـ[redacted]ـتف ؞ تكلبن ءسن

ابنت ؞ يمتوا ؞ يطلبسكن ؞ متم طغبن

كو قم غدا ؞ ءسن يمث لاقبن ؞ يمث يم ع

يام فم فمن ؞ مكذو ؞ بكاجن ؞ كاجن ؞ ورد ؞

مكن ؞ عر اما ؞ ءسن ؞ ابنت يمث ؞ اى بتقجيب

ءسن قيشغ ؞ غدا ؞ يغيام ؞ ملاقمن ؞ ءسن

اكث ؞ بكداكـ[redacted]ـذو ؞ بكقجراب ؞ ءسن

قث ؞ الشكيدابشن ؞ اوامن ؞ كعم نغجرك

ءسن ابنت ؞ يكوم ؞ وبجم ؞ بكرامن قمو ؞

ya che, 'Ba ki ba ni dīarki in yi keauta da ita?' Sai ta che, 'Haba [7] mālam, ina da dīa? Ai kai ke da abinka, kirāye ta, ka yi magāna da ita.' [8] Sai mālam ya kirāyi yārinya, ya che, 'Ina-sō in dauke ki, in yi keauta, [9] nā gaia ma uwarki, ta che in kirāye ki, in gaia maki.' Ta che, '[10] Ashā mālam, ai ba uwana ke da ni ba, kai kai ke da ni, kō kare, kō nāman dāji, ka dauke ni, ka ba shi, shi ke nan.' Sai ubanta ya che, 'Ala shi yi maki albarka.' Sai ya je, ya gaia ma kadangare. [11] Ashē dan sarki ne. Sai ya je gida, ya gaia ma ubansa, sai ubansa ya che, 'Mādala.' Ya bāda bāwa gōma, (k) kuyanga gōma, sānia gōma, kōmi duka gōma gōma, aka-kai ma ubanta. Kāna aka-bāda zanūa, aka-je aka-damra amre, aka-kāwō amarīa.

(and) said, 'Will you not give me your daughter, to make a present of (to the lizard)?' And she said, 'As for that, O learned one, do I possess a daughter? No, you are a master of your own property. Call her (and) speak with her.' Then the Doctor called the maiden, and said, 'I wish to take you away and make a present of you. I have told your mother, (and) she said I must call you (and) tell you.' She replied, 'O learned father, no, it is not my mother who possesses me, it is you, you possess me. Be it a dog or a wild beast, take me and give to him. That is all I have to say.' And her father said, 'May Allah bless you.' Then he came and told the lizard, in reality he was a chief's son. Then he went home (and) told his father, and his father said, 'Indeed!' And he gave him ten slaves, ten female slaves, ten cattle, and everything imaginable, ten of each, and took them to her (his future wife's) father's. Then he gave her clothes, (and) they came and were married, (and) he took away his bride.

يبث بالكبا ون ديمرك :. اريكو تم :. دراف :. اسر قبث
حبكن: مالم :. امدا دييمن: اايكو: بكدا ابنكك :. ــ
[redacted] كرابث :. كم مغمن دراف :. اسر مالم :. بكرا ابق
يادرفم: يبث امداسو :. امدوبكمك :. انم بكو تم
مدا غيم مغوك :. مبث :. انكرابك :. انغيا مك
مبث :. اشا مالم :. اي بدا غوا امدا :. بكمد فيب :. كم
بكمد فم: كوكبرن: كوفدا مندابم :. كدو بكمر
كبدالثن شيبكمفمن سر امنت :. يبث ال: شيمك
البرك :. سر يحكن: بغيا مكد فغمبن: ابشل دون
اسركيمبن سر يحمن غدا :. بغيام :. امبسن :.
اسر: امفسن يبث مادله :. ييا كبداو: غوم :. كد
كينغن: غوم :. اسد فيا غوم :. كوم :. دك
غوم :. غوم :. اككيم :. ابنت :. كداو: اكباد
ظغو: اكجن: اكد مر: امبرا ككاو: امرتا :.

Akwai wani bāwa ubansu, sūnansa Albarka, kuturū ne,
sai ya je gidansu, ya che shi-na-sō(n) wachan, da aka-ba kada-
-ngare, ta kia. Sai uwanta ta che, 'Me ta ke yi da kuturū?'
Sai dīarta ta che, '[12] Ina-sonsa, dan sarki ne.' Sai su-ka-che
anba shi. Su-ka-damra masu amre, har aka-kai ta gida-
-n miji, gōna, ba su ga kōwa ba, har ranan kadangare
da aka-ba shi maata, dīar Baura, sai ya che, [13] yaa je gewaiya
gōna. Ya hau dōki da kade [14] ana-gūda, su-ka-je,
ya che, 'Albarka na gida?' Sai ya fitō, ya gane shi, sai
ya kōma da gudu gida, ya che, 'Kāwō ma dan ubangijina, rua.'
Sai [15] maatar ta che, 'Ubangijinka?' Ya che, 'I,' 'Ashe kai bāwa ne?'
Ya che, 'I.' Ita kūa ta-na-daka. Sai ta aje tabarīa,
ta-na da chiki, sai ta shiga dāji. Mafārin shiga dāji
ke nan. [16] Kungurus kan kūsu.

Now their (the lizard's) father had a certain slave, by name Albarka, a leper, and he went to their house, and said he was in love with that one, whom they had given to the lizard (and who) had refused him. But her mother said to her, 'What will you do with a leper?' But her daughter said, 'I love him, he is the son of a chief, (in disguise).' So they said she was to be given to him. They were married (and all the ceremonies performed) even up to taking her to her husband's home; it was in the fields. And (the pair) did not see any one, till one day the lizard, who had been given the daughter of Baura for a wife, said he was going for a walk round the farms. He mounted his horse amid clapping and sounds of joy. They came (and) he said, 'Is Albarka at home?' Then he (Albarka) came out (and) saw him, then he ran back in haste to the house (and) said, 'Bring out water for my master's son.' But the wife said, 'Your master?' He replied, 'Yes.' 'You are indeed a slave?' He said, 'Yes.' Now she was pounding, then she put down the pestle. She was with child. Then she entered the bush. That was the first person who went to the bush (became mad). That is all. Off with the rat's head.

أكن ونبداو ؞ أبنقسن ؞ لسونقسن ؞ البرك ؞ وكثرونس
سن يجن ؞ غد فلسن يبث ؞ شنلسوا ؞ وثمد أكبا ؞ كد
نغبرن ؞ تقفن ؞ سن عواتت ؞ تبث بتقفسن ؞ د كثرو =
سن دييرت ؞ تبث ؞ إنا سنقسن ؞ ع فلسن كيبنن ؞ لسن سكبث
أنبا الثون لسكد مر ؞ مسن امجرن ؞ حم أككيت ؞ نمد
نمج ؞ نعومن ؞ بسن غكوراب ؞ حم ونمر كدم نغبرن
؞ داكبا اشن مامتن ؞ د ميم بجورن ؞ لسن يتث ؞ يدا جن ؞ تمونتن
نغونلن يعودوك ؞ د كجكج ؞ أقا غود ؞ سكجن
يبث البرك ؞ نقا غدا ؞ هن يجنوا ؞ يغجشن لسن
يكوم د غد ؞ غدا ؞ يبث كداو ود نا بسنغجهدا روا ؞
سن مدنن تمشن ؞ أبنغجنك ؞ يبث اي ؞ أبشن كجبا راقسن
يبث اي ؞ اتكو ؞ تنادك ؞ سن نا جن ؞ تبر يد ؞
تنادن نك ؞ سن فنشغ ؞ داج ؞ مبدا ونشغا دا ج ؞
بجنفرن فنغمرسن ؞ كم كوسن